Content Analysis
for the Social Sciences
and Humanities

Content Analysis
for the Social Sciences
and Humanities

OLE R. HOLSTI
Department of Political Science
University of British Columbia

ADDISON-WESLEY PUBLISHING COMPANY
Reading, Massachusetts · Menlo Park, California · London · Don Mills, Ontario

ISBN 0-201-02940-5
EFGHIJ-AL-787654

To ERIC

Preface

This book is an introduction and guide to content analysis as an approach to documentary research. It was written for the investigator who is considering using content analysis, but it is not a "cookbook" which provides a step by step formula for every research question. A single book can neither anticipate every problem that may arise in the almost infinite variety of questions one might wish to answer from documentary data, nor could it provide ready solutions for them. Illustrations are intentionally drawn from a broad spectrum of research areas and disciplines, but emphasis will be placed upon general principles applicable to classes of research questions rather than upon the impossible task of developing research outlines for every specific question.

Several other caveats should be stated. Content analysis has proved to be a valuable research method in many areas of inquiry. It has also been used to produce shelves full of unimaginative studies which appear to have been motivated by little more than the ease with which they could be carried out. According to one critic, "In reviewing the work in this field, one is struck by the number of studies which have apparently been guided by a sheer fascination with counting" (Cartwright, 1953, p. 447). The fault lies not with the method but with the users. Content analysis is of little help to the investigator who begins with a trivial problem. Nor is it a panacea for all investigations; it is, rather, a tool which may be used badly or well, foolishly or thoughtfully, on problems ranging from trivial to important. Significant research ultimately depends upon substantive knowledge of one's field and creative imagination. Any guide to research methods, including this one, is a poor substitute for either of these indispensable qualities.

Second, this book should not be read as an advocate's brief for a single approach to social inquiry. Any blanket rejection of content analysis, especially when combined with an uncritical position toward alternative techniques (e.g., Haas, 1966), deserves to be viewed with great skepticism, but extravagant claims for its merits are equally unwarranted. Indeed, any investigator contemplating the use of content analysis in his research is well advised to ask himself first whether some other technique may not satisfy his data requirements better or at lower cost.

Some introductory words about the plan of the book may be in order. In Chapter 1 we will consider some basic issues which emerge from efforts to define content analysis, classes of research questions for which content analysis is likely to prove useful, and a brief summary of major trends in content analytic research. This chapter addresses itself to what content analysis is and what it is not, and to where it fits in among the many analytic tools available to the social scientist and humanist. Chapter 2 identifies three broad purposes for which content analysis may be used, and discusses the basic research designs appropriate to each. This is the "core" of the book, and much of what follows in subsequent chapters is intended to explicate in greater detail the points introduced in this chapter. Within the framework developed in Chapter 2, a review of some existing studies will be undertaken in Chapters 3 and 4. The review is intended to illustrate the broad range of research questions for which content analysis may prove useful. At the same time we will use this literature to consider the basic question with which any user of content analysis must come to grips: What steps can the analyst take to minimize (but never completely eliminate) the risks of drawing erroneous conclusions from his data? The reader who is less interested in a broad survey of research in many fields than in guidance on a specific research problem may want to skim over these two chapters rather quickly, or to read only those sections which describe how others have approached research similar to his own. Chapter 5 discusses some of the many *categories* (e.g., subject matter, values, attitudes,) into which content data may be "coded," *units* (e.g., words, themes, paragraphs) which may be placed in the categories, and *systems of enumeration* (e.g., frequency, space, intensity) which may be used to describe attributes of documents. Choice of categories, units, and systems of enumeration represent three interrelated decisions which every content analyst must make in light of his specific research problem. This discussion is not designed to make these decisions for the analyst, but rather, to assist him by spelling out some of the assumptions which underlie alternative choices. Chapter 6 examines three problems basic to content analysis, or to any other type of research method: *sampling,* the choice of documents or parts of documents to be analyzed; *reliability,* the accuracy, dependability, stability, consistency, and predictability of results (Kerlinger, 1964, p. 429); and *validity,* the degree to which the analyst is measuring what he thinks he is measuring. The final chapter introduces the most important recent innovation in content analysis, the development of programs by which a substantial proportion of the most tedious research chores—categorizing and counting—can be accomplished by high speed electronic computers. The exciting prospects for some, but by no means all, types of documentary research will be illustrated. Equally important, the limitations of computers and the very real pitfalls which await the uncritical user, are discussed.

Before concluding, it may be worth stressing the underlying themes of this book. Content analysis opens up for the social scientist and humanist a wide variety of *opportunities* for systematic use of the most pervasive form of evidence about human affairs—the content of communication. The broad range of opportunities will become more evident as we review the variety of applications in which content analysis has proved useful. At the same time the investigator planning to undertake content analyses of his own needs to be aware of the many *dangers* which await the unwary, unimaginative, or unthinking user. Content data in many forms are plentiful, but their very availability may tempt some into aimless "fishing expeditions" motivated by the hope that "something interesting may turn up." Language is universal, but it is also complex; it "offers many alternative ways in which concepts may be expressed" (Stone, *et al.*, 1966, p. 7). Hence efforts to analyze motives, values, attitudes, and other interesting but elusive variables necessarily require imaginative and often painstaking efforts to validate inferences drawn from content data. Quantification of documentary materials may yield important and interesting data about many aspects of human experience and behavior, but the temptation to count things for the sake of counting, unless resisted, is almost certain to yield precise findings which are either meaningless, trivial, or both. If this book leaves the reader with a realistic sense of both these opportunities and dangers, it will have served its purpose.

I am indebted to many persons for their generous assistance and cogent advice. Robert C. North and Joanne K. Loomba collaborated with me on an earlier review of the content analysis literature, portions of which Gardner Lindzey and Elliot Aronson have generously permitted me to use in the present book. Andrew Quarry, Richard R. Fagen, K. J. Holsti, William Paisley, Kenneth C. Prewitt, and Philip J. Stone read all or parts of the manuscript, pointing out many ambiguities, inconsistencies, and errors which otherwise would have found their way into the book. Tradition requires that the author accept responsibility for shortcomings that remain. My debt to Phil Stone also extends to his generous assistance and collaboration on problems of computer content analysis during the past six years. The content analysis system described in Chapter 7 was originally programmed by Mrs. Anne Armour Enea and Horace Enea, and later revised several times by Kuan Lee. The many contributions, far beyond the call of secretarial duty, of Mrs. Violet Lofgren and Mrs. Arlee Ellis are too numerous to list exhaustively. My wife, Ann, also assisted in typing many drafts despite many other demands on the time of a wife and mother. The final draft was typed by Mrs. Joan Ippen with such accuracy that proofreading her copy was never much of a challenge.

For permission to quote short passages from their publications, I wish to thank Addison-Wesley, the American Statistical Association, Cambridge University Press, Chandler Publishing Company, Charles C. Thomas, Cornell University Press, Her Majesty's Stationery Office, Holt, Rinehart and Winston, Inc., *Human Relations, Journalism Quarterly,* The Journal Press, Meredith Press, The M.I.T. Press, *The New Republic, The Observer,* Prentice-Hall, Princeton University Press, *Public Opinion Quarterly,* The RAND Corporation, University of California Press, University of Chicago Press, University of Illinois Press, University of North Carolina Press, D. Van Nostrand Co., *Western Political Quarterly,* and John Wiley & Sons. I am also grateful to the authors who permitted me to quote from their books and articles.

The Dean's Committee at the University of British Columbia provided financial support for preparation of this manuscript. Staff members at Addison-Wesley solicited useful comments and suggestions from scholars in disciplines other than my own, and they have amply demonstrated that relations between author and publisher can be pleasant and fruitful.

Finally, my greatest debt is to someone with no interest whatever in content analysis—the person to whom this book is affectionately dedicated. His courage and good humor in the face of adversity have been a constant source of inspiration to me.

O. R. H.

Contents

1   Content Analysis: An Introduction

*The analysis of content is a central topic
in all of the sciences dealing with man.
The capacity for speech is man's most
striking characteristic, and language is
bound up with rational thought, the
emotions, and all of the distinctively human
parts of man's internal life. . . .
Rightly viewed, content analysis is a
core problem in the study of man, and to
work at solving it could alter the social
and behavioral sciences in fundamental ways.*

         David Hays (in press, pp. 1, 21)

Communication, the most basic form of human interaction, is necessary for any enduring human relationship, from interpersonal to international. Groups, institutions, organizations, and nations exist by virtue of communication and cease to exist once communication becomes totally disrupted. Indeed, it is no exaggeration to assert that "communication is at the heart of civilization" (Kuhn, 1963, p. 151). It therefore follows that the study of the processes and products of communication is basic to the student of man's history, behavior, thought, art, and institutions. Often the only surviving artifacts that may be used to study human activity are to be found in documents.[*]

    The extensive concern with the content of communication is vividly illustrated in Cartwright's (1953, p. 422) description of social psychology:

When one stops to think of it, it is really surprising how much of the subject matter of social psychology is in the form of verbal behavior. The

---

[*] The term "document" is used here and elsewhere in this book in the broad sense of any communication (novel, newspaper, love song, diary, diplomatic note, poem, transcribed psychiatric interview, and the like), rather than in the restricted sense (official paper) of the historian or political scientist.

formation and transmission of group standards, values, attitudes, and skills are accomplished largely by means of verbal communication. Education in the schools, in the home, in business, in the neighborhood and through the mass media is brought about by the transmission of information and by the exercise of controls which are largely mediated through written or spoken words. If one is concerned with problems of social organization, the situation is similar. Supervision, management, coordination, and the exertion of influence are principally matters of verbal interaction. Social and political conflicts, although often stemming from divergent economic interests and power, cannot be fully understood without studying the words employed in the interaction of conflicting groups, and the process of mediation consists largely in talking things out. The work of the world, and its entertainment, too, is in no small measure mediated by verbal and other symbolic behavior.

Similar comments might equally well be made by a representative of any of the social sciences or humanities. As a consequence, the study of communication content has been approached from a variety of different starting points and undertaken with the tools and conceptual frameworks of several disciplines. Content analysis is a multipurpose research method developed specifically for investigating any problem in which the content of communication serves as the basis of inference. In this chapter we shall develop this point further from several perspectives: What are the defining characteristics of content analysis? For what types of research problems is it most likely to prove useful? What are the major trends in the nature of the method, and what are the purposes for which it has been used?

A DEFINITION OF CONTENT ANALYSIS

Nearly all research in the social sciences and humanities depends in one way or another on careful reading of written materials. Given the ubiquity of this process in research, what characteristics distinguish content analysis from any careful reading of documents? Definitions of content analysis have tended to change over time with developments in technique and with application of the tool itself to new problems and types of materials. Among the definitions which have been proposed are the following:

Content analysis is the statistical semantics of political discourse (Kaplan, 1943, p. 230).

"Content analysis" may be defined as referring to any technique a) for the classification *of the* sign-vehicles, *b) which relies solely upon the* judgments *(which theoretically, may range from perceptual discriminations to sheer guesses) of an analyst or group of analysts as to which sign-vehicles fall into which categories, c) on the basis of* explicitly

formulated rules, *d) provided that the analyst's judgments are regarded as the reports of a* scientific observer *(Janis, 1949, p. 55).* *

Content analysis is a research technique for the objective, systematic, and quantitative description of the manifest content of communication (Berelson, 1952, p. 18).

We propose to use the terms "content analysis" and "coding" interchangeably to refer to the objective, systematic, and quantitative description of any symbolic behavior (Cartwright, 1953, p. 424).

The term "content analysis" is used here to mean the scientific analysis of communications messages . . . . The method is broadly speaking the "scientific method," and while being catholic in nature, it requires that the analysis be rigorous and systematic (Barcus, 1959, p. 8).

Content analysis is a phase of information-processing in which communication content is transformed, through objective and systematic application of categorization rules, into data that can be summarized and compared (Paisley, in press).

This selective sampling of definitions indicates that along with a persisting consensus about some characteristics, there has been a marked tendency toward viewing content analysis as a basic research tool which may be useful in various disciplines and for many classes of research problems.

The Requirements of Objectivity, System, and Generality

Despite their diversity, definitions of content analysis reveal broad agreement on the requirements of *objectivity, system,* and *generality.* We shall consider the meanings of these requirements, as well as two others—that it must be quantitative and limited to the analysis of manifest content—which are somewhat more controversial.

Objectivity stipulates that each step in the research process must be carried out on the basis of explicitly formulated rules and procedures. Even the simplest and most mechanical forms of content analysis require the investigator to use his judgment in making decisions about his data. What categories are to be used? How is category A to be distinguished from category B? What criteria are to be used to decide that a content unit (word, theme, story, and the like) should be placed in one category rather than another? Once the document has been coded and the findings are summarized, what was the reasoning that led to one inference rather than alternative ones? Objectivity implies that these and other decisions are

---

* From H. D. Lasswell, N. Leites, *et al., Language of Politics: Studies in Quantitative Semantics,* published by George Stewart, Inc. Copyright 1965 by the M.I.T. Press. Reprinted by Permission.

guided by an explicit set of rules that minimize—although probably never quite eliminate—the possibility that the findings reflect the analyst's subjective predispositions rather than the content of the documents under analysis. Thus, one test of objectivity is: can other analysts, following identical procedures with the same data, arrive at similar conclusions? The investigator who cannot communicate to others his procedures and criteria for selecting data, for determining what in the data is relevant and what is not, and for interpreting the findings will have failed to fulfill the requirement of objectivity.

Systematic means that the inclusion and exclusion of content or categories is done according to consistently applied rules. This requirement clearly eliminates analyses in which only materials supporting the investigator's hypotheses are admitted as evidence. It also implies that categories are defined in a manner which permits them to be used according to consistently applied rules. Stated somewhat differently, they must conform to certain general canons of category construction, a point which we will consider in more detail in Chapter 5. The requirement that research be "systematic" can also be illustrated by a negative example. In a book purporting to demonstrate the intellectual inferiority of certain racial groups, the authors culled from both reputable and highly suspect sources all materials supporting the thesis of inequality, while virtually disregarding the quantitatively and qualitatively superior evidence in support of the contrary thesis (Weyl and Possony, 1963). Although these findings were presented as a "content analysis" of the literature relating race to intelligence, a "study" of this type clearly fails to satisfy even the loosest definition of systematic research.

Important and necessary as these two criteria are, they are not sufficient to define content analysis or to distinguish it from related endeavors. This may be illustrated by several simple examples. Indexes, bibliographies, or concordances are concerned with the content of certain types of documents. All three can be prepared objectively and systematically, indeed, usually more objectively and systematically than most content analyses. They may also serve as a source of data for subsequent content analyses. *The New York Times Index, Reader's Guide to Periodical Literature,* and *A Concordance to the Poems of W. B. Yeats* (Parrish and Painter, 1963) might, for example, be used in research on focus of attention in an "elite" newspaper, trends in magazine coverage of civil rights stories, or imagery in Yeats' poetry. But these sources are not themselves content analyses because an index, a bibliography, or a concordance is not undertaken with any theoretical purpose in mind. They are merely listings of terms or titles according to specified rules (e.g., by subject matter or in alphabetical order), and the list itself is the intended end product. On the other hand, content analysis includes listing the attributes of documents according to specified rules, but this represents only an intermediate step toward answering some research question.

Generality, then, requires that the findings must have theoretical relevance. Purely descriptive information about content, unrelated to other attributes of documents or to the characteristics of the sender or recipient of the message, is of little value. The findings that Alexander Hamilton tended to use the word *upon,* that 0.7% of Richard Nixon's statements in the third television debate with John F. Kennedy included evidence (Ellsworth, 1965, p. 800), or that a Greek funeral oration of the eighth century B.C. contained "achievement imagery" are, by themselves, of little importance or interest. Such results take on meaning when we compare them with other attributes of the documents, with documents produced by other sources, with characteristics of the persons who produced the documents, or the times in which they lived, or the audience for which they were intended. Stated somewhat differently, a datum about communication content is meaningless until it is related to at least one other datum. The link between these is represented by some form of theory. Thus all content analysis is concerned with comparison, the type of comparison being dictated by the investigator's theory.

The requirements of objectivity, system, and generality are not unique to content analysis, being necessary conditions for all scientific inquiry. Thus in general terms, content analysis is the application of scientific methods to documentary evidence. At this point some readers may become aware that, like the person who suddenly discovers that he has been "writing prose all his life," they have been engaged in content analysis without knowing it.

The Quantity-Quality Issue

Along with general consensus that objectivity, system, and generality are defining characteristics of content analysis, two other proposed requirements have generated considerable debate in the recent literature. First, must content analysis be *quantitative?* Second, must it be limited to the *manifest* content, or may it be used also to probe for more latent aspects of communication?

The quantitative requirement has often been cited as essential to content analysis, both by those who praise the technique as more scientific than other methods of documentary analysis and by those who are most critical of content analysis.

The former viewpoint is summarized by the assertion that, "There is clearly no reason for content analysis unless the question one wants answered is quantitative" (Lasswell, Lerner, and Pool, 1952, p. 45). There is, however, considerable disagreement about the meaning of "quantitative" as applied to content analysis. The most restrictive definitions are

TABLE 1-1

Frequency of themes

Theme	Frequency of reference	
	Candidate A (N = 10 speeches)	Candidate B (N = 12 speeches)
U.S must honor commitment to allies	15 (56%)	3 (13%)
Appeasement of aggressors leads to war	9 (33%)	1 (4%)
Peace in Vietnam must be based on compromise	3 (11%)	14 (58%)
U.S. is upholding a corrupt government in South Vietnam	0 (0%)	6 (25%)

those which require that content analysis measure the *frequency* with which symbols or other units appear in each category. Other definitions equate it with *numerical:* "Content analysis aims at a classification of content in more precise, *numerical terms* than is provided by impressionistic 'more or less' judgments of 'either-or' " (Kaplan and Goldsen, 1949, p. 83). Others are still less restrictive and include studies in which findings are reported in such terms as "more," "less," or "increasing" (Berelson, 1952, p. 17). Finally, there is a group which accepts the distinction between "quantitative" and "qualitative," but which insists that systematic documentary studies of the latter type constitute an important, and perhaps more significant, form of content analysis. We can illustrate these viewpoints in more detail by examining a hypothetical study of campaign speeches on the Vietnam issue by congressional candidates.

Some of the earlier definitions of content analysis required that inferences from content data be derived strictly from the *frequency* with which symbols or themes appear in the text (e.g., Leites and Pool, 1942, pp. 1-2; Janis, 1943, p. 429). Using frequency counts we might, for example, tabulate how many times certain themes relating to American policy in Vietnam appear in each candidate's speeches. Reporting the number of statements in each category by all candidates (as in Table 1-1) would satisfy the requirements of many research designs.

Restricting content analysis to this single system of enumeration, however, presents a theoretical and a practical problem. Underlying this definition is the assumption that frequency is the only valid index of concern, preoccupation, intensity, and the like. Often this may in fact be a valid premise, but there is also ample evidence that measures other than frequency may in some instances prove more useful. The related practical problem is that this view places a number of standard content analysis

TABLE 1-2

Presence of themes

Theme	Number of speeches in which theme occurs	
	Candidate A (*N* = 10 speeches)	Candidate B (*N* = 12 speeches)
U.S. must honor commitments to allies	10 (100%)	3 (25%)
Appeasement of aggressors leads to war	8 (80%)	1 (8%)
Peace in Vietnam must be based on compromise	1 (10%)	9 (75%)
U.S. is upholding a corrupt government in South Vietnam	0 (0%)	4 (33%)

methods on the borderline of acceptability, and it removes some of the most imaginative content analysis studies from our consideration. A pioneering application of content analysis, the RADIR (Revolution and the Development of International Relations) studies, combined frequency and nonfrequency techniques. Each editorial in the sample taken from a series of "prestige newspapers" during a 60-year period was coded according to the appearance or nonappearance of certain key symbols (Lasswell, Lerner, and Pool, 1952). Thus at the coding stage an editorial received the same score ("present") whether a symbol occurred once or a dozen times. The findings were then summarized by tabulating the number of editorials in which each symbol was present. Similarly, we might score each category relating to American policy in Vietnam as "present" or "absent" in a speech, and then tally the number of speeches in which any theme occurred, rather than the frequency with which any content unit appeared. The results might then be reported as they are in Table 1-2 above.

The technique of "contingency analysis," in which the coding of material depends on the absence or presence of the attribute within the document or section of the document, rather than on the frequency of its presence, provides another method of scoring (Osgood, 1959, p. 63). Inferences are then based on the proximity of two or more content attributes within the text. In our study of campaign speeches we might be concerned with discovering what terms occurred in conjunction with references to Vietnam, rather than in the frequency with which these symbols occurred. The results might then resemble Table 1-3.

Finally, each speech might be given a single score which most closely characterizes its major theme. In this case we make a single qualitative judgment about the entire document without tabulating the frequency

TABLE 1-3

Contingency analysis of terms

Other symbols	Number of sentences in which other symbols occur	
	Candidate A ($N = 49$ sentences referring to Vietnam war)	Candidate B ($N = 62$ sentences referring to Vietnam war)
Commitment	32 (65%)	7 (11%)
Allies	29 (59%)	5 (8%)
Appeasement	14 (28%)	4 (6%)
Peace	8 (16%)	39 (63%)
Compromise	4 (8%)	20 (32%)
Corrupt	0 (0%)	18 (29%)

TABLE 1-4

Major theme of speeches

Major theme of speech	Candidate A ($N = 10$ speeches)	Candidate B ($N = 12$ speeches)
U.S. must honor commitments to allies	5 (50%)	0 (0%)
Appeasement of aggressors leads to war	1 (10%)	0 (0%)
Peace in Vietnam must be based on compromise	0 (0%)	7 (58%)
U.S. is upholding a corrupt government in South Vietnam	0 (0%)	0 (0%)
None of the above	4 (40%)	5 (42%)

with which any content attribute appears. But we may still report our findings quantitatively, as in Table 1-4.

These four examples, all using hypothetical data for illustrative purposes only, by no means exhaust the ways in which content data may be presented.* They should, however, indicate that the term "quantitative" may take on many meanings, no one of which will be most suitable for every type of research. Each of the four methods used to present our findings yielded somewhat different results, although the differences are not as dramatic as they sometimes are. On occasion, two systems of

---

* For a further discussion of other techniques of quantification (e.g., scaling for intensity of expression), see Chapter 5.

enumeration will lead to diametrically opposite conclusions.* Therefore, the important question for the analyst to ask himself is not: "Am I being quantitative?" but rather: "What is the theoretical relevance of the measures I am using?"

The case for designing content analysis to yield numerical data—although not necessarily solely in terms of frequency—is a powerful one. Foremost among the arguments is the degree of precision with which one's conclusions may be stated. Descriptions such as "45 percent" or "27 times out of a possible 30" convey information more precisely than statements such as "less than half" or "almost always." In response to the question "why quantify?," Lasswell, Lerner, and Pool (1952, pp. 31-32) have pointed to a number of other questions which often remain unanswered in qualitative symbol studies:

Can we assume that a scholar read his sources with the same degree of care throughout his research? Did he allow his eye to travel over the thousands of pages of parliamentary debates, newspapers, magazines and other source lists in his bibliography or notes? Or did he use a sampling system scanning some pages superficially, though concentrating upon certain periods? Was the sampling system for the Frankfurter Zeitung, if one was employed, comparable with the one for the Manchester Guardian? Were the leaflets chosen simply because they were conveniently available to the scholar, or were they genuinely representative of the most widely circulated propaganda leaflets.

A further advantage of quantification is that statistical methods provide a powerful set of tools not only for precise and parsimonious summary of findings, but also for improving the quality of interpretation and inference. In our hypothetical study of the Vietnam issue we might want to know if there is any relationship—and if so, how strong it is—between electoral success and a candidate's position toward American policy in Vietnam. Or, further, is the relationship maintained when we hold age, party, socio-economic, or other attributes of congressional candidates constant? Statistical techniques include a number of methods by which such questions can be answered with precision. In such a study it is also likely that we would not want to analyze all speeches for every candidate in the 435 congressional districts. But if we code only a sample of them, how much confidence can we have that the results are representative of the entire group of speeches? Statistical procedures may be used to indicate how likely we are to be correct—or conversely, what is the probability that we are wrong—when we make generalizations on the basis of a sample.† In short, statistics are useful tools at many stages of

---

* See the example presented in Chapter 5, pp. 120.

† For a more extended discussion of sampling, see Chapter 6.

research, but use of statistical methods is *not* dependent on recording the frequency with which content attributes appear, or on any other single method of enumeration.

Despite the advantages of employing quantitative methods, the tendency to equate content analysis with numerical procedures has come under criticism on a number of grounds. The most general of these is the charge that such a restriction leads to bias in the selection of problems to be investigated, undue emphasis being placed on precision at the cost of problem significance (Smythe, 1952; Barcus, 1959).

Related to this general criticism is the view that one can draw more meaningful inferences by nonquantitative methods (Kracauer, 1952). Qualitative content analysis, which has sometimes been defined as the drawing of inferences on the basis of appearance or nonappearance of attributes in messages, has been defended most often, though not solely, for its superior performance in problems of applied social science. When, for example, content from propaganda sources is used to predict enemy behavior, pressure of time, inability to control variables, and the possibility that nonrecurring phenomena may provide major clues to policy often render exhaustive quantitative analyses uneconomical and difficult to design and carry out. Citing instances in which qualitative analysts were able to draw more accurate inferences from studies of Nazi propaganda during World War II than those using quantitative techniques, A. L. George (1959b, p. 7) concluded that, "Qualitative analysis of a limited number of crucial communications may often yield better clues to the particular intentions of a particular speaker at one moment in time than more standardized techniques."

In line with this reasoning, proponents of qualitative techniques also question the assumption that for purposes of inference, the frequency of an assertion is necessarily related to its importance. These critics suggest that the single appearance—or omission—of an attribute in a document may be of more significance than the relative frequency of other character-istics (George, 1959b). An example of this point is found in a study of Chinese documents prior to China's active entry into the Korean war in October 1950. The change from the passive term *fan tui* to the word *k'ang yi,* previously used as an exhortation to action against Japan and against the Chinese Nationalists, provided the first clue that Chinese leaders had decided upon overt intervention in the war (Whiting, 1960, p. 99). But even studies which identify and draw inferences from the unique aspects of each document are not simply qualitative; rather than counting fre-quencies the analysts have chosen to formulate nominal categories into which one of two scores are recorded—present or absent. The results may then be reported quantitatively as, for example, in Table 1-2.

Although the issues underlying the quality-quantity debate are not trivial ones—and we shall consider them again in the discussion of systems of enumeration in Chapter 5—the position to be taken in this book rejects the rigid dichotomy which is sometimes implied in the debate, especially by those who espouse either the view that "if you can't count it, it doesn't count," or that "if you can count it, that ain't it." Our position is based on two considerations. First, measurement theorists are generally in agreement that qualitative and quantitative are not dichotomous attributes, but fall along a continuum (Lazarsfeld and Barton, 1951). To state that references to concrete things are more likely to appear in real than in simulated suicide notes is a qualitative assertion, but it is not without a quantitative aspect; even such a statement as "In his speech accepting the 1964 Republican presidential nomination, Barry Goldwater defended extremism for the defense of liberty" can be presented quantitatively. Findings reported in this form imply ordinal and nominal scaling, and statistical methods can be used with such data. In short, all data are potentially quantifiable.

Moreover, whether stated explicitly or not, many of the most rigorously quantitative studies use nonnumerical procedures at various stages in the research. This is likely to be the case in initial selection of categories. Because content analysts are not generally agreed on standard categories, even for given classes of problems, the investigator often finds himself in the position of having to develop his own for the question at hand. Hence, before constructing categories he may want to read over a sample of his data to get a "feel" for the types of relevant symbols or themes. Prior to coding he may also read over the data to identify any idiosyncratic attributes which, if not taken into account, might adversely affect the results. After coding and data analysis have been completed, he may want to check the "face validity"* of the quantitative results by rereading parts or all of his documents. Or, conversely, quantitative results may highlight qualitative aspects of the text which might otherwise have escaped the analyst's scrutiny. A study of Richard Wright's autobiography is a case in point. The reader familiar with White's (1947) quantitative findings is probably more sensitive to many qualitative aspects of *Black Boy*.

Thus the content analyst should use qualitative and quantitative methods to supplement each other. It is by moving back and forth between these approaches that the investigator is most likely to gain insight into the meaning of his data. Pool (1959, p. 192) summarizes this point: "It should not be assumed that qualitative methods are insightful, and quantitative ones merely mechanical methods for checking hypotheses. The relationship is a circular one; each provides new insights on which the other can feed."

---

* For a further discussion of validity, see Chapter 6.

It is worth noting in conclusion that for scientific research the advantages to be gained by some type of quantification continue to be important.* But asking the right question of the data is even more important than the system of enumeration used to present the findings, a point clearly expressed by a statistician, John W. Tukey (1962, pp. 13-14): "Far better an approximate answer to the *right* question, which is often vague, than an *exact* answer to the wrong question, which can always be made precise. Data analysis must progress by approximate answers, at best, since its knowledge of what the problem really is will at best be approximate." Thus for purposes of definition there are few compelling reasons for excluding studies which fail to conform to any specified level of measurement. Rather, we take the view that there are various levels and types of measurement possible with verbal data (as there are with other types of data) and that each carries with it certain assumptions (which may or may not be warranted in a specific instance).

The Manifest-Latent Issue

A second major source of disagreement among those defining content analysis is whether it must be limited to *manifest* content (the surface meaning of the text) or whether it may be used to analyze the deeper layers of meaning embedded in the document. Do the requirements of objective and systematic methods restrict the analyst merely to reporting characteristics of the document, and if not, at what point in the research process may he extend his analysis to the latent meaning of the text?

The manifest-latent issue can be considered at two levels. The requirement of objectivitiy stipulates that only those symbols and combinations of symbols actually appearing in the message be recorded. In other words, at the *coding* stage of research, the stage at which specified words, themes, and the like are located in the text and placed into categories, one is limited to recording only those items which actually appear in the document. "Reading between the lines," so to speak, must be reserved to the interpretation stage, at which time the investigator is free to use all of his powers of imagination and intuition to draw

---

* These advantages extend to the types of statistical tests which may be used with the data. In general, the higher the level of measurement attained, the more powerful the permissible tests. Extended discussion of statistical analyses lies outside the scope of this book. The interested reader can turn to any of the many standard texts available. For a discussion of statistical issues relevant to content analysis data, see Stone *et al.* (1966). It should be pointed out, however, that statisticians themselves are not agreed on some of the important issues. For example, there are those (e.g., Siegel, 1956) who take the position that most social science data do not meet the requirements of the more powerful parametric statistics. Others take a less restrictive view and suggest that such tests should be used in preference to nonparametric statistics even when it is clear that not all the assumptions of the former have been met (cf. Kerlinger, 1964).

meaningful conclusions from the data. This is vividly illustrated by the example of a mental patient who announced: "I am Switzerland" (cited in Shneidman, 1961). The inference that the patient is stating his desire for release from hospital confinement—by equating Switzerland with freedom—clearly depends on more than the lexical attributes of the sentence. But if we restrict our attention to coding operations, content analysis is limited to manifest attributes of text.

The second aspect of the manifest-latent issue concerns the *interpretation* of results. This debate is essentially one concerning the dimensions of communication which may properly be analyzed (Morris, 1946). Earlier definitions tended to limit content analysis to questions of semantics, the relationship of signs to referents, and to questions of syntactics, the relationship of signs to signs (Kaplan, 1943; Janis, 1949; Berelson, 1952). The restriction against analysis of the pragmatical dimension of language, the relationship of signs to those that produce or receive them, was usually based on the difficulty of drawing valid inferences about the causes or effects of communication directly from content data.

As has been the case in the quantitative-qualitative debate, the recent trend has been in the direction of a broader definition (Cartwright, 1953, p. 424; Barcus, 1959, p. 19). Nearly the entire volume of papers from the Work Conference on Content Analysis of the Social Science Research Council was addressed to using messages for purposes of answering questions about the causes or effects of communication (Pool, 1959). This trend toward a broader view of content analysis is evident in Osgood's (1959, p. 36) definition:

. . . we define content analysis as a procedure whereby one makes inferences about sources and receivers from evidence in the messages they exchange . . . . (W)hen the interest of the content analyst lies in making inferences about the source of a message, he must rely upon encoding dependencies, that is, the dependencies of message events upon psychological processes in speakers and writers. When his interest lies in making inferences about the effects of a message upon its receivers, on the other hand, he relies upon decoding dependencies, that is, the dependencies of events in listeners and readers (their meanings, emotions, attitudes, and the like) upon the content and structure of messages.

When used for these purposes content analysis is closely related to the field of psycholinguistics (Osgood and Sebeok, 1954; Jaffe, 1966).

The differences between the broader and more restrictive views are actually not as great as suggested at first glance. Both Kaplan (1943, p. 223) and Janis (1943, p. 437) excluded pragmatical content analysis because inferences about sources from the content of documents they write or receive can rarely be validated solely by analysis of the messages themselves. That is, inferences were limited to describing attributes of documents; inferences from content data to attributes of those who produced them or effects upon those who received them were excluded.* On the other hand, proponents of a broader definition are generally aware of the dangers of inferring personality traits, intentions, values, motives and other characteristics of communicators without some independent sources of corroborating evidence; hence they usually assume that content analysis data will be compared, directly or indirectly, with independent (i.e., noncontent) indices of the attributes or behavior which are inferred from documents.

For present purposes, a broad definition of the method will be adopted: *Content analysis is any technique for making inferences by objectively and systematically identifying specified characteristics of messages.*† In somewhat more succinct form this definition incorporates the three criteria discussed earlier: content analysis must be objective and systematic, and, if it is to be distinguished from information retrieval, indexing, or similar enterprises, it must be undertaken for some theoretical reason. Our definition does not include any reference to quantification because a rigid qualitative-quantitative distinction seems unwarranted for the purposes of defining the technique, for excluding certain studies from consideration as examples of systematic analysis of documentary data, or, by itself, for praise or condemnation of content analysis. Nor do we include the stipulation that content analysis must be limited to describing the manifest characteristics of messages. It is true that only the manifest attributes of text may be coded, but this limitation is already implied by the requirement of objectivity. Inferences about the latent meanings of messages are therefore permitted but, as we shall point out repeatedly in the following chapters,‡ they require corroboration by independent evidence.

WHEN TO USE CONTENT ANALYSIS

There are many ways that we can study man's behavior. We can experiment with him in the laboratory, give him a questionnaire, or interview him (survey research), observe him, probe him (projective tests), substitute for him (simulation), combine him with others (aggregate data

---

* While definitions restricting inferences from content data were widely accepted until the 1950's, many earlier studies did in fact draw conclusions, often implicitly, about the causes or effects of communication.

† This definition was developed jointly with Philip J. Stone in conjunction with his book on computer content analysis (Stone *et al.,* 1966).

‡ This point is particularly stressed in the discussions of research designs (Chapter 2), studies on the causes and effects of communication (Chapter 4), and validity (Chapter 6).

analysis), or study his artifacts (archeology) and communications (content analysis).

When should one consider using content analysis? Given the immense volume and diversity of documentary data, the range of possibilities is limited only by the imagination of those who use such data in their research. The diversity is suggested by a few of the questions that have been investigated in recent years by the use of content analysis:

What cultural differences are reflected in the songs and literature of various nations (Sebald, 1962, Lewin, 1947)?

To what extent have the political symbols of the New Deal been adopted by American conservatives (Prothro, 1956)?

What differences characterize the language behavior of schizophrenic and normal persons (Mann, 1944; Fairbanks, 1944)?

Is editorial support of a political candidate also reflected in biased news sections (Kobre, 1953; Klein and Maccoby, 1954)?

What has been the Soviet reaction to Voice of America broadcasts (Inkeles, 1952)?

Is the Riesman hypothesis about the increasing other-directedness of American society supported by changing content of consumer goods advertising (Dornbusch and Hickman, 1959)?

How is sentence length related to the comprehensibility of literature (Coleman, 1962)?

How are expressions of the "need for achievement" related to stages in the development of a civilization (McClelland, 1961; deCharms and Moeller, 1962)?

Who was the author of the Federalist Papers, No.'s 49-58, 62 and 63 (Mosteller and Wallace, 1964)?

What content characteristics distinguish best-sellers from other novels (Harvey, 1953)?

More generally, content analysis is likely to be especially appropriate for at least three general classes of research problems which may occur in virtually all disciplines and areas of inquiry.

First, it may prove useful when data accessibility is a problem and the investigator's data are limited to documentary evidence. The analyst who has direct access to his subjects may well find that other research techniques provide better data more directly and at a lower cost. When restrictions of time or space do not permit direct access to the subjects of research, they must be studied "at a distance," with the consequence that other research techniques (interview, questionnaire, observation, and the like) are not applicable. If the subject is no longer alive, he can be studied only through the record of his activities, through what his contemporaries set down about him, or through whatever writings he has left. In some instances the third category constitutes the most revealing, and occasionally the only surviving, source. Under these circumstances the options may be reduced to two—use the documentary evidence as skilfully and imaginatively as possible, or don't do the research at all. Content analysis may thus serve as a "last resort" approach to research when more direct techniques of analysis are ruled out by circumstances. Identification of unknown authors (Yule, 1944; Paisley, 1964), inferences from enemy propaganda (George, 1959a; Lasswell, 1949; Whiting, 1960), examination of decision-makers' attitudes during international crises (Holsti, Brody, and North, 1965), or studies of "need for achievement" in ancient civilizations (McClelland, 1958) illustrate this use of content analysis.

There are also occasions when even the investigator who has direct access to his subjects may prefer to collect his data through some form of content analysis. Despite their very real merits for social research, even the best experiment or survey studies the subject and his responses in a highly artificial situation. Knowledge that one is being studied may, in some circumstances, materially alter those aspects of behavior under analysis. Especially when it is important to get repeated measures of the subjects' values, attitudes, and the like over a period of time, and if one has reason to believe that continued interaction between analyst and subject may affect the nature of responses, then content analysis of the subject's statements may be a useful way to gather the required data. An important feature of content analysis is that it is a "nonreactive" or "unobtrusive" research technique (Webb *et al.,* 1966).

Content analysis of documents may also be useful as a supplementary source of data. In the words of a Chinese proverb, "The palest ink is clearer than the best memory" (quoted in Webb *et al.,* 1966, p. 111). A related application of content analysis, even when direct access to the subject poses no difficulty, is to develop an independent line of validation for data obtained through other methods. The investigator may check the results of questionnaire or interview data by comparing them with content analyses of the subject's statements.

For example, a study of public attitudes and concerns used both survey data and content analyses of letters to mass-circulation magazines (Sikorski, Roberts, and Paisley, 1967). The analyst who has used open-ended questionnaires or interviews may also find that he can best utilize such data by applying content analysis to them. In a cross-national study of *Youth's Outlook on the Future,* the investigators used two separate techniques to generate data and two forms of content analysis. A questionnaire was given to a sample of students from the United States, New Zealand, South Africa, Egypt, Mexico, France, Italy, Germany, Japan, and Israel. Content analysis was used to code open-ended items. The students were also asked to write a 1000- to 2000-word autobiography about their futures to the year 2000 A.D. These autobiographies were content analyzed to supplement the questionnaire data (Gillespie and Allport, 1955).   Another illustration of content analysis used in conjunction with other techniques appears in a study of community social structure (Janes, 1958). Names of persons and associations appearing in two local newspapers in "Illini City" were tabulated. Analysis of the data indicated that the distribution of families according to times mentioned in newspapers was a valid indicator of local class structure; it also revealed useful information on familial relationships, associational participation, and other social characteristics of the community. As a result of this study, Janes concluded that the sociologist can use such newspaper data both as a reconnaissance tool and as a supplement to other information on community structure.

These examples illustrate the "multiple operation" approach to research (Webb *et al.*, 1966, pp. 3-5). When two or more approaches to the same problem yield similar results, our confidence that the findings reflect the phenomena in which we are interested, rather than the methods we have used, is enhanced.

Second, some form of content analysis is often necessary when, given certain theoretical components of the data themselves, the subject's own language is crucial to the investigation. Those analyzing psychiatric interviews, projective tests, and many other types of documentary data often require information of a subtlety or complexity which renders casual scrutiny inadequate, even if undertaken by a skilled and sensitive reader. One would have little confidence in rough estimates of the degree of "need achievement" in Indian folklore (McClelland and Friedman, 1952), or of the type/token ratio—the number of different words in text of a given length—in the language of schizophrenics (Fairbanks, 1944; Page, 1953) regardless of the investigator's skill or training. Nor could one expect to settle genuine questions of disputed authorship using impressionistic analyses of style.

Finally, content analysis may be helpful when there are technical advantages because the volume of material to be examined exceeds the investigator's ability to undertake the research by himself. In studies of newspapers, magazines, movies, radio, literature, and many other forms of communication the analyst can rarely afford to examine all relevant data. One solution to the problem of data volume may be to analyze only a *sample* of it. Findings from the sample of documents selected for study can then be used to make inferences about the larger universe from which it was selected. But unless proper steps are taken to ensure that the sample is representative and unless relevant characteristics of the sample are described precisely, inferences about the entire set of documents will be dubious at best.

Another approach to the problem may be to employ one or more assistants. Whatever the merits of the investigator's sixth sense, when assistants are used he must be able to translate his methods of analysis into explicit rules to ensure an acceptable degree of consistency and uniformity (i.e., reliability) in his results. Failure to do so will raise serious problems and confound the analyst in drawing conclusions from his data. Consider, for example, a hypothetical study of trends in patterns of family decision-making as revealed in popular magazine fiction. Each coder is given responsibility for stories that appear in a given decade. Their task is first to identify passages in which decisions are made in the family, and then to classify them according to issue (consumer purchases, leisure activities, parent-child relations) and pattern of authority (father-dominated, mother-dominated, child-dominated, or egalitarian). Let us assume that the results reveal changes consistent with the investigator's hypotheses. But unless there is reasonable confidence that each analyst used the same rules for identifying and classifying relevant passages, it is impossible to determine whether the findings reflected changes in the content of the stories or differences in subjective predispositions between coders.

Sampling and employing assistants are not, of course, mutually exclusive solutions to the problem of data volume: they are often used together. For example, an analysis of key symbols appearing in "elite" newspapers over a 60-year period (Lasswell, Lerner, and Pool, 1952) could not have been undertaken without rules to guide coders; nor could every issue of each newspaper for the entire period have been examined. This study clearly required the use of both sampling and many research assistants. If rigorous and explicitly formulated rules for systematic sampling and reliable coding had not been used, inferences drawn from these data would have been of questionable value. Content analysis is a technique for meeting these requirements.

Content analysis is not relevant to all documentary research, however. It can rarely be used to determine the truth of an assertion, or to evaluate the aesthetic qualities of poetry.* Moreover, if the analyst uses documents

---

* It can, of course, be used to determine the truth of an assertion about the content of communication. The statement, "Lyndon Johnson made more references in his 1964 campaign speeches to the need for federal action to ensure civil rights than did his opponent," may be shown to be true or false by content analysis of the speeches made by the two candidates. Or, if the investigator specifies his criteria for "good poetry" (e.g., a high ratio of adjectives to nouns), then content analysis may be used to assess the relative merits of poems, but *only in terms of those criteria.*

to settle limited issues of fact, such as to determine whether *The New York Times* supported Humphrey or Nixon in 1968, methods other than content analysis could be used more efficiently. But the data the investigator seeks from the content of documents can rarely be reduced to such simple factual questions.

One approach to documentary research is exemplified by a research manual which suggests dependence upon "a sort of sixth sense that will alert you to tell-tale signs" (Gray, 1959, p. 36, quoted in Dibble, 1963, p. 204). The difficulty with such advice is not that it is wrong, but rather that it may be insufficient. Intuition, insight, or a brilliant flash, borne of experience, thorough knowledge of one's data, imagination, or luck are perhaps always present in creative research. The "folk wisdom" that "the facts speak for themselves" is decidedly not true. Hence there is always a place in research for such intangible qualities as intuition and imagination. But the same idiosyncratic qualities of intuition which render it important in some stages of research, especially in originally formulating the problem and in drawing inferences from the data, makes it less useful in others. Intuition is not a substitute for objectivity, for making one's assumptions and operations with data explicit where they are open to critical purview. Nor is it a substitute for evidence. This becomes acutely apparent when two persons, both of whom rely on subjective evaluation, draw contradictory inferences from the same documents. In the absence of explicit rules of evidence and inference which can themselves be subjected to critical scrutiny, the issue is all too likely to be settled by claims of "expertise" or stridency rather than evidence. Some of what has passed for analysis of Soviet politics, and more recently, Chinese politics, suffers from precisely this problem.

There is, finally, one further limitation of intuition that is particularly relevant for content analysis: language is complex,* and even the trained analyst with keen insight may find it difficult to make maximum use of his data unless he uses systematic methods.

The limitations of relying solely on ordinary reading of documents may be illustrated by the previously cited study of Richard Wright's autobiography, *Black Boy* (White, 1947). Although the investigator was a trained psychologist, his preliminary appraisal of the book failed to uncover a number of major themes. When he did a content analysis, marking all references to values in the margin and tallying the totals for each value category, he discovered Wright's emphasis on personal safety (18% of all value judgments), failure to identify with other Negroes, and lack of interest in social goals. In general, then, content analysis will be useful whenever the problem requires precise and replicable methods for

* For a dramatic illustration of this point, see Pittenger, Hockett, and Danehy (1960), in which the entire book is devoted to an analysis of the first five minutes of a psychiatric interview.

analyzing those attributes of documents which may escape casual scrutiny. In such cases the analyst will find the objective and systematic methods involved in content analysis advantageous as a supplement to, *not as a substitute for,* the other intellectual tools he brings to bear on his problem.

TRENDS IN CONTENT ANALYSIS RESEARCH

A somewhat different perspective on what content is and how it has been used can be gained by considering some major trends in the development of the method.* The history of content analysis as a research technique dates from the beginning of the twentieth century, although scattered studies going as far back as the 1740's have been cited (Dovring, 1954). During this time the method has gone through a number of phases.

The most easily discernible trend in content analysis is an almost geometric increase in the frequency of such research. During the first two decades of the century, an average of approximately 2.5 content analysis studies appeared each year.   During the next three decades, the annual average frequencies rose to 13.3, 22.8, and 43.3, respectively. Although many of the scholars who contributed most heavily to the development of content analysis during the period from the mid-thirties through the mid-fifties (including, among others, Harold Lasswell, Irving Janis, Bernard Berelson, Daniel Lerner, Ithiel Pool, Abraham Kaplan, Nathan Leites, and Ralph White), were, for a variety of reasons, no longer engaged in content analysis research, use of the method was by no means fading out. During the 1950's the annual number of studies increased to almost 100. Stated somewhat differently, there was more content analysis research published between 1950 and 1958 than during the entire first half of the twentieth century. Even a casual survey of the literature suggests that the quantity of such research is continuing to increase.

A more revealing view of the history of content analysis can be presented when the studies are classified according to purpose, discipline or approach, and sources examined. Empirical studies of the subject matter of communication account for an overwhelming proportion of the published research. Barcus' survey of 1719 titles revealed that nearly four out of five could be so classified, the remainder being divided between methodological research (e.g., studies of sampling or reliability in content analysis), 14.2%, and studies of form or style, 6.9%. This three-fold classification underestimates the concern of content analysts for theoretical and methodological problems; unquestionably many works listed as empirical studies of content have contributed to the development of the

---

* This description relies in part on data presented in a study of content analysis from 1900 through 1958 (Barcus, 1959).

method. Nevertheless, concern for such issues has been notably more evident recently than in earlier content analysis research. During the first two decades of the twentieth century, more than 98% of the studies dealt primarily with the content of text. By the 1950's, this figure dropped to 75%, whereas one study in six was concerned with problems of theory and method.

The recent development of various techniques of computer content analysis has served as an added impetus to the consideration of these issues. The process of preparing a research design for computer analysis has forced many analysts to come to grips explicitly with issues that might otherwise have been overlooked. This trend has not been without its critics, however. On the one hand, content analysts have been accused of being overly concerned with developing techniques, to the neglect of testing significant communication hypotheses (Stephenson, 1963). On the other hand, they have been charged with a continuing lack of serious attention to theoretical and methodological issues (Krippendorff, 1966).

Another way to describe trends in content analysis research is by approach or discipline. Three disciplines have accounted for approximately 75% of all empirical studies: sociology-anthropology (27.7%), general communications (25.9%), and political science (21.5%). Using more specific categories, Barcus found that over 60% of all empirical content analysis research has been focused in five mutually exclusive areas of inquiry, each of which accounts for at least 10% of the total: the study of social values, propaganda analyses, journalistic studies, media inventories, and psychological-psychoanalytic research.

The forms of documentary data to which content analysis has been applied have also tended to become more varied. Early investigations were confined largely to media inventories and journalistic studies, most of which were analyses of daily American newspapers. On the other hand, relatively little attention was paid to the foreign press. During the 1930's newspaper research continued to account for the largest number of studies. At the same time, content analysis was increasingly being adapted for sociological, historical, and political research. The latter category included studies of propaganda—many of them stimulated by the seminal work of Harold Lasswell and his associates—foreshadowing a trend which gained added impetus after the outbreak of World War II. During the 1940's, political research using propaganda materials accounted for nearly 25% of all empirical content analysis investigations. The dominating influence of political studies during World War II is reflected in one of the definitions cited earlier, in which content analysis was characterized as "the statistical semantics of political discourse" (Kaplan, 1943, p. 230). Lasswell's *The Language of Politics*, perhaps the most influential publication of the 1940's on content analysis, represents the high water mark of focus on political documents generally, and on propaganda materials specifically. Newspapers continue to be the source most frequently examined, but whereas such research accounted for over 60% of the studies prior to 1920, the figure had dropped to less than 30% by the 1950's. The development of new mass media (movies, radio, television) has also stimulated analyses of the audio and visual media.

Although journalistic and political studies continue to appear with increasing frequency, the most discernible trend has been toward wider application within a variety of disciplines. One of the milestone publications in the history of content analysis, appearing at the end of the 1950's, reveals something of the diversity which has come to characterize the applications of the technique within such disciplines and spheres of specialized inquiry as folkloristics, biography, history, psychoanalysis, linguistics, propaganda, cognitive organization, and psychotherapy (Pool, 1959). *Trends in Content Analysis,* published in 1959, made evident not only that a new generation of scholars engaged in content analysis had emerged, but also that they were expanding the scope of research problems to which the method could be applied and were vigorously debating a wide range of critical theoretical and methodological issues. These papers also clearly indicated a shift of interest away from purely descriptive studies toward research on the causes and effects of communication content.

In recent years there have also been efforts to expand the use of content analysis to nonlexical materials. There are imaginative studies using as data pottery fragments (Aronson, 1958), children's drawings (Craddick, 1961, 1962; Badri and Dennis, 1964), art (Gordon, 1952; Paisley, 1968), gestures and facial expressions (Ekman, 1965), photographs (Wayne, 1956), cartoons (Ehrle and Johnson, 1961), vocal tone (Starkweather, 1956), music (Paisley, 1964; La Rue, 1967), and even postage stamps (Stoetzer, 1953; Warchol, 1967).

That the trends described here are continuing is evident from the papers presented to the National Conference on Content Analysis in November 1967, the first major conference devoted to content analysis since 1955 (Gerbner *et al.,* in press). Topics included consideration of models upon which theories of content analysis might be based, problems of inference from diverse forms of communication, methods of recording and notation in content analysis, norms and standard categories, and diverse computerized techniques of content analysis which have been developed during the 1960's. The broadening interest in content analysis is documented by the fact that authors of the 25 papers represented more than a dozen fields, including linguistics, communication, political science, mathematics, psychology, sociology, social psychology, English, music, medieval and renaissance studies, advertising and marketing, psychiatry, information science, and computer science.

Finally, earlier uses of content analysis were largely confined to analyses of "natural" or "available" data—i.e., data which exist without any active participation by the investigator, such as newspapers, books, government documents, and personal documents. Increasingly, however, content analysis has also been applied to verbal data produced by subjects at the behest of the investigator. This class of data may be of two somewhat different types. There is, in the first place, the research method generating only verbal data, which may then be subjected to content analysis. The psychiatric interview and various projective instruments, such as the Thematic Apperception Test, are representative examples. A second type of data is the by-product of other standard techniques of social research. The investigator may find that he can more objectively and systematically use these data if they are content analyzed. Among the latter we may include responses to open-ended questions generated in survey research (Scheuch and Stone, 1964), written messages derived from a simulation study (Brody, 1963), or verbal communication produced during group interaction (Bales, 1950; Mills, 1964). The result of this trend toward analysis of more diverse data has been a softening of rigid boundaries between content analysis and other techniques of social research. Coding open-ended questionnaires, for example, overlaps both content analysis and survey research.

In summary, the history of content analysis reveals a series of interrelated and continuing trends toward:

* Increased use of content analysis,

* Heightened concern for theoretical and methodological issues,

* Application to a broader spectrum of problems, especially those focusing on the antecedents and effects of communication,

* Increased use for testing hypotheses, as opposed to purely descriptive research,

* Greater diversity in the materials studied,

* Use in conjunction with other techniques of social research,

* Content analysis by means of computers.

The final development—use of computers for undertaking many of the more laborious chores associated with content analysis—has been mentioned only in passing. We shall return to a further consideration of its implications in Chapter 7.

2 Content Analysis Research Designs

All communication is composed of six basic elements: a *source* or sender, an *encoding process* which results in a *message*, a *channel* of transmission, a *detector* or recipient of the message, and a *decoding process*. Content analysis is always performed on the message, be it a novel, diplomatic note, editorial, diary, or speech. The results of content analysis may, however, be used to make inferences about all other elements of the communication process. To the classical formulation of these questions— "who says what, to whom, how, and with what effect?" (Lasswell, Lerner, and Pool, 1952, p. 12)—we shall add one more: "why?" A schematic representation of the relationship between these questions, our definition of content analysis, and the communication process appears in Fig. 2-1.

Each of these six questions may be subsumed under research designed for three different purposes. The investigator may analyze messages to make inferences about the characteristics of text, the causes or antecedents of messages, or the effects of communication. These three categories differ, as summarized in Table 2-1, with respect to the questions which will be asked of the data, the dimension of communication analyzed, and the types of comparisons. For purposes of research designs, the core of Table 2-1 is the third column, in which the types of comparisons relevant to various research questions are specified.

THE FUNCTION OF RESEARCH DESIGNS

Before considering the problems and implications inherent in each of these categories, a few general comments about research designs may be in order.

A research design is a plan for collecting and analyzing data in order to answer the investigator's question. A good research design *makes explicit*

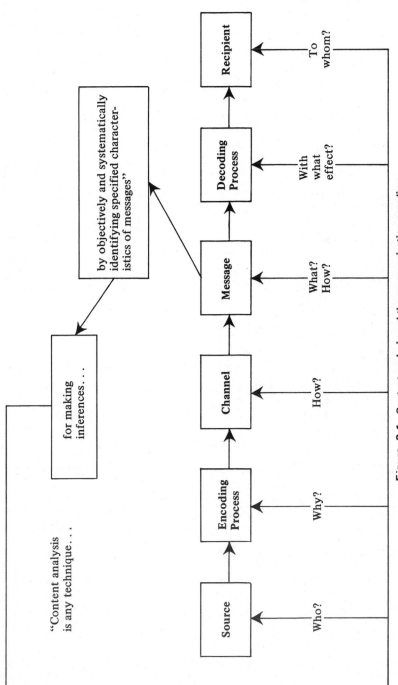

Figure 2-1 Content analysis and the communication paradigm.

TABLE 2-1

Content analysis research designs

Purpose	Branch of semiotics	Types of comparisons	Questions	Research problem
To describe characteristics of communication	Semantics (sign/referent) Syntactics (sign/sign)	Messages source A 1. Variable X across time 2. Variable X across situations 3. Variable X across audiences 4. Variables X and Y within same universe of document	What?	To describe trends in communication content To relate known characteristics of sources to the messages they produce To audit communication content against standards
		Messages, source type A/ Messages, source type B	How?	To analyze techniques of persuasion To analyze style
		Messages/standard 1. *A priori* 2. Content 3. Noncontent	To whom?	To relate known characteristics of the audience to messages produced for them To describe patterns of communication
To make inferences as to the antecedents of communication (the encoding process)	Pragmatics (sender/sign)	Messages/nonsymbolic behavioral data 1. Direct 2. Indirect	Why?	To secure political and military intelligence To analyze psychological traits of individuals To infer aspects of culture and cultural change To provide legal evidence
			Who?	To answer questions of disputed authorship
To make inferences as to the effects of communication (the decoding process)	Pragmatics (sign/receiver)	Sender messages/recipient messages Sender messages/recipient behavioral data	With what effect?	To measure readability To analyze the flow of information To assess responses to communication

and integrates procedures for selecting a sample of data for analysis, content categories and units to be placed into the categories, comparisons between categories, and the classes of inference which may be drawn from the data.* It thus implies that the investigator has clearly thought out the rationale for his inquiry, that he is able to specify the type of evidence needed to test his ideas, that he knows the kinds of analyses he will make once the data are gathered and coded, and the inferences they permit him to make. In short, a good design ensures that theory, data gathering, analysis, and interpretation are integrated.

Our earlier general warnings against "fishing expeditions" can now be stated more concretely. This type of inquiry implies the absence of a plan or strategy. Documents to be analyzed are chosen, but the reasons for their selections are not clear, even to the analyst; perhaps the rationale is no more precise than the traditional response to queries about why one climbs mountains: "Because they're there." Documents are coded, but there is no theory to guide the selection of categories and units; such important decisions are more likely than not to be made on the basis of "what's easy." Comparisons between categories may be undertaken—they may even involve sophisticated statistical analyses—but correlations between categories which are not linked by even a crude theory are more likely to be misleading than enlightening. An interpretation may be found to fit the results of content analysis but, as Merton (1957b, pp. 93-95) points out, the flexibility of *post factum* explanation—whatever is found can be "explained"—renders it virtually useless for systematic inquiry.

This point may be made somewhat differently by a homely analogy between a research design and the blueprint for a house. Without a blueprint materials are collected at the building site, but there is no guidance as to either the necessary type or quantity needed. Carpenters, bricklayers, and plumbers can assemble them, but each may have a quite different conception of the structure they are erecting. The resulting house is as likely to have been wasteful of labor and material as it is unlikely to prove functional. Both in the case of the house and in that of content analysis undertaken without a good research design, it may prove difficult to find any use for the end product.

DESCRIBING THE CHARACTERISTICS OF MESSAGES

Content analysis is used most frequently to *describe the attributes of messages,* without reference to either the intentions (encoding process) of the sender or the effect of the message upon those to whom it is directed (decoding process). Much of the research has addressed itself to some

---

* This chapter is concerned primarily with the latter two (comparisons and classes of inference) aspects of research design. Coding (categories and units) and sampling are discussed in more detail in Chapters 5 and 6, respectively.

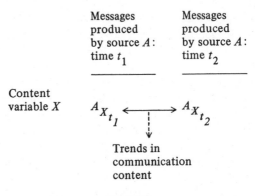

Figure 2-2

variety of the "what?" question, testing hypotheses about such matters as focus of attention, trends in communication, or cross-media differences. The investigator may also want to answer the question "to whom?," as when testing hypotheses about the way in which the content of messages will differ according to audience, or to answer questions about "how?," e.g., studies of style or of techniques of persuasion.

The type of research design will depend on the questions which the investigator seeks to answer and on his data. In order to state meaningful conclusions, however, *all* content data must be compared to some other data. To determine that an editorial used the term "freedom" X number of times is a meaningless finding by itself, as is any other unrelated fact about communication content. The dictum that "Securing scientific evidence involves making at least one comparison" (Campbell and Stanley, 1963, p. 6) is especially relevant to content analysis.

When content analysis is used to describe text, there are three basic types of comparisons that may be made. The analyst may compare documents derived from a *single source* in several ways. One application of this method is the comparison of messages over time, from which the analyst may draw inferences about secular trends (Fig. 2-2).* This is one of the most frequently used forms of content analysis. Trend studies have been undertaken to analyze values in childrens' readers (deCharms and

* The following symbols will be used in Figs. 2-2 through 2-12: A, B, C, and D indicate the source or recipients of messages; X and Y refer to content variables, and Z is a noncontent variable. Situation and time are indicated by s_1, s_2 and t_1, t_2, respectively. An arrow with two heads specifies a comparison between two categories, and an arrow with a broken line indicates the inference to be drawn from the comparison. These symbols will be used in various combinations. For example,

$$^AX_{t_1}{}^B \longleftrightarrow {}^BX_{t_2}{}^A$$

means that variable X in A's messages to B at time 1 will be compared with the same variable in B's subsequent messages (t_2) to A.

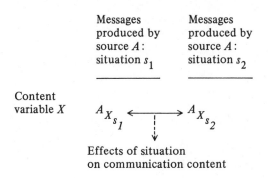

Figure 2-3

Moeller, 1962), the content of rural newspapers (Taeuber, 1932), Negro attitudes toward discrimination (Rosen, 1964), party platforms in the United States (Namenwirth, in press), research developments in psychology (Allport and Bruner, 1940), sociology (Becker, 1932), and physics (Rainoff, 1929), and many other forms of communication.

The investigator may also compare messages from a single source in differing *situations* (Fig. 2-3). This design is applicable for determining the effect of changed circumstances on specified characteristics of communications. It has been used to analyze messages generated under different conditions in simulation experiments (Brody, 1963), to determine whether newspapers that are faced with competition provide significantly better news coverage than those that have a monopoly in their circulation area (Nixon and Jones, 1956), and to study the effects of changes in cold war tensions on cohesion within the communist system (Hopmann, 1967).

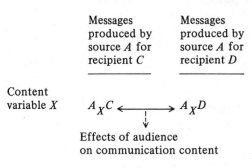

Figure 2-4

The proposition that the character of audiences affects the content and style of communication has been tested in a number of content analysis studies. In this case the research design calls for comparison of the messages produced by a single source across different *audiences* (Fig. 2-4).

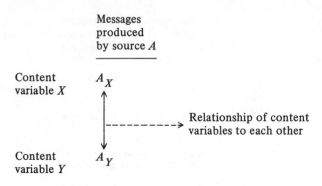

Figure 2-5

Examples of research employing this design include studies comparing John Foster Dulles' political rhetoric before groups of differing characteristics (Cohen, 1957; Holsti, 1962); fiction written for upper, middle, and lower class readers (Albrecht, 1956); and advertising in Negro and non-Negro magazines (Berkman, 1963).

Comparisons of communication content across time, situation, or audience are intermessage analyses. A research design may also be based on the relationship of *two or more variables* within a single document or a set of documents. "Contingency analysis" is one of the many techniques designed specifically for such cases (Osgood, 1959). Some form of the design depicted in Fig. 2-5 has been used to compare self-concepts with feeling toward others (Sheerer, 1949; Stock, 1949), optimism and pessimism in Protestant sermons (Hamilton, 1942), and war propaganda and welfare in political writings (Eckhardt, 1965).

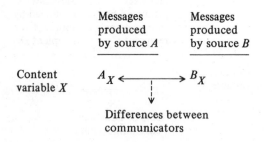

Figure 2-6

Hypotheses may also be tested by comparing the messages produced by *two or more different sources* (Fig. 2-6). Usually the purpose is to relate theoretically significant attributes of communicators to differences in the messages they produce. For example, this design has been used to examine linguistic differences in messages produced by "normal" persons

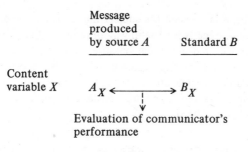

Figure 2-7

and those on the point of committing suicide (Osgood and Walker, 1959), and to identify differences in propaganda appeals of two or more orators (Shneidman, 1963), political parties (Almond, 1954), or nations (Lasswell, 1927).

Finally, content data may be compared to some *standard* of adequacy or performance (Fig. 2-7). Many analyses of the mass media have employed *a priori* standards defined, often implicitly, by the investigator's preferences. Such studies rarely satisfy even the loosest requirements of objectivity. Even when *a priori* standards are made explicit, the problems of defining such deviations as "bias" operationally have rarely been dealt with in a satisfactory manner.

An alternative to the deductive approach is to derive standards inductively from *content data.* A representative sample of messages produced by a class of communicators (e.g., college freshmen, schizophrenic patients, mass-circulation magazines) may provide norms against which the products of any single communicator may be compared. This technique has often been used in mass media research. The performance of the medium as a whole is used to construct a standard against which the content of any given newspaper, magazine, or network may be compared. For example, one might determine the average amount of foreign news in all metropolitan dailies to develop an index against which the international coverage of any newspaper may be compared. This method will not permit the analyst to determine whether performance meets some absolute standard of adequacy, but it will indicate how the newspaper performs relative to other similar sources. Thus, one could not state whether international reporting in the St. Louis *Post-Dispatch* was "excellent" or not, but one might conclude that, to use some hypothetical figures, it ranks in the top 5% of all dailies with a circulation exceeding 100,000.

A third type of standard against which content data may be compared is one defined by *noncontent indices,* such as expert opinion or aggregate data. In a study of the treatment of mental illness in the mass media (Nunnally, 1957), a pool of experts defined certain standards for accuracy in reporting. Especially when the subject matter is controversial, employment of a pool of experts is a useful way of reducing the effects of a single person's subjective predispositions, because these will be counterbalanced by others in the group. Aggregate data may also provide a relatively bias-free standard. A classic study of this type compared the incidence of minority group characters in popular magazine fiction with census data (Berelson and Salter, 1946).

INFERENCES ABOUT THE CAUSES OF COMMUNICATION

The second major classification of studies is that in which the text is analyzed in order to make *inferences about the causes or antecedents of the message,* and more specifically, about the author. Thus content analysis is employed to discover "lawful relations between events in messages and processes transpiring in the individuals who produce ... them" (Osgood, 1959, p. 36). Within the framework of Fig. 2-1, messages are examined for the purpose of answering the questions "who?" and "why?" Who was the author of a given document? What are the meanings, associations, values, motives, or intentions of the communicator that can be inferred from his messages? Whereas the description of text can be classified under semantics or syntactics, this use of content analysis is a problem in pragmatics, the relationship of signs to those who produce them.

The problem inherent in this use of content analysis is that the relationship between a person's statements and his motives, personality, intentions, and the like, is at best only vaguely understood: "There is as yet no good theory of symbolic communication by which to predict how given values, attitudes, or ideologies will be expressed in manifest symbols" (Lasswell, Lerner, and Pool, 1952, p. 49). Owing to possible differences in the ways people may express their feelings, intentions, and other traits, inferences about the antecedent causes of messages drawn solely from content data cannot be considered self-validating. Thus, however precise our measures of communication content, it is hazardous indeed to assume, without corroborating evidence from independent, noncontent data, that inferences about the author may be drawn directly from content data.

One of the more interesting debates among content analysts is that between proponents of the "representational" and "instrumental" models of communication. The former take the position that the important aspects of communication are "what is revealed by the lexical items present in it" (Pool, 1959, p. 3; cf. Osgood, 1959). Words are assumed to "represent" accurately the author's inner feelings; thus there are constant, though probabilistic, relationships between the content of communication and underlying motives of their authors. The latter argue that it is not the face meaning of a message, but "what it conveys, given its context and circumstances" that is important (Pool, 1959, p. 3; cf. George, 1959b; Mahl, 1959). In this view communication is seen as an instrument of influence; hence the content of messages may be shaped by the communicator's intent to manipulate his audience in certain directions.

The position taken here, that inferences as to the intentions or feelings of authors drawn from content data need corroboration through independent evidence, is somewhat closer to that of the instrumental school. It does not deny the existence of regularities between content and its causes; rather it accepts the view that because regularities may be of a limited type (e.g., for certain classes of communicators, in specified situations, using given media of communication) we need evidence beyond that provided by content analysis of the messages.

In order to draw valid inferences about sources from the messages they send, the content data must be compared *directly* or *indirectly*, with evidence from independent sources.

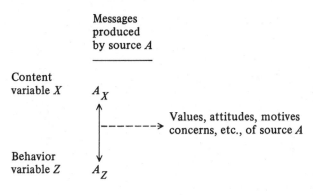

Figure 2-8

Direct comparison between content data and an independent measure of behavior (Fig. 2-8) was used in an investigation of "fertility values," as indexed by the number of children appearing in popular American magazine fiction. These figures were found to correlate with actual birth rates, as revealed by census data, during the years 1916, 1936, and 1956 (Middleton, 1960). In a study of the 1914 crisis, the degree of hostility in documents written by European decision-makers was compared to the level of violence in their military actions (Holsti, North, and Brody, 1968). In other cases, biographical data have been used to buttress findings based on content analysis of the author's writing; this technique has been used, for example, in studies of Dostoyevsky, D. H. Lawrence, and others (Kanzer, 1948, McCurdy, 1939).

Inferences based on an *indirect* relationship between symbolic and other forms of behavior are found much more frequently in the content

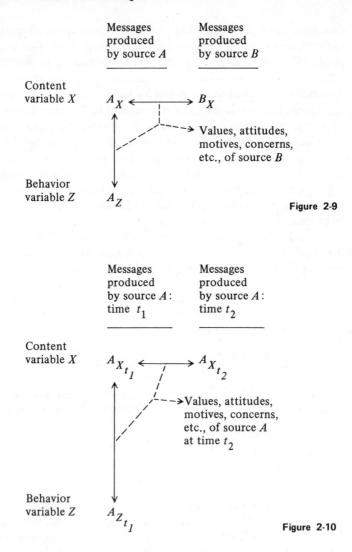

Figure 2-9

Figure 2-10

analysis literature (Fig. 2-9). The logic of such inferences can be stated as a syllogism: In a given situation, individuals whose behavior patterns are known to be z, z', and z'' produce messages with characteristics x, x', and x'', respectively. If in similar circumstances a source produces messages with attributes x'', the inference is that it was related to behavior pattern z''. In a classic example of this research design, comparison between Nazi propaganda themes and the books, periodicals, and transoceanic cables of certain domestic organizations suspected of sedition revealed significant similarities on a number of dimensions (Lasswell, 1949). The data obtained by content analysis were admitted by the court as legal evidence supporting the charge of sedition. In this case the likenesses in the messages of *two separate sources* served as the basis for inferences about the similarity of motives—support for the German war effort.

The research design may also focus on the relationship of events to symbols for a *single source* (Fig. 2-10). A psychiatrist may examine his patient's statements for attributes that have in the past provided a clue to some aspect of his behavior. In general, the investigator bases his inferences on some demonstrated relationship between events and symbols for the same or for comparable communicators. One weakness of many content analysis studies is that such a relationship between symbolic behavior and other forms of behavior was assumed rather than demonstrated.

INFERENCES ABOUT THE EFFECTS OF MESSAGES

The third major classification of content analysis studies is that in which *inferences are made about the effects of messages* (the decoding process) upon the recipient. The question "with what effect?" is, in some respects, the most important aspect of the communication paradigm. Consider just a few of the investigators and areas of research concerned with the effects of communication on some aspects of the recipient's behavior: the social psychologist studying attitude change; the political scientist or historian investigating the effects of propaganda, campaign speeches, or other types of political appeal; and the psychologist or educator investigating learning patterns. Many other examples could be cited. Nevertheless, relatively few studies have attempted to answer this question with data derived through content analysis. Probably the most systematic research on the decoding process has focused on efforts to measure the readability of text.

Earlier we pointed out that the analyst cannot assume a simple correspondence between the content of a message and the motives, values, or attitudes of those who produced them. Similarly, he cannot assume that

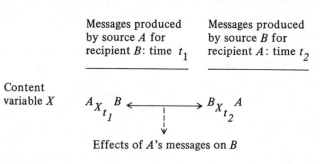

Figure 2-11

the content of a given message will have the same effect on all persons. There is strong evidence that persons interpret and assimilate the content of communication in light of their beliefs about the credibility of the source, situational, personality, and other factors. Thus, the investigator wishing to assess the effects of communication cannot confine his analysis merely to the content of the messages; his research design must also include evidence about the recipient of the communication.

As in the other types of research design, the sender's message serves as the data. Two types of comparisons may be used to measure the impact of the message. First the investigator may determine the effects of A's messages on B by content analyzing B's subsequent messages (Fig. 2-11). For example, reviews of a book have been analyzed to investigate the responses it elicits (Lerner, 1950), and the effects of hostile diplomatic messages from one nation to another have been assessed by analyzing the recipient's subsequent responses (Zinnes, Zinnes, and McClure, in press).

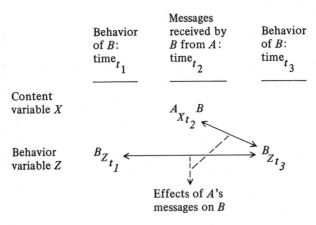

Figure 2-12

An alternative approach to studying the effects of communication is to examine other aspects of the recipient's behavior. In studies of readability, for example, various independent tests have been used to measure the extent of the reader's comprehension. Inferences as to the effects of communication are more likely to be valid if we can also compare the recipient's behavior before and after receiving the communication (Fig. 2-12). Often, however, it is possible to obtain information about the recipient only after the message is received, in which case a truncated form of the design in Fig. 2-12 is used. Needless to say, confidence in the resulting inferences are likely to be considerably weaker.

One danger in research assessing the effect of communication is the possibility of falling prey to the *post hoc, ergo propter hoc* fallacy, i.e., the fallacy of assuming that the antecedent (the content of A's message) caused the consequent (B's behavior or the content of B's message). If, to test the readability of a text, we give it to a child and later test his comprehension of it, we may be fairly certain that the prior document, the reading material, is somehow reflected in the subsequent test. Even in this relatively controlled situation we cannot be certain that extraneous factors did not creep in to confound inferences as to the readability of the text, e.g., if the material is "culture bound." Potentially more serious problems occur when these designs are used in nonexperimental studies. The difficulty derives from a lack of control over factors other than the original communications which might also be affecting the recipient of the messages. This is not an argument for eliminating research aimed at assessing the effects of communication, but only a suggestion that this type of inquiry presents special difficulties of which the analyst must be aware.

RESEARCH DESIGNS: AN ILLUSTRATIVE EXAMPLE

The research designs we have been describing represent the simplest form of each type. Designs for any actual research are likely to involve more than a single comparison. A trend study (Fig. 2-2) might be concerned with making comparisons across many rather than only two points in time, and a comparison of sources (Fig. 2-6) need not be confined to two sources. In these cases the analyst may broaden the scope of his study by adding *more comparisons of a single class.*

A more complex research design may be developed by combining *two or more classes of comparison.* For illustrative purposes, let us consider a hypothetical project designed to test hypotheses about the content of American political rhetoric during the twentieth century. More specifically, the investigator is interested in testing a hypothesis about the relationship between advocacy of domestic welfare legislation and support for interventionist foreign policies. He is immediately aware that the volume of potentially relevant data far exceeds his resources, so he decides to analyze only campaign speeches of presidential nominees. This choice not only reduces the data to a small fraction of the total, but it also ensures that the context or situation in which the rhetoric occurs is more or less constant, i.e., quadrennial electoral campaigns in the United States.

Before settling for a design that merely compares positions on welfare and foreign policy (Fig. 2-5), however, our investigator begins to worry about some factors not taken into account in his design which may confound interpretation of his findings. First, he becomes concerned about the possible effects of party affiliation; perhaps the relationship between attitudes toward welfare and foreign policies is not the same among Republicans and Democrats. Hence he decides to expand his original research design to control for the presidential nominee's party affiliation. At this point he had added a second class of comparison (Fig. 2-6) to his original design.

Our hypothetical analyst is still not satisfied, however. An impressionistic survey of presidential campaigns suggests to him that not only may there be differences between parties, but also that the positions of the parties may have changed enough to warrant comparison over time. Thus he adds a third class of comparison into his design, a trend analysis of the type described in Fig. 2-2, thereby gaining some control over the secular trends.

Finally, let's suppose that our investigator discovers, upon becoming acquainted with some social psychological literature, that the content of speeches may be affected by the nature of the audience. He reads that candidates are likely to differentiate audiences, "to see the unique and important features of any group that condition its acceptance of ideas, and then to communicate with it in terms of these special features."[*] For this reason he decides to add one further class of comparison to his research design to control for the nature of the audience. He may, for example, decide to distinguish between addresses to the "mass public," those persons with no special skills or knowledge in politics, and the "attentive public," the 10% or less of the Americans who are prone to discuss and debate political issues actively (Rosenau, 1961, pp. 35-41). Comparisons of the type depicted in Fig. 2-4 are thus introduced into our hypothetical design. In representing the research design schematically (Table 2-2), we shall use the same symbols as in Figs. 2-2 through 2-12 except that, for reasons of simplicity, Roman numerals will be used to designate data in each cell—the degree of support for welfare legislation and interventionist foreign policies.[†]

It is apparent that the original design, which permitted only a single comparison and no control over factors that might affect the relationship between campaign statements on welfare and foreign policy, has been

---

[*]From *The Political Process and Foreign Policy: The Making of the Japanese Peace Treaty*, B. D. Cohen. Princeton University Press, 1957, p. 137. Reprinted by permission.

[†]Degree of support might be measured in any of several ways, e.g., by the relative frequency of expressions of support and rejection for each policy:

$$\frac{\text{Number of support statements}}{\text{Number of support statements} + \text{Number of reject statements}}$$

Alternative systems of enumeration are discussed in Chapter 5. For illustrative purposes, we designate the trend analysis by only the first and most recent twentieth century presidential campaigns. The investigator wishing to make inferences about trends, however, would be well advised to include at least several elections between 1900 and 1968 in his research design.

TABLE 2-2

*Hypothetical research design to test hypotheses relating
attitudes toward welfare legislation and foreign policy*

| | Time t_1 1900 | | | |
| | Recipient C (mass public) | | Recipient D (attentive public) | |
Content variable	Source A (Bryan, Democrat)	Source B (McKinley, Republican)	Source A (Bryan, Democrat)	Source B (McKinley, Republican)
X (welfare) Support Reject	I	II	V	VI
Y (foreign policy) Support Reject	III	IV	VII	VIII

| | Time t_2 1968 | | | |
| | Recipient C (mass public) | | Recipient D (attentive public) | |
Content variable	Source A (Humphrey, Democrat)	Source B (Nixon, Republican	Source A (Humphrey, Democrat)	Source B (Nixon, Republican)
X (welfare) Support Reject	IX	X	XIII	XIV
Y (foreign policy) Support Reject	XI	XII	XV	XVI

enriched considerably. The research design depicted in Table 2-2 now permits four classes of comparisons; i.e., not only may we compare attitudes toward the two issues directly, we may also compare them holding each of three factors—time, party, and audience—constant. There are, therefore, four types of inferences which may be drawn from the results (Table 2-3).

TABLE 2-3

Relationship between attitudes toward two issues

Controlling for effects of	No controls	Party and time	Audience and time	Audience and party
Comparisons between data in cells number	I - III II - IV V - VII VI - VIII IX - XI X - XII XIII - XV XIV - XVI	I - V II - VI III - VII IV - VIII IX - XIII X - XIV XI - XV XII - XVI	I - II III - IV V - VI VII - VIII IX - X XI - XII XIII - XIV XV - XVI	I - IX II - X III - XI IV - XII V - XIII VI - XIV VII - XV VIII - XVI
Inferences	Direct relationship between two issues	Effects of audience on relationship	Effects of party on relationship	Effects of secular trends on relationship

This research design may seem considerably more complex than those discussed earlier. Note, however, that it does not in fact encompass any class of comparison other than those already discussed. Table 2-2 is only a combination of the basic research designs, illustrated in Figs. 2-2, 2-4, 2-5, and 2-6. *Nor does it require coding any more data than would have been the case in the simplest design.* This is not to say, of course, that one should use a more complex research design when a simpler one is sufficient. If a single class of comparison is adequate to answer the research question at hand , then this is the design that should be used. The rationale for developing a more complex design in our hypothetical case was not a case of "complexity for the sake of complexity." Rather, there was a reason to believe that without efforts to control for party, time, and audience, it would have been impossible to draw meaningful conclusions from the data. Three additional classes of comparison were introduced to permit inferences to be drawn not only as to the relationship of welfare and foreign policy in campaign rhetoric, but also the interaction of three other factors on this relationship.*

---

* As indicated earlier, this book will not attempt to describe statistical procedures applicable to content analysis data. Suffice it to say that the hypothetical design described in this chapter lends itself to "analysis of variance," a procedure described in virtually every statistics text.

CONCLUDING COMMENTS

This chapter has attempted to make explicit the linkages between our definition of content analysis, the communication process, questions which may be asked about elements of the communication process, and research designs relevant to these questions. What may appear to be an excessive concern with these issues springs from the conviction, supported by an extensive review of existing studies, that the low esteem with which content analysis is held in some quarters derives largely from its frequent use in "fishing expedition" research, i.e., research unguided by broader theoretical considerations and undisciplined by a research design. A research design is not, of course, sufficient to ensure significant findings, but it is certain that without one there can be no clear conclusions from the inquiry.

One final point is in order. Careful planning of research strategy need not impose a set of intellectual blinders to restrict the analyst's thinking to a single narrow line of reasoning. To suggest, moreover, that the discipline imposed by a research design is a weak alternative to intuitive thinking or "understanding" (Kim, 1965) is to pose a false dichotomy. It is hard to improve upon Kerlinger's (1964, p. 322) answer to these views.

In tackling a research problem, the investigator should let his mind roam, speculate about possibilities, even guess. Once the possibilities are known, the intuitive stage of thinking can enrich the research conception by leading more effectively to the analytical stage of organizing and structuring the problem. The investigator is then ready to plan his approach to the problem and to decide what research and analytical methods he will use to execute his ideas. Good research design is not pure analysis. Intuitive thinking, too, is essential because it helps the investigator to arrive at solutions that are not routine. Perhaps most important, it should be remembered that intuitive thinking and analytical thinking depend upon knowledge, understanding, and experience.

3   The Uses of Content Analysis: Describing Characteristics of Communication

Perhaps more than any other research method available to social scientists and humanists, content analysis has been marked by a diversity of purpose, subject matter, and technique. We can illustrate something of this variety, as well as some approaches to general problems common to many kinds of investigations, through examination of some questions to which it has been applied, either alone or in conjunction with other methods of social research.

One disclaimer must be made explicit at the outset: this chapter and the next one are not intended to provide a comprehensive review of the entire content analysis literature. There is little to be gained by describing more than a small sample of the countless media inventories, trend analyses, or other such investigations which make up a substantial proportion, at least quantitatively, of the literature. Only a few studies of each class are described, and then rarely in more than a brief summary. Citations of other studies, keyed to the reference section at the end of the book, are used to supplement the review, but even this bibliography can encompass only a fraction of all content analysis research.* Although we have defined the scope of content analysis broadly, its application to some of the less frequently studied aspects of communication—handwriting, nonverbal communication, or content-free communication—will be excluded. The reader interested in these might turn to articles by Wolfson (1951), Ekman (1965), and Starkweather (1956).

This summary review is organized according to the categories depicted in Table 2-1. Research is initially divided according to major purpose: to describe the characteristics of content, to make inferences about the

---

* For research completed through 1958, a comprehensive bibliography may be found in Barcus' (1959) unpublished doctoral dissertation (a listing of some 1700 titles), available through the University Microfilms subsidiary of Xerox Corporation.

causes of content, and to make inferences about the effect of content. In this chapter we shall discuss only studies of the first type. They are classified according to question and purpose of the research:

What?

- To describe trends in communication content.
- To relate known characteristics of sources to messages they produce.
- To audit communication content against standards.

How?

- To analyze techniques of persuasion.
- To analyze style.

To Whom?

- To relate known attributes of the audience to messages produced for them.
- To describe patterns of communication.

CHARACTERISTICS OF CONTENT: WHAT?

Content analysis has been used most frequently for research problems in which the question can be answered *directly* from a description of the attributes of content. In such studies the investigator is in large part freed from problems of validity, except to the extent that validity is related to sampling and reliability; the content data serve as a direct answer to the research question, rather than as indicators from which characteristics of the sources or audience are to be inferred.

To Describe Trends in Communication Content

Interest in measuring national attitudes relevant to international politics has been an important stimulus to development of content analysis techniques for trend studies. One of the earliest systematic efforts at precise measurement of *intensity* as well as direction of statements was a study of attitudes likely to manifest themselves in foreign policies (Russell and Wright, 1933). One representative editorial statement was selected from each issue in a sample of Chinese and Japanese newspapers published during the Far Eastern crisis of 1930 to 1932. The relative intensity of attitudes expressed was judged by Thurstone's method of equal-appearing intervals, an 11-point scale on which the sixth point represents evaluatively neutral statements. The results were then plotted over time and related to developments in the Sino-Japanese conflict. The same techniques were later used to trace trends in American attitudes toward China and Japan after the outbreak of war between these nations in 1937 (Wright and Nelson, 1939).

After the outbreak of World War II, Lasswell (1941) suggested that a "world attention survey" be conducted by ongoing analyses of the world's press. The purpose of the survey was to supplement our knowledge of the international environment by describing changes and continuities in public attention. Content analysis of newspapers would reveal the relative prominence (frequency) and evaluation (pro or con) of selected political symbols, including the names of leaders, nations, policies, institutions, and the like. This idea subsequently led to the most extensive survey of political symbols undertaken to that time as one aspect of research on Revolution and Development of International Relations (RADIR). Theoretically the studies centered upon "political myths"—bodies of beliefs assumed to be true by large masses of people—as indicated by such "key symbols" as "democracy," "rights," "equality," and "freedom." The project was designed to test hypotheses relating to a "world revolution" by identifying and mapping trends in the diffusion or restriction of symbols expressing major values in modern politics, and by analyzing the factors which facilitate or retard their diffusion. Editorials from one "prestige" newspaper representing each of five countries—the United States, Great Britain, France, Germany, and the Soviet Union—were analyzed for the period 1890 to 1949 (Pool, 1952a). The choice of newspapers rather than other sources of political symbols was based on both theoretical and practical considerations (Lasswell, Lerner, and Pool, 1952, p. 17):

In many countries the head of state makes few public statements, and these may be almost purely ceremonial. Party platforms often go unrevised year after year. So far as pressure groups are concerned, there are great differences in importance from state to state, and the task of gathering such fugitive material is a vast research project. The published proceedings of legislative bodies are often scanty, or altogether lacking. All states are modern enough to publish newspapers, however, so that comparable channels can be used for comparative purposes. Further, we can be relatively sure of who controls and who reads the news. In nearly all states some papers are understood to be leading organs of the party in office and of the government. Where the party system is competitive, the principal organ of parties and factions can be identified. Even with the coming of radio and television, the daily paper continues to occupy an important position in the media (and newspaper content is more accessible to study than are broadcasts).

Editorials appearing on the first and fifteenth day of each month were coded for the presence of 416 key symbols. These included 206 geographical terms (countries, international organizations, and minority groups) and 210 major ideological and doctrinal symbols (democracy, equality, proletariat, communism, nazism, nationalism, fatherland, and the like) relating to world politics in the first half of the twentieth century. Each time a symbol appeared it was scored as present, and attitudes that were expressed toward the symbol—approval, disapproval, or neutrality— were also recorded. Findings were based on the *number of editorials* in which symbols appeared, not the frequency with which the symbol itself appeared. Thus whether the term "peace" occurred once or six times in an editorial, it was recorded only once.

Data from 19,553 editorials were used to trace changing foci of attention and attitude, as indexed by key symbols, for the 60-year period. Among the many findings which emerged from these studies are the following representative examples.* The modern international system can be characterized by two primary trends: proletarian doctrines are replacing traditional liberalism, and with the increasing threat of war there has been a corresponding growth in militarism and nationalism (Pool, 1952a, p. 84). Expression of hostility toward other nations is related to insecurity; editorials in the "prestige papers" of dominant nations are generally less hostile toward others than are those of insecure or unsatisfied nations (Pool, 1951, p. 62). Symbols of representative government appear less frequently where such institutions are an accepted part of the tradition than in those nations where they are disputed (Pool, 1952b, p. 72).†

Somewhat similar studies, following the Lasswellian tradition in analysis of political symbols, have examined trends in Soviet May Day slogans (Yakobson and Lasswell, 1949), symbols used by the Communist International (Leites, 1949), and response of Communist propaganda to defeat in elections and strikes (Leites and Pool, 1949).‡

Although the RADIR studies stand out as an important landmark in the history of content analysis, relatively few investigators were encouraged to follow in this tradition. The immense labor associated with surveys of this scope was the primary inhibiting factor. As Lasswell and his colleagues themselves prophesied at a time when the computer age was in its infancy, further work of the type they had undertaken would probably be dependent upon development and adaptation of computing machinery for content analysis (Lasswell, Lerner, and Pool, 1952, p. 63).

---

* The RADIR studies, long out of print, are being republished in a single volume of the M.I.T. Press *Symbols* series.

† The latter finding illustrates a point made earlier and to be discussed in more detail in Chapter 5: frequency counts may not always be useful as *direct* measures of values, attitudes, and the like. In the above example, high frequency of references to representative government were actually *inversely* related to the acceptance of such institutions.

‡ These studies appeared in *Language of Politics,* a revised edition (1965) of which has been republished by the M.I.T. Press *Symbols* series.

One important area of inquiry left relatively untouched by the RADIR studies is that of differences and trends in meaning, beyond approval or disapproval, of such symbols as "democracy" or "peace" (Stedman, 1951; Rainey, 1966). This is an area in which a variety of content analysis methods might usefully be applied to supplement traditional approaches to textual exegesis.

Trend surveys have not been confined to political research. Various types of literature have been examined to reveal trends in religious values. The hypothesis that the decade after 1929 saw the replacement of the "social gospel" with a theology of "social pessimism" was tested through content analysis of Protestant sermons. A sample of sermons appearing in *The Christian Century Pulpit* was coded for themes relating to faith, the nature of man, science, education, and social problems. When plotted over the period 1929 to 1940, the results clearly revealed the ascendancy of pessimism (Hamilton, 1942).

Forty-six inspirational best sellers published between 1875 and 1955 were analyzed in order to identify themes and trends in American popular religion (Schneider and Dornbusch, 1958). Constant themes during the period included the views that: religion promotes success, the individual can make changes beneficial to himself by religious means, and man is inherently good. A number of other themes increased substantially in the more recent literature: religion is linked to national political aspirations, and religion promotes mental and physical health. On the assumption that individuals are motivated to purchase books which coincide with their own values (a premise well supported by independent evidence), and in view of the best-seller status of this literature, inferences regarding trends in popular religious values can also be drawn from these findings.

These studies illustrate trend analyses in which a sample of relevant material is compared continuously over a period of time. In other cases the investigator may simply base his comparisons on two points in time. The validity of assertions identifying anti-intellectualism as an important American characteristic was tested by Hage (1959). Media analyzed were newspapers published during the 1828 Jackson-Adams and 1952 Eisenhower-Stevenson campaigns, in each of which an "intellectual" ran unsuccessfully against a military hero. Issues, candidates' traits, and their positions on the issues were recorded for two newspapers during each campaign. In 1952, the press was more prone to discuss the campaign in terms of issues rather than personalities. Comments about Stevenson's intellectualism were predominantly favorable, although significant differences appeared between the "quality press" (favorable) and the "mass press" (unfavorable). The press of 1828 dealt with Adams' intellectualism and Jackson's unreflective traits strictly along partisan lines. In 1952, on the other hand, all segments of the press—mass and quality, pro-Stevenson and pro-Eisenhower—commented favorably on the latter's nonintellectual attributes. The results suggested considerable anti-intellectualism in the press during both campaigns. Whether these findings depict two isolated instances of anti-intellectualism or a persisting aspect of American culture cannot, of course, be determined from a study limited to two electoral campaigns separated by a century and a quarter.*

A special application of the trend study is the analysis of professional publications to index changing foci of scholarly interest. Articles in the *American Journal of Sociology,* for instance, were classified by central topic to describe trends in the discipline (Becker, 1930, 1932; Shanas, 1945). As Berelson (1952, p. 34) has pointed out, however, studies based solely on a few professional journals may distort the actual focus of research interest. Changes in classification of articles on the borderline of two disciplines might affect the results of studies covering a long time span. An additional problem is that of editorial policy. For example, articles on social reform accounted for 13% of all space in the *American Journal of Sociology* at the turn of the century, but no such article was published after 1935 (Shanas, 1945). Does this finding indicate changing professional interests, a shift in editorial taste, or perhaps establishment of a separate journal for the specific purpose of presenting policy-oriented research?

Owing to a broader research design, a study of changing interests in American psychology over the half century prior to 1938 is less vulnerable to this criticism. Articles appearing every tenth year in 14 journals rated most "significant" by members of the profession were coded for 32 categories reflecting the type of subjects used, topics, techniques of investigation, and modes of conceptualization. Each article was thus listed under a number of categories, usually ranging from 5 to 15 (Allport and Bruner, 1940). Use of more than a single journal and coding into multiple categories minimized potential distortion.†

---

* Other trend analyses have examined various aspects of journalism, with heavy emphasis on American newspapers. Trends in general dailies, country weeklies, comics, and Presidential news have been described by Mott (1942), Taeuber (1932), Barcus (1961), and Cornwell (1959), respectively. Considerable research has also been devoted to surveys of other sources, including movies (Dale, 1935), radio (Albig, 1938), television (Smythe, 1953), propaganda (Kris and Leites, 1953), popular heroes in magazines (Lowenthal, 1944; Winick, 1963), child development materials (Ojemann *et al.,* 1948), political platforms (Namenwirth, in press), and presidential nomination acceptance speeches (Smith, Stone, and Glenn, 1966).

† Other studies have examined trends in fields as general as physics (Rainoff, 1929), journalism (Tannenbaum and Greenberg, 1961b; Webb and Salancik, 1965), and botany (Stevens, 1932), and as specific as content analysis (Barcus, 1959), and Freud's dream theory (Herma, Kris, and Shor, 1943).

Trend inventories have varied widely in purpose and quality. Such studies can be useful for identifying major changes across long periods of time, and are relatively easy to undertake; on the other hand, surveys depending on gross categories often conceal more information of interest than they reveal. According to one source, "The most valuable use of studies of content . . . is in noting trends and changes in content. Systems of classification may be inadequate and unstandardized; nevertheless, if a system is used consistently over a time period valuable facts may appear" (Albig, 1938, p. 349, quoted in Berelson, 1952, p. 29). This seems a dubious premise upon which to stake very much research effort. At least three serious objections can be stated against this view. The first is a point made several times earlier in this book. Analyses conducted in the hope that "something interesting may turn up" are certainly not hard to find in the content analysis literature, but not only is this an expensive way to do research, it is also more likely than not to yield insignificant results. Second, if categories are "inadequate," then, irrespective of the precision of measurement, the results will also be inadequate; a content analysis cannot be better than its categories. Finally, unstandardized categories rule out the possibility of valid comparison, because the analyst cannot be certain that his findings actually reflect changes in communication content rather than lack of uniformity in the categories used for coding them. It follows, therefore, that trends inferred from such findings are unlikely to be valid.

To Relate Known Characteristics of Sources to the Messages They Produce

Hypotheses of the form "sources with characteristic A are likely to produce messages with attributes w and x, whereas those with characteristic B are likely to produce messages of types y and z" have been tested in many disciplines and from various theoretical orientations. Sources may be two novelists, political candidates, or newspapers; different media, such as radio and magazines; or communication sources in two or more different countries.

The relationship between ideological orientation of media and the nature of their news reporting has been an area of considerable research interest in Europe and the United States. As early as 1910 Max Weber urged that (quoted in Krippendorff, 1966, p. 5):

. . . we will have to start measuring, plainly speaking, in a pedestrian way, with the scissors and the compass, how the contents of the newspapers has quantitatively shifted in the course of the last generation . . . between feuilleton and editorial, between editorial and news, between what is presented as news and what is no longer offered . . . and from the quantitative results we have to move toward qualitative ones. We have to

pursue the style of presentation of the paper, the way in which similar problems are treated inside and outside the papers, the apparent expression of emotions in the papers.

More recently Gerbner (1964, p. 495) has suggested that all analysis of the mass media must proceed with a sensitivity to the ideological framework of the media: "all editorial choice patterns in what and what not to make public (and in what proportion, with what emphasis, etc.) have an ideological basis and a political dimension rooted in the structural characteristics of the medium." The general proposition that "all news are views" was tested by an examination of nine French newspapers of the political left, the right, and the commercial press. Reporting of a nonpolitical incident—the shooting of a schoolboy by a teacher—was subjected to a propositional analysis. On the basis of significant differences among newspaper types the author concluded that "There is no fundamentally non-ideological, apolitical, nonpartisan news gathering and reporting system" (Gerbner, 1964, p. 508).

Interest in the role of the press in electoral campaigns has been strong, especially since the American presidential elections of 1936 and 1940, in which the vast majority of the press supported Alf Landon and Wendell Willkie, the two Republican nominees, in their losing campaigns against Franklin D. Roosevelt. Several studies have sought to determine whether editorial support is systematically related to other aspects of campaign coverage such as the amount of space devoted to stories about each candidate. Evidence from such investigations is mixed, depending largely upon which newspapers and elections are analyzed. Blumberg (1954) examined 35 American dailies during the 1952 campaign and found little evidence of bias in news coverage. This finding was supported by Markham and Stempel (1957). Studies of 15 "prestige" dailies during the 1960 and 1964 campaigns indicated that "as a group they gave the Democratic and Republican campaigns virtually equal amount of space in their news columns" (Stempel, 1961, p. 157; Stempel, 1965). On the other hand, Hage (1959) found a general anti-intellectual bias in press coverage during the 1952 election, and analyses of dailies in Florida and California revealed that endorsed political candidates received better news coverage (Kobre, 1953; Batlin, 1954). A similar finding emerged from a study of the British press, which concluded that, with the exception of *The Times:* "There could be no doubt in the reader's mind as to which side the different newspapers supported. News and comment were inextricably mixed in the 'news' reports and special articles" (Royal Commission on the Press, 1949, p. 359).

Studies of editorial bias have tended to rely upon measures of space allocated to opposing positions on controversial issues. A serious limitation of such investigations is that they tap only a single dimension of bias. Some rough equality of space allocation may be a necessary condition of unbiased coverage, but probably it is not sufficient. During the 1940 campaign the press and radio *focused* on Roosevelt by a margin of 3 to 2, but *favored* Willkie by better than 2 to 1 (Lazarsfeld, Berelson, and Gaudet, 1944, p. 117). The more subtle, and probably more important, methods of slanting news have received less attention than measures of space. One exception is an analysis of eight major daily newspapers during the 1952 campaign. Newspapers were rated on 18 indices, including size and tone of headline, placement of stories, number of biased remarks, number of pictures, and total column inches of stories on various pages. These measurements gave strong indication of systematic bias in favor of the endorsed candidate (Klein and Maccoby, 1954). These findings also introduce a point which we will consider in more detail in Chapter 5: different categories and types of measurement may yield substantially different results. Hence the analyst must be certain that the assumptions underlying the indicators he selects are warranted for the problem at hand.

Differential coverage of "civil rights" stories has also been related to various characteristics of newspapers, including geographical location, ownership (Negro, white), and political orientation. The findings have generally supported hypotheses of systematic quantitative and qualitative differences in news coverage (Broom and Reece, 1955; Carter, 1957; Breed, 1958).

A number of studies have sought to identify the correlates of strong news coverage. The hypothesis that local newspaper competition is related to more adequate news coverage has received some attention. A comparison of 97 newspapers revealed no significant difference in allocation of nonadvertising space related to the presence or absence of competition. A second test of 260 newspapers matched for circulation and other characteristics replicated the analysis, and the data again rejected the hypothesis (Nixon and Jones, 1956). Similar conclusions were reached by Willoughby (1955, p. 204). Adequacy of news coverage during the 1960 presidential campaign was related to various characteristics of newspapers in a survey of 90 dailies (Danielson and Adams, 1961). From this research a "news potential index" was developed which, on the basis of five newspaper attributes, predicts the adequacy of news coverage. According to the formula, a newspaper is rated as 1 or 0 for each of five attributes: weekly "news hole" of 2,500 inches or more, editorial staff of 75 or more, subscription to three or more news services, publication seven days a week, and morning publication. The adequacy of news coverage can be predicted from the number of these attributes which a newspaper possesses.

Studies comparing content across two or more mass media have been relatively infrequent. In this respect development of new modes of communication has had less impact on content analysis research than might be expected. This can be attributed in part to the problem of devising coding units, other than simple time and space measures, which can be compared. A strong bias toward analysis of the more easily accessible printed materials has also restricted comparative research, with the consequence that there are very few general statements that can be made about the mass media as a whole.

One example of a cross-medium study is Asheim's (1950) analysis of what happens to a book when it is adapted into a movie. An "index of deviation," based on the proportion of space devoted to main story lines and subplots in 24 books and movies, revealed that fidelity in adaptation ranged from 89% for *Pride and Prejudice* to 38% for *The House of Seven Gables.* Book and film endings were classified as "happy" or "unhappy;" in 21 cases the type of ending was accurately portrayed in the film although details of the action were altered in three of them. The study also revealed that chronological sequence was followed more closely in the film than in the book, and that the incidence of violence, brutality, and sadism was reduced in the film.

Mental health content of the mass media has been the subject of a number of comparative studies (Taylor, 1957; Nunnally, 1957; Gerbner and Tannenbaum, 1960). Space allocations differed considerably, broadcasting media (radio and television) carrying more relevant material than printed media (magazines and newspapers). However, the content of assertions about mental health was almost identical across all media. The three most frequently appearing themes were: the mentally ill look and act differently, mental health problems originate in environmental stresses, and the problem is a serious one (Taylor, 1957).

Documents produced by political action groups have frequently been analyzed. Comparative analysis of Communist publications was used to develop a model against which perceptions and experiences of former party members (determined by interviews) could be compared (Almond, 1954). The American business community (Lane, 1951; Bernstein, 1953), political parties (Benson, 1961; Namenwirth, in press), right-wing organizations (Wilcox, 1962; Abcarian and Stanage, 1965), and Washington lobbyists (McPherson, 1964) are among other groups whose publications have been examined.

Content analysis has also been employed with a variety of materials to discover international differences in the content of communication. A comparative study of newspapers in 17 countries during a seven-day period in March 1951 was conducted under auspices of UNESCO (Kayser, 1953).

The morning newspaper with the largest circulation in each country was analyzed for a period of time selected in advance of actual publication. Comparisons were made of both format and content: the front page, space allocation, origin of news, and coverage of specific events during the week. A supplementary analysis compared four "prestige" papers published in Moscow, Paris, London, and New York.*

An examination of 15 "prestige" newspapers published on November 2, 1956, during the dual crises in Hungary and Suez, revealed differences in coverage of these events which were ascribed to the degree of involvement in one event or the other, or to instrumental handling of the news. News of the Suez invasion crowded Hungary out of these newspapers; even in the West, "attention was so overwhelmingly on Suez that the full significance of what was happening in Hungary was never made clear" (Schramm, 1959, p. 138). A less comprehensive study compared Indian and German coverage of the concurrent crises on the Sino-Indian border and in Cuba during October, 1962 (Roat, 1963).

Cross-national content analyses have not been confined to printed media. Wolfenstein and Leites (1950), in a study of plot configurations of British, French, and American movies, found that British movies emphasized that danger lies in the nature of man himself, especially in his impulses of destructiveness; many of the themes of Shakespearean drama were preserved, although cloaked in a modern idiom. French movie plots revealed human wishes opposed by the nature of life itself which in the end defeats all, including the virtuous, and both old and young suffered inevitable disappointments in love. In American movies, hazards of life were found in the situation, rather than in the nature of the individual or life itself. Winning was stressed, although not always achieved easily, and disappointment in love was denied.

In a cross-national study of student attitudes about the future, Gillespie and Allport (1955) asked subjects to prepare their autobiographies for the second half of the twentieth century. Analysis revealed a number of common values, including travel and cultural aspirations, racial equality (except in the Afrikaaner sample of South Africans), a family frame of reference, the number of children desired and expected, attitudes toward child training, moral values, scientific curiosity, and occupations.

Two studies compared the literature and songs of youth groups in Nazi Germany and the United States. Youth literature in the two countries yielded 1000 expressions of various organizational goals (Lewin, 1947). Frequency count of major themes revealed that the German literature

---

* Other cross-national studies have compared aspects of the press in the Middle East (Abu-Lughod, 1962), Australia-New Zealand (Budd, 1964), the United States-Great Britain (Hart, 1965; 1966), and Soviet-controlled Berlin (Davison, 1947).

placed significantly greater stress on national loyalty, national identification, and determination, whereas American Boy Scout materials emphasized altruism, religion, and creativity. A parallel study of children's
songbooks yielded similar results (Sebald, 1962). German sources stressed
national loyalty, obedience, and heroic death, and paid less attention to
the beauty of nature, play, and Christianity. Content analysis of such
materials can reveal important international differences at a specified point
in time, but further inferences, unsupported by independent data, are
often open to question. A case in point is Sebald's generalization, based on
Nazi songbooks issued in 1940, but without a parallel analysis of
literature before or since the Hitler era, that the modal character of
Germans is basically authoritarian.*

To Audit Communication Content Against Standards

Historically a major impetus toward development of content analysis was a
concern for judging various types of literature against certain standards.
Dovring (1954) cites an interesting example of content analysis in
eighteenth century Sweden. Publication of a collection of 90 hymns, the
Songs of Zion, aroused concern among officials of the Lutheran state
church who feared that the hymns were adversely affecting public opinion.
Content analyses, based on the frequency with which certain themes
related to Christ appeared, led opponents of the hymns to conclude that
they threatened the doctrines of the established church. Content analysis
was also used by the other side in the controversy to show that many
words which were condemned when they appeared in the *Songs of Zion*
were praised when they appeared in other hymnals.

The more direct antecedents of content analysis may be found in
studies of the American press around the turn of this century, some of it
stimulated by concern over the spread of yellow journalism. Newspapers
were no less a target of "muckrakers" and reformers than many other
institutions during this era in American history. Three early "scientific"
studies of the New York press illustrate the nature of these investigations.
Speed (1893) undertook an analysis of four New York newspapers—the
Tribune, World, Times, and *Sun*—for the years 1881 and 1893. On the
basis of the number of column inches devoted to editorial, religious,
scientific, political, literary, gossip, scandals, sporting, fiction, music and
drama, crime and criminals, art, and historical news, he concluded that
there had been an unprecedented "sacrifice of quality for quantity" in

---

*Content analysis has also been used to examine cross-national or cross-cultural
differences in the content of television programming (Gardiner, 1962), magazines
(Ginglinger, 1955), textbooks (Walworth, 1938), folktales (Colby, Collier, and Postal,
1963); sermons (Parker, Barry, and Smythe, 1955), and magazine photographs
(Wayne, 1956).

these newspapers. In a similar analysis of the New York press, Tenney (1912) compared English, German, Italian, and Yiddish language newspapers on the amount of space devoted to political, economic, cultural, amusement, crime-accident, and personal-social news. Finding the press generally deficient, he suggested that newspapers be required, by law, to publish data regularly on the percentage of attention given to each subject matter category. Matthews (1910) studied a single New York daily newspaper. Over 10,000 items were coded into four categories: *trivial* (light, inconsequential matter), *demoralizing* ("all such items as when read will leave one's character not quite as clean as it was before reading"), *unwholesome* (of the same type as "demoralizing," but not necessarily injurious to character), and *worthwhile*. The analysis revealed that less than 40% of the items were of the last category.

Clearly these early studies of the press were almost wholly devoted to measuring space allocation for various subject matter categories; many of them have justly been criticized for subjective and arbitrary procedures. Interest in standards of the mass media has been sustained, however, and many serious technical problems of the early investigations have been resolved.

A more objective analysis of press performance was that of the *New York Times* by Lippmann and Merz (1920). As a test case they selected coverage of news items from Russia during and after the revolution (1917 to 1920). As a standard against which to measure the performance of the *Times,* their assessment included only Russian events which unquestionably occurred: failure of the July 1917 offensive in Galicia, overthrow of the Kerensky Provisional Government by the Bolsheviks in November, 1917; the Russian-German peace treaty of Brest-Litovsk in March, 1918, failure of the White Generals' (Kolchak, Denikin, and Yudenitch) campaigns against the Bolsheviks, and maintenance of power by the Bolsheviks through March, 1920. Analysis revealed that coverage of these events was inadequate and misleading: "In the large, the news about Russia is a case of seeing not what was, but what men wished to see . . . . The Russian policy of the editors of the *Times* profoundly and crassly influenced their news columns" (Lippmann and Merz, 1920, pp. 3, 42).

The standard of "social norms" was used in a study of goals and goal achievement as portrayed in television programs for child, adult, and mixed child-adult audiences (Larson, Gray, and Fortis, 1963). Each act by a character that was identifiably connected with a specific goal was coded. Goals were classified into categories such as power and prestige, property, self-preservation, affection, sentiments, and psychological goals. Means to achieve the goals were coded as socially approved (legal), or socially disapproved (nonlegal, violent, or escape). Results revealed that means with the *least* likelihood of success were those classified as socially approved. There was no essential difference in this respect between those programs viewed primarily by adults and those for younger audiences.

A study of three major American news magazines—*Time, Newsweek,* and *U.S. News & World Report*— against the standard of "responsibility in mass communication" indicated that the "neatly reconstructed picture of the world" they present is often biased, distorted, or factually false (Bagdikian, 1959). While apparently strong evidence of systematic bias was presented, the absence of explicit coding categories or sampling methods raises some questions about the findings. A rigorous study of the same news magazines during the period of the 1960 presidential nominating conventions revealed that Republican candidates as a group received only slightly more favorable treatment than their Democratic counterparts (Westley *et al.,* 1963.) But when the data were re-examined according to individual candidates, each magazine was found to have treated the conservative candidates (Richard Nixon and Lyndon Johnson) more favorably than the liberal ones (Nelson Rockefeller and John F. Kennedy).

An analysis of six types of bias (attribution bias, adjective bias, adverbial bias, contextual bias, outright opinion, and photographic bias) revealed that *Time* used each technique extensively to describe recent American Presidents. *Time's* presentation of Truman was totally negative, Eisenhower was depicted in an unambiguously favorable light, and only Kennedy was described in somewhat balanced terms (Merrill, 1965). "Repeated distortion and misinformation" were also discovered in public affairs articles in *Reader's Digest* (Christenson, 1964).

Walter Lippmann, who co-authored the study of bias in the *New York Times,* has himself been the subject of analysis (Weingast, 1950). His treatment of New Deal policies in his column "Today and Tomorrow" during the first six years of Roosevelt's administration revealed, despite Lippmann's reputation as a leading American liberal, an increasing opposition to the New Deal in general as well as to specific aspects of it. For the period 1932 to 1938, Lippmann's treatment of topics was as follows: Roosevelt (11% favorable, 38% neutral, 51% unfavorable), New Deal in general (9%, 20%, 70%), first Agricultural Adjustment Act (7%, 30%, 63%), National Industrial Recovery Act (5%, 11%, 84%), Tennessee Valley Authority (38%, 50%, 12%), National Labor Relations Act (0%, 0%, 100%), Social Security (25%, 45%, 30%), and wages-and-hours legislation (0%, 6%, 94%).

Ash (1948) examined 50 periodicals over a period of 10 months to determine whether the public was given a fair opportunity to learn both sides of the controversial Taft-Hartley Labor Act. The analysis uncovered almost unanimous support for the act; moreover, those few anti-Taft-Hartley items which did appear were largely confined to low-circulation periodicals. High-circulation news magazines failed to print any items opposing the act, and the general magazines were similarly one-sided. When item counts were adjusted for circulation, 55.7% of the material favored the act, 1.8% opposed it, the remainder being neutral. However, no attempt was made to test the relevance or justice of the arguments, pro and con.

Another aspect of distortion was studied by Cony, who tested the hypothesis that, "Newspapers emphasize conflict to the extent that reality is twisted out of shape and a false picture of society as a jungle is presented to the reader" (1953, p. 15). The data revealed conspicuous differences among a sample of five newspapers; but, although 1952 was a time of considerable conflict, a substantial amount of space (31% to 46%) was devoted to reporting cooperative behavior.

The most common weakness of studies using an *a priori* standard stems from the absence of a clearly defined basis for judgment, rather than from technical problems of applying content analysis to the data. What constitutes "adequacy" in the coverage of local news? Or, how close to "equal time or space" must the media come to be considered "fair?" It is doubtful whether unbiased reporting of every controversial situation calls for equal presentation or evaluation, as is sometimes assumed by indices of bias. Often the investigator's own values serve as the standard of comparison; by itself, this need not cast doubt on whatever findings emerge. The more serious problem is that frequent failure to define such terms explicitly makes it difficult to interpret findings. In his study of country weeklies, for example, Willey (1926, p. 111) concluded that, "The Connecticut weekly newspapers are deficient in the amount of local news material they print." Yet his data revealed that space allocation to local news ranged from 4% to 92% and more than half the newspapers devoted over 50% to local news.

One answer to the difficult problem of defining standards against which to audit sources is to make comparisons against other sources; i.e., general norms for classes of communicators are developed inductively. The investigator may then rank sources along one or more dimensions. This technique has been used to rate radio commentators (Budlong, 1952), and reporting of specific events by magazines, newspapers, radio, television, and wire services (Rosi, 1964; Klapper and Glock, 1949; Sussman, 1945; Lang and Lang, 1955; and Rucker, 1960). A more precise method, the technique of "successive approximations," was used to construct a "socialization-sensationalism" index. Six rough indicators were first applied to a large number of newspapers to identify those with highest scores on socialization *(Christian Science Monitor, Wall Street Journal)* and sensationalism *(New York Daily News, New York Daily Mirror).* Detailed analysis of these newspapers yielded a more precise scoring

TABLE 3-1   Incidence of occupations in various mass media

	Jones (1942) movies	Arnheim (1944) radio serials	Berelson and Salter (1946) magazine fiction — Type of character			Johns-Heine and Gerth (1949) magazine fiction — Published in the		Spiegelman et al. (1953a) comics — Type of character		Head (1954) television — Type of character		De Fleur (1964) television
			Americans	Anglo-Saxon and Nordics	Others	1920's	1930's	Sympathetic	Unsympathetic	Protagonist	Antagonist	
Upper Status												
Business-managerial	—	33%	—	—	—	31%	29%	—	—	10%	5%	4%
Professional	—	73%	—	—	—	24%	25%	—	—	10%	4%	16%
Others and unclassified	46%	40%	59%	29%	20%	—	—	8%	8%	—	—	1%
Middle Status												
Upper middle class	—	31%	—	—	—	—	—	29%	13%	—	—	—
Small business	—	—	—	—	—	—	—	—	—	—	—	7%
Clerical	—	—	—	—	—	—	—	—	—	—	—	7%
Skilled labor	—	19%	—	—	—	—	—	—	—	—	—	3%
Law enforcement	—	—	—	—	—	—	—	—	—	24%	1%	29%
Military	—	—	10%	19%	9%	—	—	—	—	7%	2%	5%
Lower middle class	—	—	—	—	—	—	—	31%	46%	—	—	—
Others and unclassified	32%	—	19%	23%	20%	19%	17%	—	—	—	—	1%
Lower Status												
Unskilled labor	—	—	—	—	—	—	—	—	—	—	—	8%
Servants	—	—	—	2%	—	—	—	—	—	—	—	6%
Criminals	—	—	1%	2%	—	—	1	32%	33%	7%	70%	—
Others and unclassified	17%	6%	11%	27%	36%	—	—	—	—	—	—	2%
Unclassified (housewives, etc.)	5%	65%	—	—	—	26%	29%	—	—	42%	18%	11%
Total	100%	*	100%	100%	100%	100%	100%	100%	100%	100%	100%	100%

*More than 100%; serials coded for number of settings in which different occupations appear.

system of 23 categories which, when applied to front page headlines, can be used to rate any newspaper (Kingsbury and Hart, 1937).

Finally, content data may be evaluated against *noncontent indices.* In their study of the incidence and portrayal of "majority" and "minority" (e.g., Jews, Negroes) Americans in popular fiction, Berelson and Salter (1946) used census data as a standard of "reality" against which the sources were judged. De Fleur (1964) investigated the portrayal of occupations to children on television. The incidence of characters appearing in 250 half-hour segments revealed considerable over-representation of professional occupations, and a concomitant under-representation of skilled labor, craftsmen, and related workers. Background settings, interaction, patterns, and characteristics of various occupations were compared with preferences stated by children on questionnaires. Little distortion was discovered iri the television portrayal of dominant-submissive interaction among occupations. But, when television portrayals were compared with census data for the viewing area, the authors concluded that "television presents *least often* and as *least desirable* (from the child's standpoint) those occupations in which its youngest viewers are most likely to find themselves later" (De Fleur, 1964, p. 70). Findings from similar studies of radio serials, magazine fiction, movies, and television are summarized in Table 3-1.

Expert opinion has served as a second type of noncontent standard against which to audit communication content. Questionnaire responses of professional psychiatrists and psychologists provided criteria against which conceptions of mental health problems of laymen and the mass media were compared (Nunnally, 1957). The study revealed that rather than providing a bridge between professional and public views, the printed and broadcasting media presented ideas about mental health which were even further removed from the experts than were those of the average person.

A set of Lasswellian symbols was divided by a panel of experts on American culture into those consistent with, and opposed to, the American creed. The content of five Negro newspapers was assessed against this standard. Over 5000 occurrences of relevant symbols were coded; only 3% of anti-American symbols were approved by the Negro press, and a similarly small proportion of symbols integral to the American creed were disapproved (Brooks, 1959).

A different approach was used to assess the adequacy of coverage of the National Coal Board press conference on December 22, 1947, by British newspapers. Background notes to the press included 33 major points of information about production, marketing, education, and the like. Nine newspapers were then analyzed to determine how many of these items were reported or commented upon editorially (Royal Commission on the Press, 1949, pp. 268-271). This method yielded precise results, but its use is probably limited to those events about which there can be little ambiguity as to "what happened."

CHARACTERISTICS OF CONTENT: HOW?

To Analyze Techniques of Persuasion

Content analysis usually focuses on the substance (the "what?" question) of messages. It has also been used to analyze form or style (the "how?" question). For the last three decades and particularly during World War II, considerable research has focused on propaganda, "the manipulation of symbols as a means of influencing attitudes on controversial matters" (Lasswell, 1942, p. 106). Often the purpose has been to infer intentions of communicators from propaganda content, a type of analysis to be discussed in Chapter 4. The remaining research has aimed at developing a theory of form, style, and structure of persuasive communication.

A pioneering study in this area was Lasswell's analysis of propaganda techniques during World War I, in which four major objectives of propaganda and appropriate techniques of appeal for each goal were identified: to mobilize hatred against the enemy, to preserve the friendship of allies, to preserve the friendship and, if possible, to procure the cooperation of neutrals, and to demoralize the enemy. Lasswell (1927, pp. 195-199) concluded that while all four themes were present in the propaganda of every nation, they were applied with varying degrees of success; much German propaganda turned out to "boomerang," partly owing to the lasting impression that Germany was the aggressor, partly because of the ineptness of the appeals. On the other hand, British propagandists were successful in picturing humanitarian war aims, and the French were able to portray the Germans in satanic terms, such as "Hun," and "Boche." More quantitative methods were used to examine the organization, media, techniques, and symbols of Communist propaganda in Chicago during the depression of the 1930's (Lasswell and Blumenstock, 1939). That the Lasswellian influence in propaganda studies continues to the present is evident in two recent books (Dovring, 1959; Barghoorn, 1964).

Several sets of categories for describing and analyzing propaganda have been proposed. One scheme, developed at the Institute of Propaganda Analysis, enumerates content (name calling, testimonial, bandwagon, etc.) and strategic (stalling, scapegoating, etc.) techniques which have been identified in propaganda (Lee, 1952, pp. 42-79, 210-234). A somewhat different set of categories emerged from a comparative study of British and German radio broadcasts to the United States during 1940 (Bruner,

1941). A tentative list identified nine dimensions for describing propaganda: dissolvent-unifying, negative-positive, temporal, personal-impersonal, stratified-homogeneous, authoritative-casual, colloquiality, immediate-remote, and repetitiousness.

"Value analysis," a set of categories for studying personality from written materials, was used to examine the propaganda style of Hitler and Roosevelt (White, 1949).* A number of similarities were found; both stressed traditional grandeur, and both often used black-white dichotomies. Hitler also appears to have used an indirect approach to the preparation of the German people for war by emphasizing the theme of persecution by outsiders. The same method and categories were found useful for distinguishing writings by political figures of various ideological persuasions: Khrushchev, Stalin, Hitler, Mussolini, Goldwater, Hoover, Churchill, Kennedy, and Franklin Roosevelt (Eckhardt, 1965), and for testing the "mirror-image" hypothesis in speeches by Kennedy and Khrushchev (Eckhardt and White, 1967).†

A study of the picture magazines *USSR* and *American Illustrated,* which are produced by the Soviet Union and the United States for readers of the other country, revealed how persuasive literature is often framed in the value context of the audience. Both the American and Soviet magazines placed greater emphasis on values often attributed to the other nation; i.e., *USSR* emphasized such aspects of Soviet life as industrial growth and a high standard of living, whereas *American Illustrated* stressed cultural and aesthetic interests of its citizens (Garver, 1961).

A different conception of propaganda, stressing omissions and selectivity in presentation of factual materials rather than use of demagogical tricks or misuse of logic, was tested in examining arguments in Swedish newspaper editorials relating to the acquisition of nuclear weapons (Ohlström, 1966).

Although the most pervasive form of persuasive communication—advertising—has received comparatively little attention from content analysts, research has not been limited to official governmental propaganda. For example, campaign biographies, a form of persuasive literature which appears on the American political scene quadrennially, have been analyzed. The basic theme, to fashion an image of the ideal citizen of the Republic, has remained the same since 1824. Moreover, "rival candidates appear in campaign biographies to be as alike as Tweedledum and Tweedledee" (Brown, 1960). Considerable research has also focused on

---

* For a detailed explanation of value analysis, a technique which is not limited to the study of propaganda materials, see White (1951).

† Techniques of other propagandists which have been examined by content analysis include Father Coughlin (Lee and Lee, 1939), and Gerald L. K. Smith (Janowitz, 1944).

public letters, such as those written to Congressmen (Wyant and Herzog, 1941); magazines (Sikorski, Roberts, and Paisley, 1967); newspapers in the United States (Foster and Friedrich, 1937; Toch, Deutsch, and Wilkins, 1960), the Soviet Union (Inkeles and Geiger, 1952, 1953), and Communist China (Wang, 1955); and to a magazine by radical right wingers (McEvoy, 1966).

Rosi (1964) employed both quantitative and qualitative techniques to examine the contribution of 50 periodicals and the *New York Times* to the debate on the cessation of nuclear testing during the period from 1954 to 1958. A more intensive analysis of the *Saturday Review, National Review, U.S. News and World Report,* and the *Bulletin of the Atomic Scientists* revealed certain similar patterns of persuasion. All but the *Bulletin* tended to judge the issue on only a single dimension, either national security *(National Review, U.S. News),* or humanitarian concerns *(Saturday Review).* All four minimized political methods of action, either because of a distrust of negotiation and an emphasis on military strength, or because of faith in nonpolitical means such as world opinion or moral regeneration. Finally, all but the *Bulletin* tended to speak in one-sided generalities, dealing with implications of a test ban in an oversimplified and doctrinaire manner. In this respect these periodicals dealt with the issue in a manner very similar to that of the mass-interest magazines.

The most evident weakness of propaganda analysis has been the absence of systematic research to relate categories of appeal, techniques, and dimensions (and combinations of these) to effects. What types of appeals are most effective? Under what circumstances? For which subject matter categories? For what types of audiences? One exception is a detailed investigation of Kate Smith's war bond drive during World War II. Content analysis was used to identify characteristics of her appeals which might be expected to elicit particular responses from the audience. The validity of inferences based on content data was then checked by interviewing the audience (Merton, 1946). Foster and Friedrich (1937) suggested that analysis of letters to the editor provides a continuing measure of the effects of propaganda. Although they provided evidence to support the validity of such an index, the idea does not appear to have been followed up with subsequent research. Thus, questions about how technique and content of appeals are related to effects have remained largely unanswered.*

To Analyze Style

Studies of style have differed widely in method and have ranged from investigations of the single author to analyses of an entire language. Word counts have yielded concordances of individual authors, including Yeats

---

* Other studies on the effects of communication are discussed in Chapter 4.

(Parrish and Painter, 1963) and Matthew Arnold (Parrish, 1959), and have been used to describe continuities and discontinuities in the Russian language (Josselson, 1953). Relative frequencies of various parts of speech (e.g., verb-noun-adjective ratios) have been used to describe constant and varying characteristics of poetic style across five centuries (Miles, 1951), and structural components have been used to examine folktales (Propp, 1958) and mythology (Levi-Strauss, 1964).

The relationship between attributes of style and commercial success in fiction has been the focus of several content analysis studies. Using both content and noncontent factors, Berreman (1940) found that best sellers and poor sellers could effectively be distinguished by the amount of publicity the book received. But the amount of publicity was less useful in making fine distinctions, as would be required to distinguish between top best sellers and books which sold only somewhat less well. He found that such content factors as setting, theme, and treatment of theme were important in cases of well-advertised books which sold poorly and those that sold well despite limited marketing effort. A somewhat similar study was later undertaken by Harvey (1953). After novels were coded for many content attributes, a statistical technique was used to discriminate the best and poorest selling novels. A formula using four factors—readability, central male character's level of emotion, his affectionate attitude toward other central characters, and a sentimental theme—yielded a formula which predicted sales success 82% of the time.

An interesting application of content analysis to style in a nonlexical medium is Gordon's (1952) study of art evaluation. A group of experts and laymen was asked to assess 10 paintings of various styles, content, color, and texture. Verbal criticisms of the judges were then coded to discover the determinants of excellence in painting. This research, based on a concrete task rather than abstract philosophizing about art, was found to yield less dependence upon nebulous qualities (e.g., "beauty," "taste," "feeling") than other techniques, and provided a precise and replicable method of analysis.

Generalizations about qualitative features of literature have been tested by content analysis.* Jane Austen's *Persuasion,* Emily Brontë's *Wuthering Heights,* and George Eliot's *Middlemarch* were examined to illustrate the thesis that "metaphorical language reveals to us the character of any imaginative work ... more tellingly perhaps than any other element" (Schorer, 1949, p. 560). Skinner analyzed the pattern of alliteration—the appearance of two or more syllables beginning with the same consonant near each other—in Shakespeare's sonnets. After adjustment for the number of occurrences deriving from repetition of the same

---

* See also literary studies by Raben (in press) and Sedelow and Sedelow (in press).

words, the frequency of alliteration did not differ significantly from chance, "so far as this aspect of poetry is concerned, Shakespeare might as well have drawn his words out of a hat" (Skinner, 1939, p. 191).

A related aspect of style, in which the character rather than the word or phrase serves as the recording unit, is letter redundancy. Paisley (1966) content analyzed 39 samples from English translations of Greek texts covering three time periods, 18 authors, and nine topics. Letter redundancy was shown to vary systematically with authorship, topic, structure, and time of composition.

Political rhetoric, especially that of American Presidents or Presidential candidates, has been a favorite subject for study. One approach is illustrated by a study of Woodrow Wilson's speeches (Runion, 1936). Categories were developed around grammatical aspects of discourse—sentence length, sentence structure, and figures of speech. Following in this tradition is Wolfarth's (1961) comparison of John F. Kennedy's inaugural address with those of all preceding Presidents. Much of the analysis is devoted to word and sentence counts, with considerably less attention to policy content or presentational style of the addresses.

Some of the more imaginative studies of rhetorical style have developed categories other than word counts, sentence length, and the like. A study of broadcast addresses by Eisenhower and Stevenson during the 1956 campaign related substantive and stylistic categories (Knepprath, 1962). Styles of the two candidates were compared for subject matter, form of reasoned discourse, use of "loaded terms," and types of motive appeals. Shepard (1956), examined various content attributes of Henry J. Taylor's radio talks for General Motors. The issues and symbols which Taylor discussed were identified, and his treatment of them was coded as favorable, neutral, or unfavorable. Assertions were further coded as factual or interpretive and for the type of evidence presented: statistics, examples and comparisons, analogies and figurative language, testimony, or none. The data revealed that Taylor's discussion centered largely on controversial issues in a manner favorable (90%) to Republican and conservative policies and unfavorable (88%) to those of Democrats and liberals, with heavy reliance upon unsupported assertions.

An interesting analysis of political rhetoric is found in a study of the 1960 presidential campaign designed to test the assertion that in their televised debates John Kennedy and Richard Nixon "made clearer statements of their positions and offered more reasoning and evidence to support their positions than they did in other campaign situations" (Ellsworth, 1965, p. 794). Statements made during the four debates and four other campaign addresses—the acceptance and farm speeches of both candidates—were coded. The data clearly revealed a higher incidence of analytic, evidential, and declarative content during the televised debates

(52% to 74%) than during the other addresses (8% to 28%). Further analysis of the data also revealed other interesting findings. When the debates as a whole were compared with closing statements, at which time no rebuttal by the opponent was possible, the latter were found to include significantly less "rational" content; i.e., the prospect of "imminent rebuttal" appears to have contributed to a higher proportion of reasoned argument.

A similar technique of coding was used to test the hypothesis that ideological distance between candidates increases the amount of policy discussion in campaign addresses (Ellsworth, 1967). Twenty speeches from the 1960 and 1964 campaigns were coded for the relative frequency of analytic, evidential, and declaratory themes. Although candidates in 1964—Lyndon Johnson and Barry Goldwater—were assumed to be farther apart ideologically than were Kennedy and Nixon four years earlier, the data revealed no significant difference in the amount of policy content. Without necessarily disproving White's (1965) contention that the 1964 election was more heavily issue oriented than that in 1960, the findings indicated that ideological differences did not produce heightened policy content in at least one form of political communication—the campaign speech. Reanalysis of the data did, however, indicate that the ideological content of political rhetoric—defined as statements regarding "the nature or character of man, society, government, or the relationship between them"—was significantly higher in 1964 (33.5%) than in 1960 (22.1%).

A quite different analysis of style is found in Horton's (1957) study of the dialog of courtship in popular songs. The lyrics of over 80% of the popular songs published in 1955 were found to fit into a series of "acts" depicting the course of romance: Prologue (wishing and dreaming), Act I (courtship), Act II (the honeymoon), Act III (the downward course of love), and Act IV (all alone).

CHARACTERISTICS OF CONTENT: TO WHOM?

To Relate Known Attributes of the Audience to Messages Produced for Them

Studies to relate audience attributes to message content are often undertaken with a view to testing some form of the general proposition that communicators tend to cast their messages in the idiom of the intended audience. They have also tended to center on messages produced to change attitudes.

Two previously cited studies demonstrated that John Foster Dulles effectively identified the distinguishing characteristics of his audience and directed his political appeals to those attributes. Both during his efforts on behalf of the Japanese Peace Treaty of 1951 (Cohen, 1957) and during his later tenure as Secretary of State (Holsti, 1962, pp. 150-154, 183-187), the content of Dulles' rhetoric was guided in part by the nature of those to whom his appeals were addressed.

An examination of two mass-circulation magazines, *Life* and *Ebony,* supported the hypothesis that differences in advertising are based on the socio-economic levels of the two audiences (Berkman, 1963). When the offered product or service was predicated on the Negro's present lower status, the advertising was in a form appropriate to that status. On the other hand, when the advertised items reflected the status to which the Negro was thought to aspire, there was little essential difference in the two magazines, except for the substitution of Negro models in *Ebony,* two-thirds of the advertisers selling to middle class markets used identical ads in the two magazines.

Albrecht (1956) analyzed short stories in large circulation magazines with lower *(True Story, True Confessions),* middle *(American, Saturday Evening Post),* and upper *(Atlantic, New Yorker)* status readers, recording the distribution and evaluation of 10 "family values." To avoid the assumption that values found in popular fiction necessarily reflect those most widely held in a society, the investigator used an independent source—data in a sociology journal—as his source of categories. These included values relating to life goals, affection, family size, sex, happiness, monogamy, divorce, division of labor, status, and child rearing. Stories produced for each status level strongly supported American family norms (as revealed by the sociological data). The degree of approval of some specific values differed significantly from level to level, however; middle level stories conformed most closely to basic family norms, thereby supporting the general view that American values tend to be middle-class values. The data also indicated that stories produced for the lower class were most conservative in attitude and those in upper-class magazines were most liberal with respect to family values.

Interpretations of findings relating audience attributes to communication content are generally of three basic types: that authors *write differently* for dissimilar audiences, that the literature *reflects* basic value differences of the audiences, or that such materials *shape* the values and predispositions of the audience. These are not mutually exclusive aspects of the communication process, but rather, represent three types of inferences which have been drawn from content data. The first interpretation presents the fewest problems of validity and can be made directly from attributes of the content. The second explanation is a variation of the theme, often debated with respect to the mass media, that producers of communication are only giving audiences "what they want." This may or may not be true, and generally can be confirmed only by means other than content analysis. That is, this type of explanation is no longer concerned only with the "what?" or "how?" questions, rather, it is directed at the causes of communication—the "why?" question. As indicated earlier, such inferences require either direct or indirect confirmation with independent data. The third interpretation is concerned with the effects of communication and it, too, is tenuous unless supported by data other than the description of the content.

To Describe Patterns of Communication

Content analysis has on occasion been used in studies of a sociometric nature. A central problem in sociometry concerns the patterns and content of communication between individuals or groups, including such questions as who communicates what with whom, through what channels? The analyst may also be interested in the effects of situational or structural changes on these aspects of communication.

Several techniques for scoring verbal interaction among group members have been developed. *Interaction process analysis* uses 12 content categories for classifying responses in six problem areas: communication, evaluation, control, decision, tension reduction, and reintegration (Bales, 1950). *Sign process analysis* is another technique for systematically recording what is said in the course of group interaction. The scoring scheme abstracts and records the distribution of positive, negative, and neutral assertions about objects, which are grouped into subsets according to locus (internal or external), sex, and status (Mills, 1964, p. 103). The Leary (1957, p. 65) content analysis approach identifies eight interpersonal processes: managerial-autocratic, competitive-narcissistic, aggressive-sadistic, rebellious-distrustful, self-effacing-masochistic, docile-dependent, cooperative-overconventional, and responsible-hypernormal. Use of the Bales, Mills, and Leary techniques is not limited to descriptive studies of communication patterns. They have also been used to draw inferences about communicators; e.g., the Leary system was developed for diagnosis of personality.

Content analysis studies of communication patterns have also been undertaken at other levels. Analysis of documents written by leaders of the Dual Alliance and Triple Entente nations during the summer of 1914 indicated that as war approached, there was a significant increase in messages exchanged within alliances and decrease in intercoalition communication, with concomitant changes in the content of messages (Holsti, 1965b). The Leary scoring system was used in an analysis of messages produced in 17 "Inter-Nation Simulations." The data revealed that after all members of an alliance had obtained nuclear weapons, the modal pattern of communication changed from a "wheel" configuration to an "all channels" pattern; at the same time expressions of hostility in interalliance messages decreased significantly (Brody, 1963). A combination of these two approaches may be found in a study comparing patterns and content of messages in simulation and historical data (Zinnes, 1966).

CONCLUSION

By far the greatest number of studies in the content analysis literature is undertaken with a view to describing the content of some set or sets of communications. A small sample of this literature has been reviewed in this chapter to illustrate the broad range of problems to which this method has been applied. Such research presents the fewest problems of inference because validity does not require comparison with data outside those under analysis; the research question can be answered directly from a description of communication content.

Yet it would be a mistake to think that the investigator undertaking a description of communication content can merely assume the validity of his findings or that he is free, in designing and executing his research design, from making decisions which may significantly affect their validity. Lack of proper attention to any of several problems may vitiate the findings of an otherwise carefully designed study. These include careful formulation of the question in theoretical terms prior to coding and analysis so that the interpretation process is not reduced to finding some explanation to fit the data; preparation of a sampling design that reduces the universe of relevant data to manageable proportions without introducing biases which preclude valid generalizations from the sample back to the universe; construction of categories which meet both the theoretical requirements of the problem at hand and the general canons of category construction; and precise operational definition of categories so that coding can be done with an acceptable level of reliability. The first of these is a restatement of the now familiar warning against fishing expedition research. The issues of categories, sampling, and reliability are basic to any systematic research; they will be considered in greater detail in Chapters 5 and 6.

4 The Uses of Content Analysis: Making Inferences About the Causes and Effects of Communication

THE ANTECEDENTS OF CONTENT: WHY?

Among the most interesting and challenging research problems are those about the causes and effects of communication. What motives, values, beliefs, and attitudes are revealed in a person's writing or speech? What can we learn about a culture by examining documentary evidence? What stylistic idiosyncrasies are unique to a particular author? What is the relationship between exposure to information and cognitive or attitudinal changes? These are but a few of the questions to which content analysis has frequently been applied.

Many definitions of content analysis explicitly exclude its use for purposes of inferring the antecedents or causes of content. Nevertheless, such inferences often have been drawn from content data. One major goal of propaganda analysis, for example, has been to make inferences about values, intentions, and strategy of communicators. As indicated earlier, research on the pragmatic dimension of communication has become a major aspect of content analysis studies. The problem, then, is no longer whether content analysts *should* make inferences concerning the cause of communication, but rather, given the trend of research, what steps the investigator can take to enhance confidence in the validity of his inferences. Studies selected for review in this chapter were chosen in part to illustrate a variety of research applications and in part to examine alternative approaches to the problem of validation. As in the previous chapter, studies are organized according to the categories in Table 2-1:

Why?
- To secure political and military intelligence.
- To analyze psychological traits of individuals.
- To infer aspects of culture and cultural change.

Who?
 . To determine authorship.

With What Effect?
 . To measure readability.

 . To analyze the flow of information.

 . To assess responses to communication.

To Secure Political and Military Intelligence

An important impetus to the development of content analysis was a large scale propaganda research effort during World War II. Social scientists, many of whom made significant theoretical and methodological contributions to content analysis, were engaged by the Federal Communications Commission, Library of Congress, and Justice Department to study these materials.

The most difficult problem, because of the constraints within which the propaganda analyst operates, is that of establishing criteria for inference. The FCC used both *direct* and *indirect* techniques. The first method operates from a *representational* model of communication; i.e., the investigator assumes that words in the message are valid indicators of intentions, irrespective of circumstance. Inferences regarding intentions, expectations, and situational factors are drawn *directly* from attributes of propaganda, based on a past correlation of conditions or events and content characteristics. The direct method is illustrated by a study to determine the degree of collaboration between German and Italian propaganda agencies. Because the content of German and Italian broadcasts were consistently different, analysts concluded that there was no collaboration between the two countries. This inference was proved correct by evidence which became available after the end of the war (Berelson and De Grazia, 1947).

The single step approach to propaganda analysis has been criticized for two deficiencies: past regularities are often based on a very few cases, and the method is insensitive to changes in propaganda strategy, which may render past correlations invalid.

An *instrumental* model of communication, in which it is assumed that the important aspect of the message consists in what it conveys, given context and circumstances, underlies the indirect method of inference.* The initial step in the indirect method is to establish the propaganda goal or strategy underlying the characteristics of content. A series of

---

* For a further discussion of the representational and instrumental models, see Pool (1959) and Mitchell (1967).

interconnected causal imputations are derived from this point (George, 1959a, p. 41):

Situa-   Elite   Elite   Elite   Propa-
tional ◄──── esti- ◄──── expec- ◄──── inten- ◄──── ganda ◄── Content
factor   mate   tation   tion or   strat-
                                       policy   egy

In the indirect method, then, the process of inference is broken up into a number of smaller steps. The relationship of the two methods of inference to one another is summarized by George (1959a, p. 43):

It is [recommended], first, that the direct approach be utilized in hypothesis formation for whatever it is worth (which depends upon the number and quality of the tentative, incompletely confirmed one-to-one correlations that are available) and that the indirect method be utilized in the assessment, or testing, of the inferential hunches derived from the direct approach. Second, it is recommended that such transitions from the direct to the indirect approach be made quite deliberately, in full awareness that the indirect method requires logic-of-the-situation reasoning and the use of generalizations other than the one-to-one type of correlation between a content indicator and an aspect of the elite's political behavior or situational milieu.

Despite many difficulties facing the analysts, documentary material on the Nazi conduct of the war indicated that FCC inferences were accurate in an impressive number of cases. For a two-month period (March-April, 1943), 101 out of 119 inferences made by the German section were scored as correct. Of methodological interest is the finding that frequency and nonfrequency indicators were about equally successful (George, 1959a, pp. 264-266).

To Analyze Psychological Traits of Individuals

It is a widely held belief among social scientists and humanists that symbolic behavior of the individual can provide important psychological data about personality, values, beliefs, intentions, and other characteristics of the communicator. Personal documents—defined by Gordon Allport (1942, p. xii) as "any self-revealing record that intentionally or unintentionally yields information regarding the structure, dynamics, and functioning of the author's mental life"—may take many forms, ranging from a diary or intimate letters to autobiographies and speeches addressed to a wide audience. The motives for producing personal documents may vary from psychotherapy to hopes of literary fame. Personal documents may also be produced specifically for research purposes. To obtain data for testing five hypotheses about the effects of social catastrophe, Allport,

Bruner, and Jandorf (1953) held a prize competition for the best essay on "My Life in Germany Before and After January 30, 1933," the date Hitler and the Nazis came to power. The competition drew over 200 responses averaging more than 100 pages in length. Finally, investigators' purposes in analyzing personal documents have differed widely despite the common goal of making inferences about the communicator.

Written materials have been content analyzed to infer personality traits of their authors. The letters of an Irish woman, Jenny Gove Masterson, were subjected to *personal structure analysis,* a system developed to aid the clinician "as a supplement to his more or less brilliant insight, a technique offering evaluation and analysis which will have the virtue of objectivity and will also reveal aspects of the material that may have eluded his scrutiny" (Baldwin, 1942, p. 163).* The procedure was grounded on the assumptions that frequency of an item in the case material is a measure of its importance in the personality. From a table of frequencies and correspondences, three well-integrated but independent ideational clusters were isolated. These revolved around Jenny's attitudes toward self and son, jobs, and death. Baldwin's study has been replicated using a technique of computer analysis (Paige, 1966).

Although critical of Baldwin's statistical analysis, Andrews and Muhlhan (1943) employed a modified version of personal structure analysis to study congruent idea patterns in the personal diary of a young girl. As in Baldwin's study, independent checks were used to test the validity of content analysis data, with satisfactory results. These studies are of methodological and theoretical as well as substantive interest; they are among the first in which inferences were drawn not only from frequency counts but also from associational structures of the communicator, as measured by the conjunction or clustering of two or more symbols. The method of *contingency analysis* employed in both of these studies has been further developed by Osgood (1959).†

In the previously cited study of the effects of social catastrophe on personality (Allport, Bruner, and Jandorf, 1953), intensive analysis of 90 life histories indicated that: individuals are unable to realize the imminence of catastrophe, catastrophe does not produce radical changes in personality, attitudes swing away from the middle of the road toward both extremes in crisis, aggression is not the most natural response to frustration, and even Nazis engaged in persecution occasionally engaged in acts of kindness.

A number of categories have been used to analyze themes, plots, and characters of novels to infer psychological traits of their authors. As in

---

* The text of these letters may be found in Allport (1946).

† For a further discussion of contingency analysis, see Chapter 5.

other studies of this type, the analyst assumes that key psychological traits of the writer must manifest themselves in his writing. Novels by D. H. Lawrence (McCurdy, 1939), the Brontë sisters (McCurdy, 1947), Charles Kingsley (Deutsch, 1947), Dostoyevsky (Kanzer, 1948), and Knut Hamsun (Lowenthal, 1949) have been analyzed, as have Shakespeare's plays (McCurdy, 1953).

Unlike descriptive studies of literary style, such as those discussed earlier, the validity of inferences about psychological traits of authors cannot be established merely by developing adequate analytic categories. A number of methods have been used to validate content data. Investigation of the author's biography may provide at least a partial check on the validity of inferences drawn from the data; i.e., are events and experiences in the writer's life consistent with psychological inferences drawn from content data? This method was applied in the studies of the Brontës, Dostoyevsky, Lawrence, and Shakespeare.

An interesting variation of the validity problem, validation by prediction, is illustrated in Lowenthal's 1937 study of Knut Hamsun. Hamsun's novels revealed themes consistent with fascism: stress on race and natural community, pantheism, and reduction of women to reproductive functions. From these data Lowenthal concluded that Hamsun was intrinsically a fascist, a conclusion borne out a few years later by Hamsun's collaboration with the Nazis during World War II (Lowenthal, 1949).

Investigations of this nature have not been limited to fictional materials. A study of Richard Wright's autobiography, *Black Boy,* was described earlier to illustrate the point that content analysis of documentary materials may reveal information that would have escaped even the skilled analyst using more impressionistic techniques (White, 1947). Quite different kinds of documents, Justice Robert Jackson's legal opinions, were analyzed and related to other aspects of his behavior in an effort to reconstruct continuities and changes in his legal philosophy (Schubert, 1965). Several hypotheses derived from theories of attitude change were tested by an analysis of John Foster Dulles' statements about the Soviet Union. Data derived from over 400 speeches, press conferences, interviews, congressional hearings, statements, and letters supported the general hypothesis that Dulles consistently interpreted new information about Soviet policies, intentions, and capabilities in a manner consistent with his beliefs about the fundamental nature of the Soviet system (Holsti, 1967).

Political rhetoric has been analyzed to infer personality traits of the speaker from logical and cognitive characteristics of his verbal production (Shneidman, 1963). Theoretical bases of this approach are the premises that all humans engage in thinking or reasoning, that there are many styles of reasoning (not only those that follow Aristotelian logic), and that from

TABLE 4-1

*Idiosyncrasies of reasoning and cognitive
maneuvers in the rhetoric of John F. Kennedy,
Richard M. Nixon, and Nikita Khrushchev*

Idiosyncrasies of reasoning	Kennedy	Nixon	Khrushchev
Irrelevant premise	8.7%	4.9%	2.2%
Argumentum ad populum	3.4	12.0	22.6
Complex question	0.0	1.9	21.5
Derogation	0.9	4.9	11.8
Stranded predicate	6.6	7.1	5.4
Truth-type confusion	2.2	6.4	0.0
Cognitive Maneuvers	Kennedy	Nixon	Khrushchev
To enlarge or elaborate the preceding	7.9%	6.0%	0.6%
To smuggle debatable point into alien context	5.8	8.4	0.0
To be irrelevant	7.3	9.6	16.8
To allege but not substantiate	4.4	6.3	4.6
To introduce new notion	0.0	0.0	2.3

the idiosyncratic characteristics of a person's logical processes one can infer other attributes of that individual.

The text is first coded into two category sets. *Idiosyncrasies of reasoning* include 32 categories grouped under five headings: idiosyncrasies of relevance, idiosyncrasies of meaning, arguments containing suppressed premises or conclusions, idiosyncrasies of logical structure, and idiosyncrasies of logical interrelations. *Cognitive maneuvers* consist of 65 styles of thought development, e.g., to switch from normative to descriptive mode, or to render another's argument weaker or stronger by paraphrase.

To illustrate the method, Shneidman (1961; 1963) examined the logical styles of Kennedy and Nixon on their first two television debates, and that of Khrushchev in speeches delivered after the collapse of the Paris "Summit" conference and at the United Nations. A partial comparison of "idiosyncrasies of reasoning" and "cognitive maneuvers" in the rhetoric of Kennedy, Nixon, and Khrushchev appears in Table 4-1.

The second step in the analysis is to construct, for each idiosyncrasy of reasoning, the logical conditions under which the idiosyncrasy is controverted or cancelled or, to use the author's term, *contralogic*.

TABLE 4-2

Illustrations of method of annulling (or controverting) logical idiosyncrasies

Idiologic. Samples of specific ways of thinking, in terms of idiosyncrasies of logic	Contralogic. Logical conditions under which the logical idiosyncrasy (column 1) is controverted or annulled	Psychologic. Psychological state consistent with the logical condition (2) which would annul the idiosyncrasy (1)
Example from Bleuler, von Domarus and Ariety: "Switzerland loves freedom; I love freedom; therefore I am Switzerland." Fallacy: identification in terms of attributes of the predicate (or undistributed middle).	If one supplies the implicit premise that Switzerland is the only member of the class of freedom lovers (and if I loved freedom, then it would follow, without logical error, that I would have to be Switzerland.	The reasoning reflects a psychological state in which the range of attention is constricted and narrowed (to one member of a class). Psychological symptoms: intense concentration, oblivion to ordinary stimuli, hypesthesia, acute withdrawal, and at its extreme, catatonia.
Example from Binswanger's "The Case of Ellen West." At 16 her motto is "Aut Caesar aut nihil" (Either the greatest or nothing). Before her death she says "If I cannot remain young, beautiful, and then, then rather—nothingness." Fallacy: dichotomization.	If one supplies the implicit assumption that the aspects of the universe under discussion are organized in a binary manner, then it follows logically that the alternative to leading a perfect *life* is death.	The reasoning reflects a psychological state in which the basic identifications are confused, the basic attitudes toward self-control are ambivalent, and there is a general polarized approach to concepts and people, with unhappy vacillations between the extremes of the dichotomized polarities. Psychological symptoms: obsessions, abulia, fixed ideas, anxiety, general impotence, rumination, suicide.
Example from Wertheimer: Question to the young Gauss: "What is the sum of $1+2+3+4+5+6+7+8+9+10$?" Response: correct answer (55) in amazingly short time. Fallacy: none.	One can do the task correctly and quickly if one sees (makes the assumption) that (a) there are pairs of numbers ($1 + 10$, $2 + 9$, etc.) each of which totals 11; (b) there are 5 such pairs; (c) 5 times 11 equals 55. The principle is represented by the formula: $n + 1 \times n/2$	The reasoning reflects a psychological state in which there is a high intelligence, active curiosity, open mind, freedom to explore intellectually, inquiring mind that is original but not destructive, freedom from fear of teacher (or authority generally? Of father?) The psychological label for this state is "genius."

Inferences regarding psychological characteristics of the communicator are
then drawn from the contralogic as illustrated in Table 4-2 (Shneidman,
1961, p. 22; see also the comprehensive coding manual which has been
prepared by Shneidman, 1966).

Shneidman's inferences regarding the personalities of Kennedy, Nixon,
and Khrushchev appear to have considerable face validity. For example,
Khrushchev is characterized in these terms (1961, pp. 61-62):

*He feels that others are prone to misunderstand his position and yet he
desires acceptance and will even sacrifice other needs or ends to achieve it.
He is moody and needful of approval. But with his pessimism about
resolving differences, he enjoys conflict and struggle, as much for its own
sake as a means to an end . . . He trusts his own instinct, his "natural
feel" for things. He is painstaking in certain areas, but in general is
impatient and suspicious of detail or subtlety.*

Pending considerable further research, the psychological correlates of
logical styles are only working hypotheses. Nevertheless, as a method of
studying style, this technique represents a substantially more sophisticated
approach than earlier attempts to analyze political discourse through
content analysis (Hayworth, 1930; Runion, 1936; McDiarmid, 1937).

The utility of content analysis in psychiatry stems from the view that
"psychiatric disorders, regardless of their etiology, are ultimately mani-
fested as disorders of social communication" (Jaffe, 1966, p. 689). Sound
recording of psychotherapeutic interviews has opened an entirely new
field, and a vast source of personal documents for analysis. Much of this
research has been directed toward developing and validating measures for
diagnosis, and for evaluation of psychotherapy. A partial listing of such
indices follows.

The *type-token ratio* (TTR), measures variability in the communicator's working vocabulary. A score is based on the number of different
words found in samples of standard length: 100, 200, 500, or 1000 words
(Johnson, 1944). The hypothesis that speech variability increases with
successful therapy has generally been supported. A test of 12 schizophrenics and 12 college freshmen revealed that the mean TTR for the
schizophrenic patients was significantly lower; also, the stability of their
TTR scores in successive samples was significantly lower than that of the
college freshmen (Mann, 1944; Fairbanks, 1944). In addition, the language
of the patients was characterized by a more negative tone, preoccupation
with the past, and more frequent self-references. Roshal (1953) tested the
hypothesis that language variability, as measured by TTR scores for both
100- and 200-word samples, is related to adjustment. Difference in TTR's
between the first and final interview were significantly higher for the
group in which therapy was judged to be more successful using both

measures. Further clinical applications of the TTR are described in Gottschalk (1961).

The *adjective-verb ratio* scores the number of adjectives per 100 verbs (Boder, 1940). This measure has been found to differentiate the language structure of "normal" subjects from that of schizophrenics. Normal subjects have more adjectives per verb, as well as more adjectives per noun (Mann, 1944).

The *discomfort-relief quotient* (DRQ), derived from learning theory, measures the amount of drive borne by the patient (Dollard and Mowrer, 1947). The DRQ is computed by dividing the number of discomfort (drive) words by the total number of discomfort and comfort (relief) words. Tests with the DRQ have produced rather mixed results. In some cases it has been significantly correlated with measures such as palmar sweating, but in others no relationship with success in therapy was noted. A comparison of DRQ ratings with a scoring system to measure motivation and conflict found that the latter index recorded changes in therapeutic progress, whereas the DRQ ratio did not change (Murray, Auld, and White, 1954).

The *positive-negative-ambivalent quotient* (PNAvQ) resembles the DRQ except that, unlike the DRQ, only the patient's self-evaluations are scored (Raimy, 1948). DRQ and PNAvQ scores were computed for 17 interviews, with strong evidence that the two scores are highly correlated (Kauffman and Raimy, 1949). However, this finding was not confirmed by a second study.

The hypothesis that there is a positive correlation between the extent to which an individual expresses acceptance of and respect for himself and the degree to which he expresses these feelings toward others has been investigated (although not with the PNAvQ). Although the samples studied were small (10 subjects), in both cases the data supported the hypothesis (Sheerer, 1949; Stock, 1949).

A measure of *defensiveness* was developed on the premise that defensiveness follows perceptions of threat, defined as an experience perceived to be inconsistent with a value or concept of self or the environment (Haigh, 1949, p. 181). A defensive reaction is one in which perceptions are distorted to reduce awareness of perceived incongruence. It is inferred from such patient responses as denials, rationalizations, and projections.

Scales for thematic analysis of *hostility* and *anxiety* found in verbal samples have been developed. One is a weighted scale for measuring three types of hostility classified on the basis of direction—outward, ambivalent, and inward (Gottschalk, Gleser, and Springer, 1963). A second scale is based on a system of weighted scoring for six categories of anxiety—death, mutilation, separation, guilt, shame, and nonspecific anxiety (Gleser, Gottschalk, and Springer, 1961).

A measure of *speech disturbance* has been found to correlate significantly with anxiety and conflict in therapeutic interviews. The ratio is calculated by dividing the number of speech disturbances by the number of words in the sample (Mahl, 1959).

On the theory that "motivation and psychological conflict play significant roles in shaping and distorting language responses," a general approach to the study of normal and pathological speech by word associations has been developed ((Laffal, 1965, p. x). The subject's entire vocabulary (rather than only certain types of words, as in the DQR, PNAvQ, or adjective-verb ratio), is coded into 114 categories for which extensive definitions and scoring rules are presented.*

Content analysis research in psychotherapy has yielded rather mixed results. In some cases, contradictory findings have been obtained using the same measure with different samples of subjects. In others the small sample of subjects has tended to raise questions about the generality of findings. The primary difficulty has often rested not with the analytical scheme for scoring responses, but with the absence of clearly defined criteria of "success" (Auld and Murray, 1955, p. 389). This is a restatement of the recurring problem in using content data to make inferences about communicators and audiences: content data are not self-validating and clear measures of the dependent variables that they are intended to index are often lacking.

Another problem is that the proliferation of content analytic studies has not been matched by efforts to replicate or integrate methods and findings. The author of the most recent general review of such research concluded that (Marsden, 1965, p. 315):

System after system has been developed and presented in one or two demonstration studies, only to lie buried in the literature, unused even by its author. Moreover, few variables or notions about therapeutic interviews have received anything approaching programmatic or extensive content-analysis investigation. This has resulted in redundancy; systems were developed with apparent unawareness that other approaches to the same problem, or efforts to apply the same approach to other problems, had already been reported. Happily, some recent studies suggest that this pattern may be changing.

Nevertheless, the psycholinguistic approach to therapeutic materials appears to offer a fertile area for research. Rarely has the richness of

---

* Content analysis systems have also been developed for systematic examination of Rorschach (Elizur, 1949, Lindner, 1950), and Thematic Apperception Tests (Shneidman, 1951; Hafner and Kaplan, 1960; Arnold, 1962). Research relating other language categories to psychotherapy is reviewed in Mowrer (1953), Snyder (1953), Auld and Murray (1955), and Marsden (1965).

communication been so dramatically illustrated as in an extensive linguistic and paralinguistic content analysis limited to the first five minutes of a psychiatric interview (Pittenger, Hockett, and Danehy, 1960). Some of the possibilities in this area of research are also suggested in an extensive, multimeasure psycholinguistic analysis of two interviews. Minute-by-minute readings on heart rate and skin temperature were related to a number of verbal measures, including the TTR, speech disturbance ratio, and rating scales for anxiety and hostility (Gottschalk, 1961).

Use of language measures for purposes other than psychotherapy can be illustrated by a study comparing genuine suicide notes with ordinary letters and simulated suicide notes (Osgood and Walker, 1959). Among many content analysis methods used were the TTR, DRQ, and adjective-adverb/noun-verb measures, all of which differentiated real suicide notes from the letters. Only the latter measure, however, was successful in distinguishing real from simulated notes. Content analyses of real and simulated suicide notes are also reported in Gottschalk and Gleser (1960), Stone and Hunt (1963), and Ogilvie, Stone, and Shneidman (1966).

Most of the above studies have been in-depth analyses of single individuals rather than classes of communicators, in part because intimate personal documents for larger groups are rarely available. There are, however, some exceptions. For a study of business values during the early period of American industrialization, Cochran (1953) obtained and analyzed over 100,000 letters written by presidents of Class I railroads.

Content analysis has also been used to assess psychological variables in the context of political decision-making, particularly in the area of foreign policy. One approach, a continuation of the Lasswellian tradition, has emphasized elite values and ideology. In the absence of direct measures, Soviet and American publications representing political, economic, labor, military, scientific, and cultural elites were examined to identify major values. Themes regarding the economy, social and internal political affairs, and external relations were coded into more than 40 category sets. An investigation of elite foreign policy attitudes for the same period focused on perceptions of the international system, power relationships, and operational codes. Although Soviet and American value preferences were found to be symmetrical in some respects, and incompatible in others, the data also revealed that elites in both nations displayed a strong tendency to act and speak in such a way as to magnify differences between them (Angell, Dunham, and Singer, 1964).

A second approach to foreign policy studies has focused on analysis of documents written by officials holding key decision-making roles. The basic assumption is that foreign policy decisions, like all decisions, are in part a product of the policy-maker's perceptions, that if men define situations as real, they are real in their consequences. Again, the choice of content analysis is based largely on the inability in most cases to use observational methods to assess the perceptions, attitudes, and values of foreign policy leaders at the time of decision. When these more direct techniques are not applicable, systematic analysis of diplomatic documents provides an indirect method to bridge gaps in time and space. Themes, which have been classified into categories such as friendship, hostility, capabilities, time pressure, and alternatives, have served as the unit of analysis (North *et al.*, 1963).

An initial study tested two basic hypotheses about the relationship between perceptions of threat and perceptions of capability during an international crisis (Zinnes, North, and Koch, 1961). During the weeks prior to war in 1914, perceptions of capability appeared much less frequently in decision-makers' documents as perceptions of threat increased. This study also revealed the limitations, for many purposes, of using frequency as the sole basis of inference. After the 1914 data were recoded to permit analysis on the basis of intensity as well as frequency, hypotheses relating to perceptions of capability and injury were reexamined. Decision-makers of each nation most strongly felt themselves to be victims of persecution and rejection precisely at the time when they were making policy decisions of the most crucial nature (Holsti and North, 1965).

Other analyses of the 1914 data, within the framework of a model linking actions and perceptions, have consistently shown that the more intense the interaction between parties, the more important it is to incorporate perceptual variables, as indexed by content data, into the analysis (Holsti, North, and Brody, 1968). This strong relationship between perceptions of hostility, feelings of involvement, and policy decisions has also been found in a study of Soviet and Chinese leaders during three crisis situations (Zaninovich, 1964). Related studies have tested several models of hostility in international communication (Zinnes, 1963; Zinnes, Zinnes, and McClure, in press), and have compared the 1914 content analysis data with those derived from simulation studies (Hermann and Hermann, 1967, Zinnes, 1966).

A number of prominent hypotheses in the decision-making literature were tested using documents from the 1914 crisis. The data revealed that as stress increased, decision-makers perceived time as an increasingly salient factor in formulating policy and they became preoccupied with short-term, rather than long-range, implications of their actions. Leaders in various capitals of Europe also perceived the alternatives open to themselves to decrease, and those of their adversaries to increase, as they came under more intense stress (Holsti, 1965b). On the other hand, conscious efforts on the part of American and Soviet leaders to extend decision time and keep alternatives open apparently contributed to nonviolent resolution of the Cuban missile crisis (Holsti, in press). In another study comparing events during the Cuban missile crisis of 1962 with those in the summer of 1914, some important differences emerged. During the Cuban crisis both sides tended to perceive rather accurately the nature of the adversary's actions, and then proceeded to respond at an "appropriate" level. Thus, unlike the situation in 1914, efforts by either party to delay or reverse the escalation were generally perceived as such, and responded to in a like manner (Holsti, Brody, and North, 1965).

To Infer Aspects of Culture and Cultural Change

Anthropologists, sociologists, and others have traditionally examined societal artifacts to describe constant and changing characteristics of cultures. Content analysis may prove especially useful in such studies because various forms of documents often constitute the major surviving source of evidence about past cultures. For example, in order to measure socio-economic influences on the range of problems investigated by seventeenth century English scientists, Merton (1957a) examined the minutes of the Royal Society for the years 1661-1662 and 1686-1687. Research of this type can also be illustrated by a series of studies centering on hypotheses relating *need of achievement* and *inner/other direction* to major stages in cultural development.

A person with high *n* achievement is someone who wants to succeed, who is energetic and nonconforming, and who enjoys tasks which involve elements of risk. *N* achievement has been defined operationally as "a sum of the number of instances of achievement 'ideas' or images" (McClelland, 1958, p. 520). The hypothesis that "a society with a relatively high percentage of individuals with high *n* achievement should contain a strong entrepreneurial class which will tend to be active and successful particularly in business enterprises so that *the society will grow in power and influence*" was tested by scoring samples of literature from the periods of growth (900 to 475 B.C.), climax (475 to 362 B.C.), and decline (362 to 100 B.C.) of Greek civilization (McClelland, 1958). As an index of economic power and influence, the location of vase remains was used to construct maps of the area within which Greece traded in the sixth, fifth, and fourth centuries B.C.; these figures, 1.2, 3.4, and 1.9 million square miles, respectively, were interpreted as measures of the growth, climax, and decline of Greek power and influence. The amount of *n* achievement imagery found in various kinds of literature during these three stages in Greek history is revealed in Table 4-3. When compared to trade area, the findings supported the hypothesis that expressions of *n* achievement index stages in the development of a civilization.

An independent check on these results was made by analyzing inscriptions on vases produced in various eras of Greek civilization.

TABLE 4-3

*Number of n achievement images per 100 lines
by type of sample by time period*

Period	Man and his gods	Estate manage-ment	Funeral cele-brations	Poetry	Epi-grams	War speeches	Aver-age
Growth, 900-475 B.C.	2.01	3.54	7.93	2.87	4.72	7.38	4.74
Climax, 475-362 B.C.	1.21	0.82	5.94	0.38	2.36	5.55	2.71
Decline, 362-100 B.C.	0.81	0.00	2.54	0.16	1.57	3.00	1.35

Aronson (1958) found that doodling styles can be used to discriminate persons with high n achievement from those with low n achievement. An objective scoring system for lines, shapes, and spaces of spontaneous doodles has been cross-validated against several groups of subjects. Without serious modification, the same scoring system was applied to inscriptions on Greek vases. The results substantiated the other findings; signs of high n achievement were significantly more frequent in the period of growth and less frequent in the period of climax. The same system of content analysis has also been used in a cross-cultural study relating child training practices to n achievement in Indian folktales (McClelland and Friedman, 1952).*

According to some students of American culture, there has been a notable trend from the "Protestant ethic" or inner-direction to a "social ethic" or other-direction (Riesman, Glazer, and Reuel, 1950). On the assumption that inner- and other-direction could be measured by achievement motive and affiliation motive (as defined by McClelland, 1958), respectively, children's readers for the period 1800 to 1950 were content-analyzed to determine whether these psychological variables index observed cultural change in the United States. Hypotheses tested were: that there has been a decrease in the incidence of achievement motivation and moral teachings, that there has been an increase in occurrence of the affiliation motive, and that incidence of the achievement motive has been positively correlated to an independent measure of achievement (the number of patents issued, corrected for changes in population). The first hypothesis was not supported; achievement motivation in the readers increased steadily throughout the nineteenth century and began to decline only around the turn of the century. Changes in achievement imagery

---

* For other examples, see McClelland (1961).

were, however, highly correlated with the number of patents granted, which also reached a peak at the end of the nineteenth century and have declined since that time. The other two hypotheses were also supported by the content data (deCharms and Moeller, 1962).

A somewhat different test of the hypothesis of increasing other-direction was provided by a content analysis of advertising in the *Ladies' Home Journal* for the period 1890 to 1956 (Dornbusch and Hickman, 1959). Other-directedness was measured by eight separate types of appeals in advertising, including testimonials of celebrities, collective endorsements ("housewives like product X"), positive and negative interpersonal satisfactions, and the like. The null hypothesis—that there was no difference in the proportion of other-directed advertisement before and after the midpoint of 1921—was rejected; all eight indices of other-directedness appeared with significantly greater relative frequence after 1921.

These studies illustrate some of the many possible ways in which content analysis of social and historical documents can be used to test hypotheses. At the same time it should be pointed out that there are many pitfalls, aside from such technical problems as coding reliability, to be avoided. A most important problem, one rarely resolved beyond doubt, is the selection of materials which do in fact represent the culture, or at least some significant segment of it. Do newspapers, drama, or literature of a period, taken collectively, represent merely a manifestation of the authors' personalities, or do they reflect the more general milieu?

A partial solution to the problem is to rely on materials which meet the criterion of popularity, as was done in the study of achievement motivation in Greek literature. The rationale for this approach has been spelled out in a cross-cultural study of themes in popular drama (McGranahan and Wayne, 1948, p. 430):

> Our first assumption in this study is that popular drama can be regarded as a case of "social fantasy"—that the psychological constellations in a dramatic work indicate sensitive areas in the personalities of those for whom the work has appeal; their needs, assumptions and values are expressed ("projected") in the drama. The successful play must be attuned to the audience.

A second approach involves examining materials which explicitly perform the function of transmitting and instilling social norms. For example, editorials in the Cuban newspaper *El Mundo* were analyzed because, "The controlled Cuban press—in addition to providing a direct channel to the public—is also of prime importance in 'feeding' the other agencies of political training" (Fagen, 1967, p. 207). In this study, major themes about Cuban friends and enemies were related to four international and domestic events: the Bay of Pigs invasion, Castro's "I am a Marxist Leninist" speech, Cuba's exclusion from the Organization of American States, and the Cuban missile crisis. Socialization materials, which may take very different forms across culture and time, have been widely used in content analysis research; e.g., folktales (McClelland and Friedman, 1952, Colby, 1966b), children's readers (deCharms and Moeller, 1962), youth manuals (Lewin, 1947), songs (Sebald, 1962), and textbooks (Walworth, 1938).

A third method is to use one or more independent indices against which to correlate content data. In their comparative study of German and American drama during the 1927 season, McGranahan and Wayne (1948) used six separate sets of data, both content and noncontent, to support their conclusion that there were real and persistent differences in the psychology of Germans and Americans. A sample of plays from the 1909-1910 season was analyzed to determine whether differences could be attributed to Germany's defeat in World War I. Another test compared German audience reactions to movies which had been successful or unsuccessful in the United States. Each supplementary test supported findings based on content analysis, thereby increasing confidence in them.

To Provide Legal Evidence

During World War II the United States government asked Harold Lasswell to analyze certain materials and to testify about their content in four cases of suspected criminal sedition. The purpose was to demonstrate that statements by the accused publishers conformed to enemy propaganda themes. Materials ranged from over 200 books in English and Russian in the *Bookniga* case to 11 issues of the periodical *The Galilean,* published by William Dudley Pelley. Eight tests (see Table 4-4) were developed to analyze the materials, the results of which were accepted in evidence by the court (Lasswell, 1949, pp. 177-178).

The most outspoken critics (St. George and Dennis, 1946; Hughes, 1950) of the content analysis data presented in the sedition trials hardly qualify as dispassionate observers. Yet some of their specific objections are not wholly without merit. It has been pointed out that, "There is almost no theory of language which predicts the specific words one will emit in the course of expressing the content of his thoughts" (Lasswell, Lerner, and Pool, 1952, p. 49). In the absence of such a theory, a posture of considerable skepticism is warranted toward use of content analysis data for other than descriptive purposes in legal proceedings.

TABLE 4-4*

Tests to analyze materials in sedition trial

Test	Description
Avowal	Explicit identification with one side of a controversy.
Parallel	The content of a given channel is compared with the content of a known propaganda channel. Content is classified according to themes.
Consistency	The consistency of a stream of communication with the declared propaganda aims of a party to a controversy. The aims may be official declarations or propaganda instructions.
Presentation	The balance of favorable and unfavorable treatment given to each symbol (and statement) in controversy.
Source	Relatively heavy reliance upon one party to a controversy for material.
Concealed source	The use of one party to a controversy as a source, without disclosure.
Distinctive-ness	The use of vocabulary peculiar to one side of a controversy.
Distortion	Persistent modification of statements on a common topic in a direction favorable to one side of a controversy. Statements may be omitted, added, over-emphasized or under-emphasized.

*From H.D. Lasswell, N. Leites, *et al. Language of Politics: Studies in Quantitative Semantics,* published by George Stewart, Inc. Copyright 1965 by M.I.T. Press. Reprinted by permission.

A form of content analysis intended to yield only descriptive information has been used by the Federal Communications Commission to determine whether radio station owners conform to prescribed standards (*Content Analysis,* 1948, p. 910). In its annual survey, the FCC compares station logs with ideal ratios between commercial and local live, sustaining, and public issue programs. In one case the American Jewish Congress sought to deny an application by the *New York Daily News* for an FM broadcasting license on grounds of unfavorable bias against minority groups. In a split opinion the Commission ruled that both the qualitative and quantitative data contained "technical deficiencies . . . so serious as to vitiate any real value the analysis might otherwise have had." At the same time, the Commission ruled in unambiguous terms that content analysis is an acceptable evidentiary technique if the data are deemed to be of adequate quality (*Content Analysis,* 1948, p. 914).

On the whole, content analysis has been used sparingly as a source of legal evidence. Literary infringement cases are perhaps the legal area in which it might be used most suitably. Existing tests suffer from precisely those deficiencies which can be remedied through careful content analysis (Sorensen and Sorensen, 1955, p. 264):

> *To distinguish the ideas, plots, title, phraseology, characters and locale, all of which are not infringible from the "original form of expression, language or thought sequence and literary style" is simply too difficult a job for the ordinary observer making a superficial comparison.*

> *Meanwhile, copyright counsel have no way of knowing whether the judge read all of the works, scanned part of each, used his own sampling system, or how much weight, if any, he may give to the exhibits submitted.*

The tests developed in the sedition cases, as well as those developed by "literary detectives" (described below), might well provide data better than impressionistic scanning.

THE ANTECEDENTS OF CONTENT: WHO?

Among the earliest uses of systematic documentary analysis were those designed to settle questions of disputed authorship. Who wrote *The Imitation of Christ?* Was James Madison or Alexander Hamilton the author of *The Federalist Papers* Nos. 49-58, 62, and 63? These are two of many problems of literary detection which have been investigated by content analysis. The belief that each person's style contains certain unique characteristics is an old one and methods of inference from statistical description of content attributes go back at least to the nineteenth century (Mendenhall, 1887). But because there are so many possible characteristics of style which might be used to discriminate between authors, the major task is that of selecting proper indicators. The problem must often be started from scratch in each inquiry, as reliable discriminators in one case may fail in another. For example, sentence length, often thought to be a useful index, proved useless in the case of the *Federalist Papers*—the known writings of Madison and Hamilton averaged 34.59 and 34.55 words per sentence, respectively; hence even a precise measure of sentence length in the disputed papers would not enable one to settle the question of their authorship.

Frequencies of various classes of nouns were used to determine whether Thomas à Kempis or Jean Gerson wrote *The Imitation of Christ.* Five independent tests, based on the incidence of approximately 8200 nouns each, yielded the results in Table 4-5.* On this basis Yule (1944)

---

* From G. U. Yule, *The Statistical Study of Literary Vocabulary.* Copyright 1944 Cambridge University Press. Reprinted by permission.

TABLE 4-5

*Incidence of special nouns in The Imitation of Christ,
and known writing of Thomas à Kempis and Jean Gerson*

Test	The Imitation of Christ	Thomas à Kempis	Gerson
1	671	709	912
2	376	365	823
3	59	58	162
4	6	7	21
5	0	1	24

concluded that Gerson was not the author. Although it is impossible to prove that *The Imitation of Christ* was written by Thomas à Kempis, these data are clearly consistent with the hypothesis of his authorship.

The frequency of 265 words in known writings of Madison and Hamilton served as the test for 12 *Federalist Papers* whose authorship was disputed (Mosteller and Wallace, 1964). The data strongly supported the claim of Madison's authorship. The weakest odds in Madison's case were 80 to 1 on *Paper* No. 55; No. 56 was next weakest, at odds of 800 to 1 for Madison. Politically important but infrequently appearing words turned out to be far less effective discriminators than the high frequency function words. This finding is consistent with one generalization which has emerged from other studies of the unknown communicator in painting, literature, and music, it is the "minor encoding habits," the apparently trivial details of style, which vary systematically within and between communicators' works (Paisley, 1964).

Other statistical methods for identifying authors from content characteristics have emerged from studies of the "Quintus Curtius Snodgrass Letters" (Brinegar, 1963), and the "Junius Letters," a series of political pamphlets written from 1769 to 1772 (Ellegård, 1962).

The potential pitfalls of authorship studies can be illustrated by Morton's (1963) research into authorship of the 14 Epistles attributed to Paul. The author claimed to have identified seven elements of style which could be used to discover the unique elements of any person's style. "The brain," he asserted, "has fingerprints in the form of word patterns. No one writes and speaks exactly as you do." On the basis of tests on Greek texts of known authorship, seven discriminators of style were identified: *sentence length,* frequency of the *definite article, third person pronouns,* and the aggregate of all forms of the *verb to be;* and frequency of the words *and, but,* and *in.* After analysis of the Epistles in terms of these criteria, Morton concluded that they were written by six different authors, and that Paul himself had written only four major Epistles. He added, "Theologians all over the Christian world have now to face the implications of this discovery. They must revise their view of the life of Paul, they must revise the history of the early church, and they must jettison doctrines that have now been shown to be without foundation."*

Ellison (1965) subsequently applied these presumed discriminators of style to texts of known authorship, however, and cast serious doubt on their general validity. He concluded that *Ulysses* was written by five different authors, none of whom wrote *Portrait of the Artist as a Young Man*. Indeed, even different sections of Morton's own article were found to contain quite distinct styles as characterized by his seven indicators. While Ellison's critique of the Morton study did not prove that Paul wrote all of the Epistles attributed to him, it clearly cast doubt upon the latter's findings to the contrary, as well as upon the utility of his indicators of style.

The specific lesson to be drawn from this controversy relates to the difficulties which may confound the literary detective. There is also a lesson for content analysts other than literary detectives in this episode. The major source of difficulty in Morton's study was his assumption that a relationship between content of communication (in this instance, seven elements of style) and its antecedents (identity of the author), found to be valid in the case of some Greek texts, would be valid for all documents and authors. It is precisely because such premises are often of doubtful validity that inferences from content data to their antecedents are no better than the criterion against which they are compared. That is, Morton's use of the research design in Fig. 2-9 appears to have failed because the relationship between A_X and A_Z was not sufficiently general to permit inferences from B_X—the Epistles—about their authorship.†

THE RESULTS OF COMMUNICATION: WITH WHAT EFFECT?

The basic format of content analysis research designed to study the effects of communication is: If messages have attributes A_X, B_X, and C_X, then the prediction is that the effect on the recipient will be A_Y, B_Y, and C_Y. Content analysis describes the relevant attributes of the independent variables $(A_X, B_X, \text{and } C_X)$, but, as indicated earlier, any direct inference as to effects from content is at best tenuous. When a government controlled

---

* From A. Q. Morton, A Computer Challenges the Church, *The Observer*, London. Copyright 1963 by The Observer. Reprinted by permission.

† In addition to settling a number of long-standing controversies, authorship studies have yielded some important statistical by-products. Yule's investigations resulted in the K measure, now used in linguistics, stylistics, and related areas of inquiry, and Mosteller's work on the *Federalist Papers* is of as much interest to statisticians as to historians because of its original contribution to Bayesian statistics.

newspaper such as the Chinese *People's Daily* is analyzed to measure elite attitudes (Eto and Okabe, 1965), problems of inference are somewhat limited. The assumption that this source reflects leadership views—i.e., the antecedents of communication—is plausible and can be verified by independent analyses of content or noncontent indices. But it would not necessarily follow that the same source could be used to measure its effects upon mass opinion in China.

That effects of communication are related not only to attributes of content but also to other factors is well established (cf. Klapper, 1960, Bauer, 1964; Hovland, Janis, and Kelley, 1953). For present purposes it will suffice to summarize very briefly a few of the major research findings on this point. There is, in the first place, ample evidence that persons tend to seek out information which supports *preexisting attitudes* and to avoid contradictory communications. It has been demonstrated that self-exposure to literature on the smoking-health issue was much stronger among nonsmokers than among smokers (Cannell and MacDonald, 1956), and that pro-United Nations literature reached mainly those who initially supported the U.N. (Star and Hughes, 1950). Moreover, because pre-existing attitudes are often derived from groups to which one belongs, persons who are strongly motivated to maintain their membership (e.g., in a political party) are highly resistant to message content which contradicts group norms. There are also strong indications that the effects of communication are related to the *perceived credibility of the communicator;* the higher the credibility of the source and the more he is esteemed, the more likely is the content of the message to have an effect on the audience. Finally, research on attitude change indicates that persuasibility exists as a *personality factor* independent of content (Janis *et al.*, 1959). That is, certain personality types are more readily affected by the content of messages than others. For example, persons with low self-esteem tend to be more easily persuaded, whereas those with psychoneurotic symptoms are highly resistant to the effects of communication. These conclusions can be restated within the framework of content analysis research: owing to the possible effects of factors other than message content, including audience predispositions and decoding habits, the effects of communication cannot be inferred directly from the attributes of content (what) or style (how) without independent validation.

This problem was anticipated in an early proposal to measure public opinion by quantitative newspaper analysis. Woodward's (1934) research design incorporated systematic efforts to test the relationship between public attitudes and newspaper content. Often, however, this relationship is simply assumed to be a positive one. For example, frequencies of British and American place names in colonial American newspapers were tabulated to index sentiments of national identity (Merritt, 1966).* But the absence of evidence demonstrating that the appearance of these symbols either reflected or shaped public views calls into serious question inferences drawn from the content data. In short, the burden of proof is on the investigator to present evidence that audience attitudes can indeed be inferred directly from communications produced for that audience. As indicated in Figs. 2-11 and 2-12, measures of effects may be derived from analyses of subsequent messages produced by the recipient to determine if they are consistent with the predicted effect, or from noncontent indices of the recipient's behavior.

To Measure Readability

The most systematic content analysis research measuring effects of communication has centered on correlating attributes of style with ease of comprehension. Characteristics of text which have often been tested include various aspects of vocabulary (diversity, hard words, long words, abstract words), sentence structure (length, type, number of prepositional phrases or indeterminate clauses), and human interest elements (personal pronouns, colorful words).

There have generally been two approaches to identifying and validating elements of readability. The first has been to identify the distinguishing attributes of materials prejudged to have a certain level of difficulty, e.g., adventure stories and philosophical writings. This approach assumes that the investigator can judge, *a priori*, the level of difficulty of such materials, often a dubious premise. A more reliable technique has been to use independent tests to determine reading comprehension of subjects.

One of the earliest systematic studies on readability was undertaken by Gray and Leary (1935). They found that 24 of 44 language variables were significantly correlated with comprehension scores. After eliminating some variables which were highly correlated with others, five were selected to index readability: the number of different words, uncommon words, personal pronouns, prepositional phrases, and the average length of sentences.

Flesch (1943) and Lorge (1944) developed formulas based on three factors—sentence length and two measures of vocabulary. The Flesch system was later revised, with formulas to measure both *reading ease* and *human interest* characteristics of text. Subsequent research has focused in large part on developing easier methods of scoring the vocabulary factor in Flesch's formula. One method is to count only those words falling outside

---

* This choice of indicators to measure feelings of national identity is discussed further in the next chapter.

a standard 3000-word list (Dale and Chall, 1948). Another study demonstrated that incidence of one-syllable words is so highly correlated with the Flesch vocabulary factor that it may be used in its place, with a considerable saving of scoring time (Farr, Jenkins, and Patterson, 1951).

While readability research has consistently pointed to the importance of vocabulary load and sentence length (Brinton and Danielson, 1958), the limitations of these measures must be recognized. These formulas measure only some aspects of *style,* not other important elements of readability—content, organization, and format (Kearl, 1948). Second, readability measures cannot be applied mechanically; e.g., it is true only to a point that the shorter the sentence, the more readable the text. Finally, these formulas are geared to the effect of style on the general audience; little allowance is made for the reader's experience and expectations, each of which can have an important bearing on the extent to which the text is understood (Waples, Berelson, and Bradshaw, 1940, pp. 135-145). For example, a repair manual or other piece of specialized writing may be quite readable to those familiar with its technical vocabulary, and unintelligible to all others.

The *Cloze procedure,* which represents a radical departure from traditional approaches to readability, overcomes the first two of these limitations. The text is initially mutilated by removal of every fifth, seventh, tenth, or *n*th word, after which the reader is asked to supply the missing words (Taylor, 1953). The index of readability is based on the percentage of blanks correctly filled in. The advantage of the method is that it is effective in cases where other methods break down; i.e., when idiosyncratic use of language (for example, the writings of James Joyce or Gertrude Stein) produces invalid readability scores. Although originally developed to measure readability, because the Cloze system is sensitive to semantic, associational, grammatical, and syntactical determinants of verbal behavior, it has subsequently proved useful in personality (Honigfeld, Platz, and Gillis, 1964) and psychiatric research (Fillenbaum and Jones, 1962; Salzinger, Portnoy, and Feldman, 1964).

Other attributes of style whose effects have been studied, and for which measures have been developed, include *sensationalism* (Tannenbaum and Lynch, 1960), and *abstraction* (Gillie, 1957; Haskins, 1960).

To Analyze the Flow of Information

The effect of communication is sometimes analyzed by comparing the source and content of incoming information with that of outgoing information. Starting with the basic assumption that "abandonment of neutrality in favor of the belligerent which supplies the greater amount of news" was a factor in American entry into World War I, Foster (1935, 1937) examined the flow of news to the United States from the outbreak of hostilities in Europe in 1914 until the American declaration of war on Germany in April 1917. Over 11,000 items appearing on the front page of the *New York Times* and in the Chicago press were coded according to origin of the news and to type of appeal contained within it which might make the reader favor American participation. The data revealed that American readers were almost wholly dependent upon news directly from, or dispatched through, the Entente powers. Thus, events such as the German invasion of Belgium were reported almost exclusively by news received from Germany's enemies. As war approached, the proportion of news from American sources increased sharply, as did news containing some appeal favoring American participation.

Content analysis was used to determine whether the Associated Press and United Press International, each of which had full-time bureaus in Havana, were responsible for charges of inadequate public information about the Cuban revolution. Stated somewhat differently, how did the content of AP and UPI dispatches about events in Cuba affect that of newspaper stories? All stories about Cuba filed during December 1958 were analyzed. Tables summarizing AP and UPI reports were compared to coverage of the Castro revolution by major newspapers published in Washington, Cleveland, and Louisville. Scores were computed for percentage of available AP and UPI information used, and the prominence (headlines, placement) with which it was displayed. On the basis of the comparison between information received by newspapers from AP and UPI and that published by them, the author absolved the news services from charges of inadequate coverage: "The newspapers received enough wire copy to tell the long, continuing story of the Cuban revolution. They made little use of this material, however, until the last six days" (Lewis, 1960, p. 646).

A form of content analysis was used to study the transmission of rumors removed six times from an original source (De Fleur, 1962). Subjects in a community were informed that prizes would be offered to those who could repeat a short advertising slogan to a team of investigators. The slogan was given to a sample of subjects, and interview responses three days later were analyzed to determine the degree of distortion in the original message. By asking subjects to identify their source of information, it was possible to determine how many steps removed each respondent was from the original source.*

---

* Other studies employing some form of content analysis to chart flow of news include Carter (1957), Schramm (1959), Hart (1961), and Galtung and Ruge (1965).

To Assess Responses to Communication

One aspect of the effects of a communication is the degree to which its symbols become assimilated by the audience. Prothro (1956) tested the hypothesis that political symbols of the New Deal have become a permanent part of the American tradition, and that not even successful spokesmen for conservatism reject them. The first Acceptance, Inaugural, and State of the Union addresses of Presidents Hoover, Roosevelt, Truman, and Eisenhower were coded for relative frequencies of *political appeals* (government aid, government regulation, national power, etc.) and *demand symbols* (peace, freedom, faith, controls, initiative, etc.). While demand symbols distinguished Hoover and Eisenhower from Roosevelt and Truman, Eisenhower's political appeals were free from any repudiation of the New Deal, thereby supporting the hypothesis.

Soviet newspapers and domestic and foreign broadcasts were analyzed to assess the effects of Voice of America broadcasts. For a four-year period beginning in 1947, mass communication materials were examined for all references to the Voice of America. A number of content analysis techniques were used to answer different questions. Frequency counts were used to measure focus of attention and distribution of Soviet references to VOA. Most foreign attacks on VOA were directed to Eastern and Western Europe, with little attention to Latin American audiences. During the four-year period there was a relative increase in attention directed to domestic audiences, especially in those publications read predominantly by the Soviet intelligentsia. Thematic analysis was used to code more than 2500 references to VOA. These data revealed that the Soviets, rather than posing a counterimage of Soviet virtues, responded by counteracting the image they assumed VOA had created of the United States (Inkeles, 1952; see also Massing, 1963).

Does the content of communication have a greater effect on the audience when it is attributed to a high prestige source? Attitudes before and after exposure to three messages attributed to Thomas Gates, Walter Lippmann, and James Conant indicated that messages with a byline do produce greater change in the direction of the message, but only when the byline is located at or near the top of the message (Tannenbaum and Greenberg, 1961a; see also Hovland, Janis, and Kelley, 1953).

Two studies have examined the effects of scholarship by analyzing published reactions to research. Lerner undertook a thematic content analysis of the published reviews of *The American Soldier*, a study of Army morale during World War II by a large team of social scientists. Responses were related to professional affiliation and other attributes of the reviewer. In his conclusion, Lerner suggested how content and predispositions combined to shape the nature and tone of reviews. That is, the book presented an important challenge to reviewers who, however, for lack of time, skill, or inclination, generally responded on the basis of preexisting attitudes. These attitudes, in turn, were found to be generally related to the reviewer's occupation (e.g., professional soldier or social scientist), prior commitment to scientific research in human affairs, and willingness to transfer responses from the book under review to the general symbol "social science" (Lerner, 1950, pp. 241-242).

A somewhat similar study examined the treatment of Freud's theory of dreams in general psychology, abnormal psychology, and psychiatry textbooks (Herma, Kris, and Shor, 1943). The investigators initially developed a list of 30 propositions basic to the theory of dreams. All available textbooks published between 1901 and 1940 were coded according to: mention of the theory of dreams; frequency of basic propositions cited; attitude toward the theory as a whole and toward specific propositions comprising the theory; and, if the theory was rejected, the basis of rejection (ridicule, moral grounds, scientific grounds, etc.). The data revealed that the theory of dreams had become a predominant interest only in texts on abnormal behavior, and that those who rejected the theory did so on grounds other than scientific.

CONCLUSION

This brief review of research on the causes and effects of communication should underscore the themes identified in the preface—that content analysis presents both dangers and opportunities for the student of human affairs. The research questions to which systematic analysis of documentary evidence has been applied include core problems in many of the social and humanistic disciplines. The rather skeptical attitudes toward content analysis, as expressed by such critics as Lazarsfeld (1941) and Cartwright (1953), have not completely lost their validity. Unimaginative studies of the "counting for the sake of counting" variety continue to appear. But these are counterbalanced by an increasing number of inquiries in which substantively and theoretically important problems are tackled with methodological sophistication and creative imagination. Certainly a number of the studies cited in this chapter can thus be described. Yet even a moderately optimistic appraisal of some trends in current research should not cause us to overlook the many pitfalls which, if not avoided, can nullify an otherwise well-designed study. Some of these have been mentioned in this chapter: questionable categories, generalization from an unrepresentative sample, absence of a well-defined criterion of the dependent variables that content data are assumed to index, and others. Having concluded our survey of studies to illustrate some of the uses of content analysis, we shall now turn to a more systematic discussion of these problems.

5   Coding Content Data

Coding is the process whereby raw data are systematically transformed and aggregated into units which permit precise description of relevant content characteristics. The rules by which this transformation is accomplished serve as the operational link between the investigator's data and his theory and hypotheses. Coding rules are thus a central part of the research design, and in preparing them the analyst makes a number of decisions:

- How is the research problem defined in terms of *categories?*
- What *unit* of content is to be classified?
- What system of *enumeration* will be used?

Although we shall consider coding under these three headings, this division is solely for purposes of exposition. It does not imply that selections of categories, units, and system of enumeration are independent decisions; rather they represent a series of interrelated choices. There is no "best" method of coding which can be applied to all research questions, but in deciding how to code his data the investigator should bear some general principles in mind. First, each alternative method of coding content materials carries with it certain assumptions about the data and the inferences which may be drawn from them. The investigator should be aware of these, because with each choice he in fact incorporates some of these premises into his research design. Second, decisions about methods of coding should be guided by the investigator's theory and hypotheses. Unless theory and technique are intimately related, even the minimal requirements of validity cannot be met. The latter point also suggests why aimless "fishing expeditions" into documentary data are not likely to prove rewarding. Without a theory, however rudimentary, to inform the analyst, he is without any guides for his coding decisions. In short, unless he can state explicitly *why* he is analyzing documents, he cannot intelligently work out a plan on *how* to do it.

CATEGORIES

General Requirements

A central problem in any research design is selection and definition of categories, the "pigeonholes" into which content units are to be classified. "Content analysis stands or falls by its categories. Particular studies have been productive to the extent that the categories were clearly formulated and well adapted to the problem and to the content" (Berelson, 1952, p. 147).

Without reference to a specific research question it is impossible to discuss substantive aspects of content analysis categories beyond giving illustrations, as we shall do later in this chapter. It is possible, however, to state some general principles of category construction. That is, categories should *reflect the purposes of the research,* be *exhaustive,* be *mutually exclusive, independent,* and be derived from a *single classification principle.** We shall return to the hypothetical research design presented in Chapter 2 to illustrate these requirements. To recapitulate briefly, that design was developed to test a hypothesis that attitudes toward domestic welfare legislation and interventionist foreign policies were related, and it included controls for the possible effects of party, time, and audience.

The most important requirement of categories is that they must adequately *reflect the investigator's research question.* This means, first of all, that the analyst must define clearly the variables he is dealing with (the "conceptual definitions"), and secondly, he must specify the indicators which determine whether a given content datum falls within the category (the "operational definition"). A good operational definition satisfies two requirements: it is a *valid* representation of the analyst's concepts, and it is sufficiently precise that it guides coders to produce *reliable* judgments. Familiarity with one's data is an important asset for developing valid and reliable categories, but even the most knowledgeable investigator may want to test his definitions on a small sample of data before coding actually begins.

To illustrate these points, we can turn to our study of presidential campaign speeches in which the two concepts to be measured were attitudes toward domestic welfare legislation and interventionist foreign policies. We might have chosen, for reasons of convenience and precision of measurement, to count the relative frequency of sentences referring to domestic and foreign policy. Alternatively, we might have constructed word lists of terms identifying the two concepts and asked coders to count how frequently words on each list appeared in the speeches. Clearly

---

* This discussion follows, with some modifications, that in Kerlinger (1964, pp. 606ff).

neither of these operational definitions would have been satisfactory for the research question. The first method fails to distinguish welfare legislation and interventionist foreign policies—the variables needed to test our hypothesis—from other domestic and international issues. The second operational definition assumes that the frequency with which certain terms are used adequately indexes attitudes toward them. It would, however, fail to distinguish between a speech permeated with praise for social security and one devoted to a long attack on Medicare. Were our problem concerned only with focus of attention to issues, the latter measure might have proved valid (as well as convenient), but for the question at hand it is virtually useless.

The point we have been making here is important enough to warrant another example, this time drawn from a published study. The purpose of the research was to measure the development of national consciousness in the American colonies during the four decades prior to the Revolutionary War (Merritt, 1966). The relative frequency of occurrence of American place names (towns, cities, and the like) in a sample of colonial newspapers was taken as an index of community awareness. These frequencies were plotted for the period 1735 to 1775, and conclusions about the development of nationalism in America were drawn from the trends that emerged. From an increase in the frequency of American place names, and a concomitant decline in the appearance of British geographical symbols, the author concluded that a well-developed sense of American community had emerged prior to the Revolutionary War.

Although coding of these proper names was done with high reliability (0.92 to 0.96), inferences drawn from the data are open to serious question. What evidence is there that the occurrence of geographical names is a valid index of nationalism? If, as is likely, one found a higher proportion of Nigerian names in the *West African Pilot* than American names in the *New York Times,* would one conclude that national consciousness is better developed in Nigeria than in the United States?

It seems not unlikely that place names in newspaper stories reflect shifts in the locus of newsworthy events more faithfully than trends in community awareness. Indeed, one might suppose that during the latter decades of the eighteenth century English newspapers also contained an increasing proportion of American place names, reaching a peak during the years from 1776 to 1783, with frequent references to such places as Boston, Concord, Lexington, Philadelphia, Trenton, and Yorktown! Doubts about the validity of these categories are buttressed by other data from the same study. When references to American place names were classified as favorable, neutral, or unfavorable, changes were virtually nonexistent, even during a period of over two decades (Merritt, 1966, p.

49). It may be, of course, that sentiments of American nationalism did in fact increase during the four decades prior to the Declaration of Independence, but owing to questionable links between the concept "national awareness" and its operational definition, this study can shed little light on the question.

One further decision the investigator must make relates to the generality or specificity of his categories. That is, how fine are the distinctions he wishes to make *within* categories? In our hypothetical example we used two categories—attitudes toward welfare legislation and foreign intervention—but we might have further subdivided them as follows:

Domestic welfare legislation: attitudes toward

1. Federal aid to education
   a) Public primary and secondary schools
   b) Private primary and secondary schools
      i) Parochial schools
      ii) Nonparochial schools
   c) Universities

2. Social insurance
   a) Social Security
   b) Unemployment compensation
   c) Others

3. Medical programs
   a) Medicare
   b) Veterans' hospitals
   c) Research grants
   d) Others

4. Other welfare programs

5. Welfare programs, type unspecified

Interventionist foreign policies: attitudes toward

1. Foreign economic assistance to:
   a) Asia
   b) Africa
   c) Western Europe
   d) Eastern Europe
   e) Latin America
   f) Others
   g) Economic assistance, area unspecified

2. Foreign military assistance

   a) Military assistance not involving combat personnel
   b) Military assistance involving combat personnel
   c) Military assistance, type unspecified

3. Other interventionist foreign policies, or type unspecified

Without much difficulty we might have made even finer distinctions; e.g., both economic and military assistance might have been coded according to the target country, thereby increasing our total number of categories to several hundred. That this process could go on indefinitely is a point we need not dwell upon further. More important is the question of costs and gains associated with proliferating subcategories. Subdivisions within categories permit the analyst to make more comparisons, and therefore, to test more hypotheses, but research costs will increase as coders have to make more and finer judgments. Reliability may also suffer as the number of categories increases.* At some point they may become so narrow that most of them will be used once or perhaps not at all; i.e., the categorized data are virtually identical with raw data. Should this prove to be the case, it is possible to aggregate categories for purposes of testing hypotheses and reporting findings. In our example we could, for example, aggregate foreign policy attitudes into those relating to economic, military, and others, or even combine all the data into a single category. On the other hand, the investigator who discovers that his initial categories are so broad that important distinctions are lost cannot disaggregate results without completely recoding the data.

In summary, every advantage of using more and narrower categories is counterbalanced by some costs. Ultimately, the choice can be made only in terms of the problem at hand. In our example, as the hypothesis was originally stated there would have been little reason to expand categories by coding foreign policies according to continent. But suppose that halfway through the study we also wanted to test two subsidiary hypotheses:

1. Candidates opposed to welfare legislation tend to support interventionist foreign policies toward Asia and isolationist foreign policies toward Europe.

2. Candidates supporting welfare legislation tend to support isolationist foreign policies toward Asia and interventionist foreign policies toward Europe.

---

* Whether this is true will depend in part on the nature of judgments coders must make. Also, many reliability formulas take into account the number and expected frequencies with which categories are used.

We could do so only if our categories distinguished target areas of intervention, or if we were willing to recode our data to include this distinction. Few analysts are completely insured against the problem of being "locked in" by their categories once coding has started, but those with a clear conception of their research goals and a carefully thought out research design are less likely to suffer from such frustrations.*

The second general requirement—that categories be *exhaustive*—means that all relevant items in the sample of documents under study must be capable of being placed into a category. The rule of exhaustiveness poses few difficulties in certain types of research. If we interview a group of city councilmen with a view to comparing occupational background with their role conceptions, it is relatively easy to develop a set of occupational categories which include all councilmen. In some types of content analysis studies it is also possible to define categories exhaustively by listing every content unit to be placed in each one. In the RADIR studies coders were supplied with a list of 416 key symbols which defined the limits of the required information. The coding process was thus reduced from a judgmental task to a clerical one. Most content categories, however, do not lend themselves easily to exhaustive definition, especially if units larger than words or symbols are used. Consider such concepts as "need for achievement," "other direction," "editorial bias," and many others of a similarly complex nature. The analyst would find it virtually impossible to enumerate exhaustively all the words and combinations of words that might denote the presence of such concepts. Nor, in our study of twentieth century presidential campaign speeches, can we readily specify precisely all the ways in which candidates can express support for or rejection of interventionist foreign policies and welfare legislation. At best we would try to define each of these concepts as precisely as possible by characterizing its major properties; these would serve as the rules by which coders would judge whether content units fall within its boundaries. The better the category definition, the more likely is it to conform to the requirement of exhaustiveness, but even the most carefully designed study is likely to fall short of completely satisfying this requirement.

The requirement of *mutual exclusiveness* stipulates that no content datum can be placed in more than a single cell. In other words, operational definitions of the investigator's variables must be precise and unambiguous. Consider again our study in which the content variables are attitudes toward interventionist foreign policies and welfare legislation. A violation

---

* This dilemma is to some extent resolved when computers are used for content analysis because reanalysis of the data usually involves only additional computer time, not recoding of the data. This point is further developed in Chapter 7.

of this rule would occur if certain types of statements could be placed into both categories, e.g., if our categories were defined so that a general statement (i.e., one without geographical referent) expressing support for massive government action to raise standards of living could be coded as support for both interventionist foreign policies and domestic welfare legislation. In this case, a positive correlation between attitudes toward the two policies is, of course, spurious.

Independence of categories, the rule that assignment of any datum into a category not affect the classification of other data, is often hard to satisfy, especially when content units are scaled along some dimension. For example, suppose that we decided to measure intensity as well as direction of attitudes toward foreign and welfare policies. We might decide to rank statements according to the Q-sort, in which items are assigned to a nine-point fixed distribution scale:

Category (scale value)	1	2	3	4	5	6	7	8	9
Percentage	5	8	12	16	18	16	12	8	5

When any content unit is assigned to a category, it affects assignment of those that follow. If we have 100 statements and the first five are placed into category 9, clearly none of the subsequent 95 statements can be assigned to that category. Similarly, after 99 statements are classified, assignment of the 100th item is completely determined.

The requirement of independence is overlooked whenever some form of ranking is used to assign values to content units. Ranking can be a useful way to treat data, but the analyst needs to be aware that his subsequent analyses, including statistical operations that may be performed, are restricted. Comparing the average (mean) intensity of two separately Q-sorted data is meaningless because by definition each is 5.00. Thus, if we performed a Q-sort on all welfare and foreign policy statements for 1900, and did another Q-sort for 1968 statements, we could not determine whether intensity of support welfare legislation had increased in the intervening 68 years.

Finally, the rule that each category must be derived from a *single classification principle* stipulates that conceptually different levels of analysis must be kept separate. Consider again our illustrative study, in which categories for a single year might have been formulated as in Table 5-1. By combining source (Democrats and Republicans) and attitude (support, reject) at a single level, these categories are in clear violation of the rule. Note also that, as formulated, these categories violate the requirement of mutual exhaustiveness. A statement by William Jennings Bryan, before a mass audience, condemning American military efforts against guerillas in the Philippines would be coded both in category I (a

TABLE 5-1

Categories for 1900

| | Mass Public | | | |
Category	Bryan, Democrat	McKinley, Republican	Support	Reject
Foreign policy	I	II	V	VI
Welfare legislation	III	IV	VII	VIII

| | Informed Public | | | |
Category	Bryan, Democrat	McKinley, Republican	Support	Reject
Foreign policy	IX	X	XIII	XIV
Welfare legislation	XI	XII	XV	XVI

foreign policy statement by a Democratic candidate) and in category VI (rejection of an interventionist foreign policy action).

It is, of course, unlikely that even an inexperienced analyst would make a mistake of the type illustrated in this rather simple example. When a complex set of categories is being developed, however, violation of this principle may be less easily recognized.

Standard Categories

One of the questions frequently debated in the literature is that of *standard categories*. The advantages of standardization are the same as in any area of scholarship: results may be compared across studies and findings will tend to become cumulative. On the other hand, the disparity of purpose which characterizes content analysis research makes standardization difficult to achieve. Some categories have been rather widely employed in descriptive studies of newspaper content (Willey, 1926; Woodward, 1930; Bush, 1961), values (White, 1951; Lasswell, 1935), political symbols (Pool, 1952a), attitudes (Osgood, Suci, and Tannenbaum, 1957), and a few other areas. There have also been recent attempts to develop standard categories for general psycholinguistic analysis (Laffal, 1965) and dream analysis (Hall and Van de Castle, 1966). But, in general, Pool's (1959, p. 213) assessment of a decade ago accurately reflects the state of the field:

It is questionable, however, how ready we are to establish standard measures . . . in content analysis. Such a measure is convenient when a considerable number of researchers are working on the same variable, and when someone succeeds in working out good categories for that variable. It is doubtful that either of those criteria can be met in most areas of content analysis.

Reasons for the general absence of standard categories are not hard to find. The premium on "originality" and the concomitant reluctance of analysts to adopt the categories of others—tendencies clearly not limited to content analysis research is probably a contributing factor. A more basic reason, however, is that there are few areas of social inquiry in which there is sufficient consensus on theory to inform the selection of categories. More specifically, we are lacking a general theory of communication from which such categories might be drawn. Finally, many of the most interesting content analyses will probably always depend on categories developed especially for the data at hand.

This state of affairs, understandable as it may be, actually has broader implications for research than might appear at first glance. It is, in the first place, closely related to the problem of identifying *norms* for important classes of communicators. More broadly, the purpose of both standard categories and norms is to improve the *quality of inferences* from content data. Let us consider both of these questions in more detail.

In Chapter 2 we discussed norms in connection with research designs for evaluating the performance of communication sources. Here we are concerned with norms in the empirical rather than the prescriptive sense, i.e., our interest is in the modal range of communication behavior for various classes of communicators. The task of establishing norms is a relatively simple one for groups whose membership is very limited. For example, in their study of the authorship of 12 *Federalist Papers*, Mosteller and Wallace (1964) were in effect faced with the task of identifying stylistic standards for two classes of sources, each with a membership of one—James Madison and Alexander Hamilton.

More commonly, social scientists and humanists are interested in larger groups. Moreover, their interests may not be confined to content attributes which are as easily defined as those used in the analysis of the *Federalist Papers*—relative word frequencies. In such cases establishment of norms is often an undertaking that exceeds the time and resources of a single investigator. But even when many analysts are working in a single area of inquiry, unless they are using identical categories results are not cumulative and, therefore, one cannot abstract norms from them. This observation can perhaps best be illustrated in the field of psychotherapeutic research. The volume of investigations, as well as the quality and ingenuity of many studies, is impressive. But, as is evident in Marsden's (1965) comments cited earlier,* the strong tendency for each investigator to develop original categories—and often to drop them after one or two studies—has been a deterrent to the replication necessary for developing standard categories and norms.

The importance of norms for any class of communicators is that they provide a benchmark against which the analyst can compare his findings. This is, of course, a specific application of the general rule that meaningful analysis requires at least one type of comparison. When comparison is to be made to an outside criterion (i.e., one which lies outside the documents under analysis) inferences drawn from the comparison can be no better than the criterion itself. Consider a few examples:

1. How does the proportion of international news in newspaper X compare with that of metropolitan dailies?

2. How does textbook X compare with those found to be readable by 10-year-old children?

3. How do changes in the pattern of patient X's verbal behavior compare with those who have undergone successful psychotherapy?

In each case the analyst draws conclusions from data about a single source (newspaper X, textbook X, patient X) in light of comparison with an entire class of communicators (metropolitan dailies, materials which 10-year-old children can read and understand, patients who have undergone successful psychotherapy). Valid inferences depend on both the analyst's data and the criterion (or norm) with which they are being compared.

Hall (in press) cites two interesting examples in which analysts, apparently unaware of norms for certain classes of individuals, were led to faulty inferences. The first study revealed that the content of dreams in a New Guinea tribe contained more misfortunes than good fortunes. Because members of this tribe hold a pessimistic view of life, the authors concluded that dream content faithfully reflected their waking life attitudes. But, as Hall points out, misfortunes exceed good fortunes in dreams of people throughout the world, including those whose attitudes toward life are optimistic. In the other study, dreams of the elderly were found to contain many themes of diminished resources to cope with problems. But inferences relating this content characteristic to age were ill-founded because the same thing is found in the dreams of the young.

There are some indications that recent developments in computer-based content analysis may serve as a major impetus toward development of standard categories. Analysts who might otherwise have adopted

---

* See Chapter 4, p. 77.

categories developed in other studies have often found that they were not defined precisely enough to permit replication. Moreover, the laboriousness of coding tended to discourage analyzing the data twice—once with one's own categories, a second time with those found useful in another study. When computers are used, operational definitions of categories must be explicit and exhaustive. It is thus a relatively simple matter for one analyst to communicate with others about his categories. Equally important, costs of reanalysis of data on IBM cards can be measured in added dollars spent on machine time rather than in the more valuable currency of a scholar's time in completing his study. Unambiguous, easily shared, and conveniently used categories do not, of course, ensure wide acceptance. But it does seem reasonably safe to predict that *if* progress is made toward developing standard categories (and as a result, developing norms), it will come about largely as a result of computer-based content analysis research. *

Categories: Some Examples

In the absence of standard schemes of classification, the analyst is usually faced with the task of constructing appropriate categories by trial and error methods. This process consists of moving back and forth from theory to data, testing the usefulness of tentative categories, and then modifying them in light of the data.

There are as many possible schemes for classifying content data as there are questions which may be asked of the data. Among the types of categories used frequently in content analysis research are the following examples. They are presented here neither as standard categories for studies of a certain class, although some were designed as such and have in fact been widely used, nor with an endorsement that they be adopted uncritically. They are intended to serve only an illustrative purpose.

Subject matter categories are probably the most frequently used in content analysis. The goal is to determine what the communication is about. Subject matter categories are usually developed specifically for the problem at hand; thus their variety is limited only by the number of different substantive questions one seeks to answer with content data. Among the many examples of subject matter categories, and the purposes for which they were used, are the following.

To identify trends in newspaper content, Mott (1942) placed news items in 12 categories:

1. Foreign news and features
2. Washington news
3. Columns dealing with public affairs
4. Original editorials

---

* Further evidence in support of this point is presented in the more extended discussion of computer content analysis in Chapter 7.

5. Business, financial, marine   6. Sports
7. Society   8. Women's interests
9. Theater, movies, books, art, etc. 10. Radio announcements and news
11. Comic strips and singles   12. Illustration (excluding comics).

In his study of American party platforms, Benson (1961) coded themes according to the following categories:

1. The general and specific role of government in a democratic republic
2. The locus of government power
   a) County   b) State   c) Nation
3. The role and power of the branches of government
   a) Executive b) Legislative c) Judicial
4. Foreign policy
5. Character self-portrait
6. Image of the opponent.

Prothro's (1956) categories for comparing values in presidential addresses were:

1. Government aid
2. Economy and efficiency
3. Bright realities (e.g., prosperity in U.S.)
4. Peace
5. Law enforcement
6. Community cooperation
7. Government regulation
8. Progress
9. Class
10. Economic unity
11. Social optimism
12. Dark realities (e.g., threats of external aggression)
13. Party
14. National power

Love songs were analyzed by Horton (1957) according to these categories:

Prologue: Wishing and dreaming

Act I: Courtship
   Scene 1: Direct Approach   Scene 2: Sentimental Appeal
   Scene 3: Desperation   Scene 4: Questions and Promises
   Scene 5: Impatience and Surrender

Act II: The honeymoon

Act III: The downward course of love

Scene 1: Temporary Separation
Scene 2: Hostile Forces
Scene 3: Threat of Leaving
Scene 4: Final Parting

Act IV: All alone

Scene 1: Pleading
Scene 2: Hopeless Love
Scene 3: New Beginnings

An example of categories in the form of a scale, i.e., in which items are given different weights, is an anxiety scale developed by Gleser, Gottschalk, and Springer, (1961):

Type of Anxiety		*Occuring To or Experienced By*	*Weight*
1. Death	a)	Self	3
	b)	Animate others	2
	c)	Inanimate objects	1
	d)	Denial	1
2. Multilation anxiety	a)	Self	3
	b)	Animate others	2
	c)	Inanimate objects	1
	d)	Denial	1
3. Separation anxiety	a)	Self	3
	b)	Animate others	2
	c)	Inanimate objects	1
	d)	Denial	1
4. Guilt anxiety	a)	Self	3
	b)	Animate others	2
	c)	Denial	1
5. Shame anxiety	a)	Self	3
	b)	Animate others	2
	c)	Denial	1
6. Diffuse or nonspecific anxiety	a)	Self	3
	b)	Animate others	2
	c)	Denial	1

Studies of attitudes, values, and the like generally use some form of *direction categories* to determine the author's treatment of relevant subjects. Among the most widely used ways of classifying direction are a three-point nominal scale or seven-point semantic differential scales:

1. Favorable   2. Neutral   3. Unfavorable

Positive	+3	+2	+1	0	−1	−2	−3	Negative
Strong	+3	+2	+1	0	−1	−2	−3	Weak
Active	+3	+2	+1	0	−1	−2	−3	Passive

Standard refers to the basis upon which the sources make judgments. The examples below represent a set of specific categories for coding the standards by which Freud's dream theory was rejected (Herma, Kris, and Shor, 1943), and a general purpose set of categories for standards of judgment in personality studies and clinical psychology (White, 1947):

Standards for rejecting Freud's dream theory

A. *Depreciation through value judgment*

 1. Ridicule and mockery
 2. Rejection on moral grounds
 3. Denial of validity

B. *Denial of scientific character of theory*

 1. Questioning analysts' sincerity
 2. Questioning verification of theory
 3. Questioning methodology

C. *Exposure of social status of theory*

 1. Disagreement among experts
 2. Fashionableness
 3. Lack of originality

Standards of judgment for personality analysis

A. *Moral*

 1. Morality   4. Obedience
 2. Truthfulness   5. Purity
 3. Justice   6. Religion

B. *Social*

 1. Pleasant personality   5. Generosity
 2. Conformity   6. Tolerance
 3. Manners   7. Group unity
 4. Modesty

C. *Egoistic*

  1. Strength   3. Intelligence
  2. Determination   4. Appearance

D. *Miscellaneous*

  1. Carefulness   3. Culture
  2. Cleanliness   4. Adjustment

A related category is that of *evidence* presented by the source in support of his assertions. An example is the category set used to analyze Henry J. Taylor's radio talks (Shepard, 1956):

1. Statistics
2. Examples and comparisons
3. Analogies and figurative language
4. Testimony
5. None.

Value categories are among the most widely used in content analysis. The examples below include sets of categories proposed as general purpose schemes by Lasswell and Kaplan (1950) and White (1951, pp. 22-32), and two others developed for a specific set of documents:

*Lasswell's value categories**

1. Power   5. Wealth
2. Rectitude   6. Well-being
3. Respect   7. Enlightenment
4. Affection   8. Skill

White's "value analysis" categories†

A. *Physiological*

  1. Food   4. Health
  2. Sex   5. Safety
  3. Rest   6. Comfort

B. *Social*

  1. Sex-love
  2. Family-love
  3. Friendship

---

* A computer content analysis "dictionary" for the Lasswell value categories has been written by Peterson and Brewer (n.d.). The format and operation of this and other "dictionaries" is described in more detail in Chapter 7.

†These categories were developed for personality studies and clinical psychology, but White (1951, pp. 44-55) demonstrates how they may be adapted to other purposes, e.g., political or propaganda research.

C. *Egoistic*
1. Independence
2. Achievement
3. Recognition
4. Self-regard
5. Dominance
6. Aggression

D. *Fearful (emotional security)*

E. *Playful*
1. New experience
2. Excitement
3. Beauty
4. Humor
5. Creative self-expression

F. *Practical*
1. Practicality   2. Ownership   3. Work

G. *Cognitive*
1. Knowledge

H. *Miscellaneous*
1. Happiness   2. Value in general

For his analysis of business values as revealed in letters written by railroad presidents, Cochran (1953) developed the following categories:

A. *General business concepts*
1. Expansion and innovation
2. Relations with competitors, suppliers, and customers
3. Internal reaction to external change

B. *Managerial problems of the railroad corporation*
1. The managerial hierarchy
2. Labor relations
3. Inter- and intracorporate relations

C. *External relations of the railroad corporation*
1. The railroad as an agency of regional growth
2. Railroads and government
3. Public relations

D. *Attitudes of railroad executives toward general problems of society*
1. Effect of formal foreign and domestic philosophies and literary works
2. Religion
3. Value of public and private education
4. Proper area for government expenditure and philanthropy
5. Proper role of government in economic and social life and personal participation in public affairs.
6. General political observations
7. Examples of personal philosophy and methods of thought

Berelson and Salter (1946) used the following value categories in their study of popular fiction:

A. *"Heart" goals*

   1. Romantic love
   2. Settled marriage state
   3. Idealism
   4. Affection and emotional security
   5. Patriotism
   6. Adventure
   7. Justice
   8. Independence

B. *"Head" goals*

   1. Solution to immediate concrete problems
   2. Self-advancement
   3. Money and material goods
   4. Economic and social security
   5. Power and dominance

Closely related to value studies are those which examine *ends and means* used to attain them. A study of goal achievement in children's television programs used categories consisting of seven classes of goals and eight classes of methods (Larson, Gray, and Fortis, 1963):

Classes of Goals

1. Property (material success)
2. Self-preservation (including status quo wish)
3. Affection
4. Sentiment
5. Power and prestige
6. Psychological (including violence, education)
7. Other

Classes of Methods

1. Legal
2. Nonlegal (yet no attempt to injure or damage)
3. Economic
4. Violence
5. Organization, negotiation, and compromise
6. Escape (attempt to avoid facts inherent in accomplishing the goal, forgetting goal, etc.)
7. Chance
8. Other

For a study of comic strips, Spiegelman, Terwilliger, and Fearing (1953a) formulated these categories:

Goals

1. Brutality
2. Vengeance
3. Power-status
4. Wealth
5. Freedom
6. Physical integrity
7. Adventure
8. Romantic love
9. Recreation
10. Comfort
11. Justice
12. Group success
13. Service-benefactor

Means

1. Industry
2. Personal charm
3. Fate
4. Authority
5. Trickery
6. Violence
7. Sponging

Traits of characters appearing in fiction and the mass media have often been coded. Occupational, ethnic, and political trait categories are illustrated in the following examples.

De Fleur (1962) used these occupational categories in his study of television:

1. Professional, technical, and kindred workers
2. Farmers and farm managers
3. Managers, officials, and proprietors (except farm)
4. Clerical and kindred workers
5. Sales workers, retail, and others
6. Craftsmen, foremen, and kindred workers
7. Operatives and kindred workers
8. Private household workers
9. Service workers (except category 8)
10. Farm laborers and farm foremen
11. Laborers (except farm and mine)
12. Occupations not reported (or unclassified)

Berelson and Salter (1946) placed characters in American popular fiction into five categories:

1. Americans
2. Anglo-Saxon and Nordic descent
3. Jews
4. Negroes
5. Other descent

The traits of ideal communists, as described in various types of party literature, were classified in the following way by Almond (1954):

A. *Goal qualities*

    1. Esoteric
    2. Exoteric

B. *Tactical qualities*

1.	Militance	5.	Activism
2.	Rationality	6.	Dedication
3.	Organization	7.	Uniqueness
4.	Leadership	8.	Confidence

Verbal interaction is a central aspect of both small group studies and analysis of psychiatric interviews. Bales' (1950) categories for studies of the former type are:

A. *Social-emotional area: positive*

    1. Shows solidarity
    2. Shows tension release
    3. Agrees

B. *Task area: neutral*

1.	Gives suggestions	4.	Asks for orientation
2.	Gives opinion	5.	Asks for opinion
3.	Gives orientation	6.	Asks for suggestion

C. *Social-emotional area: negative*

    1. Disagrees
    2. Shows tension
    3. Shows antagonism

Interaction categories for analysis of psychiatric interviews can be illustrated with those developed by Bandura, Lipsher, and Miller (1960) to study "interaction sequences," defined as a patient's statement expressing hostility, the therapist's response, and the immediately following patient's statement:

A. *Patient*

    1. Hostility: any expression of dislike, resentment, anger, antagonism, opposition, or of critical attitudes
    2. Referent:

a)	Spouse	d)	Self
b)	Children	e)	Therapist
c)	Parents	f)	Other person or object

B. *Therapist*

  1. Approach reactions: responses designed to elicit further expressions of hostile feelings, attitudes, and behavior

    a) Approval   d) Reflection
    b) Exploration e) Labeling
    c) Instigation

  2. Avoidance reactions: responses designed to inhibit, discourage, or divert hostile expressions

    a) Disapproval   d) Ignoring
    b) Topical transition e) Mislabeling
    c) Silence

  3. Unclassified

Several of the miscellaneous categories used for analysis of fiction and drama can be illustrated by those included in a comparative study of German and American theater (McGranahan and Wayne, 1948).

A. *Basic themes*

  1. Love   5. Outcast
  2. Morality   6. Career
  3. Idealism   7. No agreement
  4. Power

B. *Endings*

  1. Happy   3. Tragic or unhappy
  2. Ambiguous 4. No agreement

C. *Time of action*

  1. Contemporary (1920-1927)
  2. Historical
    a) 1789-1919 b) 1453-1788 c) Antiquity
    d) No specific time: sagas, fairy tales, symbolic fantasies

D. *Setting of action*

  1. Domestic setting
  2. Foreign or legendary setting

E. *Patterns of conflict in the love theme*

  1. Youthful love versus parents
  2. True love versus unwholesome love
  3. Love versus temporary misunderstandings
  4. Love versus ideals, higher values
  5. Idealists' love versus social norms
  6. Power conflicts for love
  7. Love versus outcast status
  8. Miscellaneous

A number of category sets have been developed to classify the *devices* used in propaganda and other forms of persuasive communication. Under this heading we may also include categories used to detect techniques of slanting news.

On the basis of his extensive studies in propaganda, Lee (1952) developed the following categories:

A. *Techniques of basic procedure*

    1. Selecting the issues
    2. Case making
    3. Simplification

B. *Omnibus symbols*

    1. Glittering generalities   2. Name calling

C. *Techniques of identification*

    1. Transfer and testimonial   3. Bandwagon
    2. Plain folks   4. Guilt and virtue by association

D. *Strategic techniques*

    1. Hot potato   9. Appeasement
    2. Stalling   10. Confusion
    3. Least of evils   11. Big lie
    4. Scapegoating   12. Censorship
    5. Shift of scene   13. Person to person
    6. Change of pace   14. Program of deeds
    7. Big tent   15. Leadership
    8. Conflict

A general set of categories for assessing bias in newspapers includes space, placement, and lexical devices for slanting coverage and treatment of political campaigns (Klein and Maccoby, 1954):

1. Number of stories
2. Column inches, all headlines
3. Type size of type A headlines
4. Tone of headlines
5. Number of type A headlines
6. Story placement in column 8
7. Number of biased remarks
8. Number of direct quotes
9. Number of pictures
10. Column inches, all pictures
11. Total column inches of stories (front page)
12. Total column inches of stories (jump page)
13. Total column inches of stories
14. Ratio of front to jump page coverage

Merrill's (1965) categories for analyzing bias in news-magazines include the following devices:

1. Attribution bias
2. Adjective bias
3. Adverbial bias

4. Contextual bias
5. Outright opinion
6. Photographic bias

Studies of *rhetorical style* are widespread in the content analysis literature. In his analysis of Woodrow Wilson's rhetorical style, Runion (1936) used grammatical classifications:

A. Sentence length

B. Classification of sentences
1. Use
   a) Declarative
   b) Imperative
   c) Interrogative
   d) Exclamatory
2. Structure
   a) Simple
   b) Complex
   c) Compound
   d) Compound-complex
3. Artistry
   a) Loose   b) Periodic   c) Balanced

C. Figures of speech
1. Metaphor
2. Simile
3. Personification

4. Rhetorical question
5. Unclassified figures

A quite different set of categories was developed by Ellsworth (1965) to study campaign speeches:

Analysis: Any statement of a *specific position* which is supported by *reasoning* and/or discussion of *consequences.*

Evidence: Any statement which *utilizes evidence* in a nonanalytic fashion to support a *specific position* specifically espoused or assumed to be espoused by the candidate.

Declaration: Any statement by a candidate which states a *specific position* where neither reason, nor a discussion of consequences, nor evidence is offered in support of the position.

To these primary categories Ellsworth added two subcategories, *criticism* and *defense,* thereby producing a category set with nine classifications.

Analysis	Analytical criticism	Analytical defense
Evidence	Critical evidence	Defensive evidence
Declaration	Declarative criticism	Declarative defense

This list of category-sets is neither exhaustive nor does it define the limits of content analysis. It is merely an enumeration of types of categories which have been employed more or less frequently. Nor are the categories at the same conceptual level. Subject matter categories can be used independently, as is done when newspaper content is classified into various types of news. But one cannot code items for direction (e.g., approval-disapproval) independently of a referent. The same is true of the "standard" category. The coder may first be asked to isolate a subject matter unit (e.g., Freud's dream theory), then classify it for direction of attitude (favorable or unfavorable), after which some judgment is made as to the standard used for acceptance or rejection (Herma, Kris, and Shor, 1943).

UNITS OF ANALYSIS

Recording Units

In addition to defining the categories into which content data are to be classified, the analyst must designate the units to be coded. The initial choice is that of *recording unit,* the specific segment of content that is characterized by placing it in a given category. Almost all content analysis studies have used one of five units.

The *single word* or *symbol* is generally the smallest unit that is used in content analysis research.* In the past, this unit has usually been avoided in mass media research involving a large volume of data. A notable exception was the RADIR studies, in which nearly 20,000 editorials were searched for the appearance of specified political symbols. More recently, computer content analysis programs have materially reduced the costs and tedium of word or symbols analyses, while at the same time eliminating, for all practical purposes, the problem of reliability. Among the classes of research reviewed in Chapters 3 and 4, words or symbols have found widest use in studies on readability (Gray and Leary, 1935; Flesch, 1948; Taylor, 1953), style (Miles, 1951, Parrish, 1959), psychotherapy (Dollard and Mowrer, 1947), and literary detection (Yule, 1944; Mosteller and Wallace, 1964).

For many purposes the *theme,* a single assertion about some subject, is the most useful unit of content analysis. It is almost indispensable in research on propaganda, values, attitudes, beliefs, and the like. A major drawback is that coding themes is usually time consuming. Another difficulty is that its boundaries are not as easily identified as those of the word, paragraph, or item. The sentence, "These clandestine Soviet actions on the imprisoned island of Cuba will not be tolerated by the American

---

* For exceptions, see Skinner's (1939) study of alliteration in Shakespeare's sonnets, in which each syllable was recorded according to its first consonant, and Paisley's (1966) analysis of "letter redundancy" in various English texts.

people," contains assertions about three nations. The coder must be able to reduce this sentence into its component themes before they may be placed in the proper categories. This process of reducing a grammatical unit into thematic units—sometimes called "unitizing"—can seriously reduce reliability unless the structural properties of the thematic unit are precisely defined.

Studies of fiction, drama, movies, radio, and other forms of entertainment materials have often employed the *character* as the recording unit. In this case the coder tallies the number of persons, rather than the number of words or themes, into the appropriate categories. Such research has focused on ethnic, socio-economic, marital, psychological, and other traits of characters as portrayed in magazines (Berelson and Salter, 1946), movies (Jones, 1942), television (De Fleur, 1964), comics (Spiegelman, Terwilliger, and Fearing, 1953a), and other products of the mass media. Characters appearing in novels or drama have also been used with various categories of traits for the purpose of drawing inferences about the personalities of authors (Kanzer, 1948; McCurdy, 1939, 1947, 1953).

In part because grammatical units such as the *sentence* or *paragraph* do not usually lend themselves to classification into a single category, they have rarely been used as recording units. The sentence about Soviet actions in Cuba, cited above, illustrates a problem that is even more severe when the paragraph is the recording unit. Should it be coded as an assertion about Soviet actions, as an expression of American policy, or as an evaluative statement about Cuban society? It is, of course, all three. The sentence or paragraph is rarely satisfactory when precision of measurement is important; in that case words or themes will probably be used. On the other hand, when only crude measurement of content attributes across a large body of data is required, coding sentences or paragraphs is likely to prove far too laborious.

The *item* is the recording unit when the entire article, film, book, or radio program is characterized. This unit is too gross for most research, and may present problems when items fall between two categories; e.g., is a war film with a comic theme classified under "war" or "comedy"? When used in conjunction with well-formulated categories that permit reliable judgments about major attributes of the book, article, and the like, item analysis can yield interesting results, as in the case of the Schneider and Dornbusch (1958) study of values in best-selling religious books.

Context Units

It may not be possible to classify a recording unit without some further reference to the context in which it appears. Attitudes toward democracy cannot be inferred solely on the basis of how frequently that word and others defining the category "democracy" appears in the communication;

TABLE 5-2

Comparison of four recording and context units

Method	Recording unit	Context unit
I	Symbol	Sentence
II	Paragraph	Paragraph
III	Three sentences	Three sentences
IV	Article	Article

the *context unit* is the largest body of content that may be searched to characterize a recording unit. Once the coder identifies the symbol "democracy" in a document he may be instructed to search through the sentence, paragraph, or even the entire document, for evidence of the author's attitude toward democracy.

Selection of recording and context units rests upon two considerations. First, which units will best meet the requirements of the research problem? This question can be answered only in light of the hypotheses and the nature of the data. The important point is that *selection of units may affect results of the analysis.* Geller, Kaplan, and Lasswell (1942b) performed an experiment comparing four different recording and context units on the same sample of editorial matter. (Table 5-2). The four methods were in agreement in indicating *direction* of bias (favorable, unfavorable, neutral), but differed considerably in revealing its *extent.* In general, the larger the recording unit, the more the degree of bias in editorials was emphasized, and as the size of context unit was increased, the number of neutral entries diminished.

The consequences which may result from choice of context units can be further illustrated in contingency analysis. In this method of content analysis, inferences are based on co-occurrences of content attributes within the same unit. If the context unit is very small, few co-occurrences will be found; on the other hand, if the entire document is the context unit, everything which appears will be contingent with everything else. Osgood very tentatively suggested that stable results can be achieved with units of 120 to 210 words (Osgood, 1959, p. 62).

A second factor which few investigators can afford to overlook is efficiency; i.e., which units give satisfactory results with the least expenditure of resources? "Satisfactory" cannot be defined in general terms, but only in light of a specific research problem. In an analysis of best-selling inspirational literature, initially themes appearing in each paragraph were coded, a task which proved disappointingly time consuming and difficult (Schneider and Dornbusch, 1958, Appendix C). A second coding method was also used: The entire book was read and assigned a single summary score for each category. A comparison of results derived by the two methods revealed that little substantive information was lost with the latter approach. Questions of efficiency can often be answered only by comparing two or more methods on the same sample of data. Unfortunately, relatively few studies have reported experiments of this kind.

SYSTEMS OF ENUMERATION

All content variables are quantifiable or else they are not variables. But there are many forms of measurement which yield quantified results. In deciding how to analyze his data and present his findings, the analyst chooses both the *unit* in terms of which quantification is to be performed, and the *system of enumeration* he will use.

The recording unit and the unit of enumeration may be identical, as was the case in a study of occupations portrayed on television; the occupation of each character was recorded and results were presented as the relative frequencies of various occupational types (De Fleur, 1964). In a similar study of soap operas, recording and enumeration units were different. The occupation of each character was initially recorded, but the results were reported according to the number of *scenes* in which any occupational type appeared; thus a scene involving three housewives was tallied only once (Arnheim, 1944). We can contrast these studies in somewhat different terms. The first one used only a single *unit* and *system of enumeration;* the *frequency* of each occupational type in television programs was recorded, and these scores served as the basis for reporting results. In the analysis of soap operas, however, two units and systems of enumeration were used. The initial recording of occupational types considered only *appearance*—did a particular occupational type appear in the scene? But for purposes of analysis and reporting, a measure of *frequency* was used—in how many scenes did each occupational type appear?

Systems of enumeration vary considerably in precision and in time required to code a given sample of data. The investigator must determine how fine are the discriminations he needs in order to satisfy the requirements of his problem; generally, the greater the need for precision, the higher will be the costs of the analysis. Often the nature of the categories and data are such that the search for maximum precision will not only entail considerably higher costs, but also may sacrifice reliability. The choice may also affect the results of the analysis. For example, editorials may be coded according to the frequency of favorable or unfavorable assertions about a specific issue. If the unit of enumeration is the single assertion, results will indicate whether the entire editorial was only slightly (50+%) or predominantly on one side or the other. If the entire editorial serves as the unit of enumeration, i.e., if the whole editorial is scored pro or con, this distinction will be lost. Consider, for instance, a hypothetical study of the effects of newspaper editorials on a school bond

TABLE 5-3

Comparison of results using different units of enumeration

Editorial	Recording unit: Number of themes	Unit of enumeration: A. Themes	B. Editorials
1	4 favorable 3 neutral 3 unfavorable	4 favorable 3 neutral 3 unfavorable	1 favorable
2	3 favorable 2 neutral 2 unfavorable	3 favorable 2 neutral 2 unfavorable	1 favorable
3	2 favorable 0 neutral 0 unfavorable	2 favorable 0 neutral 0 unfavorable	1 favorable
4	0 favorable 1 neutral 5 unfavorable	0 favorable 1 neutral 5 unfavorable	1 unfavorable
Summary		9 favorable (36%) 6 neutral (24%) 10 unfavorable (40%)	3 favorable (75%) 0 neutral (0%) 1 unfavorable (25%)

issue in which the recording unit is the theme, scored as favorable, neutral, or unfavorable. We might use either the theme (A) or the entire editorial (B) as the unit of enumeration (Table 5-3).

This rather simple example is presented to demonstrate that different units may yield strikingly different results, not to judge their relative merits. The most important aspect of the investigator's choice, therefore, is that each system of enumeration carries with it certain assumptions regarding the nature of the data and inferences which may be drawn therefrom. The first method assumes that what is important for assessing the effects of editorials is the number of favorable and unfavorable assertions about an issue, and thus, that a relatively ambivalent editorial such as No. 1 should be scored differently from No. 3. The second method incorporates the premise that the impact of persuasive messages lies in the overall impression created. Stated somewhat differently, the first view is that the effect of the whole is equal to the sum of its parts, the second position is that the impact of the whole is different from the sum of its parts.* Once again we can see the hazards of allowing methodological

* For reasons discussed in Chapter 2, inferences about the effects of editorials on voters could not be drawn directly from content data. Thus, whichever unit of enumeration was selected, the results would require validation with independent data; we might, for example, interview a sample of voters to determine the extent to which their views were influenced by editorials.

convenience, rather than substantive and theoretical concerns, to dictate the research design. This is just one more point at which it is important to confront the question: "What is the theoretical relevance of the measures I am using?"

Many early content analysis studies employed measures of *space* (e.g., column inches) to describe relative emphases in the content of newspapers. The analogous unit for film, radio, and television is *time*. The continuing popularity of space/time measures can be attributed largely to the relative ease with which they may be used to produce quantitative results. Unfortunately, these same qualities have also led to their use in innumerable studies of great apparent precision and, at best, peripheral theoretical importance.

For some purposes space/time measures may serve as an adequate substitute for other more time-consuming units.

Markham and Stempel (1957) compared newspaper political coverage as measured by the amount of space in column inches, frequency of issues mentioned, and size of headlines. The three methods yielded similar results, but measuring the relative allocation of space was done considerably more rapidly than counting issues. The limitations of space/time units derive mostly from a lack of sensitivity to other than the grossest attributes of content. Such measures are most appropriate for descriptions of mass media, but are too crude to index attitudes, values, style, and the like. For example, space measures may be useful if we wish to compare coverage of international news, but they would be of dubious value to answer questions about the degree of political bias in newspapers because a one-to-one relationship between the amount of space devoted to a subject and the manner in which it is treated cannot be assumed.

One alternative to space/time units is to search the document, or some subunit of the text, for the *appearance* of the attribute. The size of the context unit determines the frequency with which repeated items occurring in close proximity to each other are counted separately. Depending on the context unit, repetition of a given attribute within a sentence (White, 1947), paragraph (Schneider and Dornbusch, 1958), or item (Lasswell, Lerner, and Pool, 1952) does not change the tally. This method of enumeration has two important advantages. It can usually be done with relative ease and with high reliability because the coder is faced with a simple dichotomous decision: does the content unit appear or not? Moreover, it is useful if one cannot assume a linear relationship between frequency and importance of content attributes. Some investigators have labeled this type of nominal measurement as "qualitative" content analysis, although the term is somewhat misleading because data coded in this manner may be presented quantitatively (e.g., the percentage of items in which a given theme appears), as well as subjected to certain statistical tests.

The most widely used method of measuring characteristics of content is *frequency,* in which *every* occurrence of a given attribute is tallied. For example, how frequently do the folktales of various Indian tribes express need to achieve (McClelland and Friedman, 1952) or, how frequently did Madison and Hamilton use the words "whilst" or "upon" (Mosteller and Wallace, 1964)?

Much of the qualitative-quantitative debate in content analysis ultimately comes down to disagreement about the validity of frequency measures. There is a considerable element of truth in the charge that the validity of frequency counts is usually accepted as an unexamined article of faith. On the other hand, those who have compared frequencies with other measures have often concluded that the former are satisfactory (Pool, 1959, p. 194). But the merits of opposing views cannot be determined in the abstract. Rather, the analyst should consider the issue in light of his research question, because if he selects frequency measures to test his hypotheses, he incorporates two related assumptions into his research design. First, he assumes that the frequency with which an attribute appears in messages is a valid indicator of concern, focus of attention, intensity, value, importance, and so on. Second, he assumes that *each unit of content*—word, theme, character, or item—*should be given equal weight,* permitting aggregation or direct comparison.

George (1959b) and others have contended that for purposes of drawing inferences about causes and effects of communication, the first premise is often untenable. Other questions have been raised regarding frequency measures. For example, what is the relationship between distribution, or permeability, of attributes in the text and their importance (Dunphy, 1964a)? Is there a difference between two variables appearing equally often if their distribution in documents is different? Are associational structures of the type revealed by contingency analysis, which depend on appearance and contiguity rather than frequency, better measures for certain classes of research problems?

The dubious validity, for many research problems, of the assumption that each unit should be assigned equal weight has often received recognition from content analysts (cf. Stewart, 1943). Descriptions of newspaper content, for example, routinely differentiate items appearing on the front page from those printed elsewhere, either by coding them separately, or by using a system of weighting to reflect the factor of prominence. Similar devices have been used to reflect the position of items within the page and size of headlines. Ash's (1948) study of the Taft-Hartley Act illustrates a method of adjusting scores to reflect circulation. An evaluation of the act received a score proportional to the circulation of the magazine in which it appeared. These are but a few of many ways that have been used to modify frequency counts by weighting for qualitative differences.

For research dealing with values, attitudes, and related concerns, simple tabulations of frequency may prove insufficient because they fail to take *intensity* into account. In other words, the assumption that valid inferences regarding attitudes can be drawn from frequency scores, unadjusted for intensity of expression, is often untenable. Some of the problems can be illustrated by examining four Chinese statements.

1. We may find it necessary to disagree with Khrushchev's policies.

2. We must bitterly denounce Khrushchev's policies.

3. We will soon begin denouncing Khrushchev's policies.

4. We have sometimes disagreed with Khrushchev's policies in the past.

To map trends in Sino-Soviet relations, the analyst might require some method of differentiating the intensity of the four themes. A set of nominal categories such as favorable-neutral-unfavorable fails to discriminate between these assertions—all of them would be coded as unfavorable.

Measuring the intensity of content units is often one of the more difficult aspects of coding. At minimum it requires coders to take on one additional judgment. That is, after content units are placed into categories, items in each category must further be rated along some scale for intensity. Compounding the problem is the broad range of linguistic elements which may indicate intensity, making it difficult to list all criteria the coder has to consider in making his decisions. In the themes cited above there are at least five elements to be considered in judging intensity: the relative intensities of the verbs "disagree" and "denounce"; the function of the adverbial modifiers "sometimes" and "bitterly"; the element of tense—past, present, and future actions; the probabilistic character of the first theme; and the imperative nature of the second one. This list by no means exhausts the intricacies of language which may denote intensity.

One method of coding for intensity is the "paired comparison" technique developed by Thurstone. From a representative sample of content units, judges decide which of each possible pair is rated higher on a linear scale of attitudes. The judgments are then used to construct categories into which the entire set of content units are coded. In the case of the four Chinese statements, judges would be asked to make six comparisons for intensity of Chinese disagreement with Khrushchev's policies:

1 versus 2	2 versus 3	3 versus 4
1 versus 3	2 versus 4	
1 versus 4		

If their judgments are transitive—e.g., if each judgment was consistent with the formula that 2 is more intense than 3 is more intense than 1 is more intense than 4—then these items could be used to define a scale of disagreement. In actual practice one would use a good many more items to form a reasonably comprehensive and stable scale. Zinnes (1963), for example, used 11 different random samples of from 10 to 16 items each to develop a 12-point scale for rating the intensity of hostile themes in diplomatic documents. The scale was then used for rating a larger sample of 2000 themes. Another version of this procedure was used to study national attitudes, as revealed in newspapers and journals, during two crisis periods in the Far East (Russell and Wright, 1933; Wright and Nelson, 1939). An experiment demonstrated that scales derived empirically, as by the Thurstone technique, sometimes yield more satisfactory results than logical scales when relatively untrained coders were used. Differences between the two methods of scale construction were not significant when experienced and trained personnel did the coding (Exline and Long, 1965).

The Q-sort scaling technique described earlier in this chapter has also been applied to content data. Judges are instructed to place content units into a fixed distribution nine-point scale (North *et al.*, 1963).* This is a rank order method with the number of permissible ties determined by the fixed distribution. When the content units to be scaled require rather subtle discriminations, the Q-sort may be useful because it forces judges to make fine distinctions rather than to rely on one or two of the extreme points on the scale.   On the other hand, a serious disadvantage inherent in the technique is that one cannot make comparisons between two different samples of Q-sorted data because the score of any item is only meaningful in relation to other items in the same sample. Thus, for long-term trend analyses and other types of research involving several samples of data, the paired comparison technique should be used in preference to the Q-sort. Paired comparison, rank order, or any other scaling method depends, of course, on the assumption that content units are sufficiently homogeneous on a single continuum that they may be compared.

An "atomic" approach to coding for intensity, "evaluative assertion analysis," was developed by Osgood, Saporta, and Nunnally (1956; Osgood, 1959). The initial step is to translate all sentences into one of two common thematic structures:

1. Attitude object/verbal connector/common meaning term.

2. Attitude object$_1$/verbal connector/attitude object$_2$.

For example, the sentence "An aggressive Soviet Union threatens the United States," is translated to read:

The Soviet Union / is / aggressive.
The Soviet Union / threatens / United States.

---

* The Q-sort distribution is described on page 100.

TABLE 5-4
"Evaluative assertion analysis" coding

Attitude object	Verbal connector	Value	Common meaning term	Value	Product
1. Soviet rulers	are	+3	ruthless	−3	−9
2. Soviet rulers	are	+3	atheistic	−3	−9
3. Soviet rulers	are	+3	despots	−3	−9
4. Soviet rulers	have in the past pursued	+2	evil goals	−3	−6
5. Soviet rulers	may now possibly agree to	+1	some measures designed to relax world tensions	+2	+2
6. Soviet rulers	perhaps will be more willing	+1	to forego aggressive designs	+3	+3
			Total		−28

Scores are computed on the basis of values assigned to verbal connectors and common meaning terms. These range from +3 to −3 depending on their direction and intensity. The method can be illustrated more fully by coding a sample paragraph (see Table 5-4).

Soviet rulers are ruthless, atheistic despots. These men have in the past pursued evil goals. Yet there now appears some possibility that they will agree to some measures designed to relax world tensions. Perhaps they will be more willing to forego aggressive designs.

The final step is the computation of values for each attitude object, in this case a single one—Soviet rulers. Dividing the sum of the product column by the number of themes will yield a score on a scale of +9 through −9. In Table 5-4, the score would be $-28/6 = -4.67$. Alternatively, if it is desirable to obtain results that are comparable to the semantic differential scales* (with a range of +3 through −3), the sum of the product column can be divided by $3N$, N being the number of themes. In that case, the score for Table 5-4 would be $-28/3(6) = -1.56$. Extensive rules for coding and scoring have been formulated (Osgood, Saporta, and Nunnally, 1956).

---

* See page 107.

Because this method first reduces the theme to its parts and specifies which elements of the theme are to be scored, it can be used with a high degree of reliability. Coders can be trained rapidly, but the method is too laborious to use with large volumes of data, and it is uneconomical if only gross measures of attitude (e.g., pro or con) are required. It is probably most useful when the analyst requires precise data on only a limited number of attitude objects; it has been used, for example, to assess the treatment of presidential candidates by three major news magazines during the 1960 campaign (Westley *et al.*, 1963), to examine John Foster Dulles' attitude toward the Soviet Union (Holsti, 1967), and to analyze editorial treatment of India in the *New York Times* (Lynch and Effendi, 1964).*

These, then, are the coding decisions which face content analysts. In examining alternative approaches and the assumptions which underlie them, we have no doubt disappointed the readers seeking the single best method of coding documentary data. If, however, the reader has come to appreciate that coding decisions must be integrated with all aspects of the research design, the chapter has fulfilled its primary purpose.

---

* Other methods of accounting for intensity in content data are described in Jacob (1942) and Kaplan and Goldsen (1949).

6   Sampling, Reliability, and Validity

The goal of content analysis research is to present a systematic and objective description of the attributes of communication. These data may be used to make inferences about communicators or audiences. But whatever the specific purpose of the study, there are certain problems which the content analyst shares with all persons conducting systematic inquiry. What is the universe of communication to be described, and what sample is to be drawn therefrom? Do repeated measures with the same categories on a set of documents yield stable and consistent results? That is, can the study be replicated? Do the categories actually index the variables they are intended to measure? Careful attention to these questions must be an integral part of every research design if it is to meet meaningful standards of systematic investigation. A comprehensive discussion of sampling, reliability, and validity is well beyond the scope of this book; thus we will consider only some general issues of particular relevance to content analysis.

SAMPLING

Because communication materials pervade society, few analysts can escape making sampling decisions. The volume of newspapers, magazines, books, government documents, speeches, letters, and other documents is such that, whether the research problem is broad or narrow in scope, the universe of relevant materials is likely to overwhelm even the investigator well endowed with time and resources. Often the choice can be reduced to one of two alternatives: obtain the data by sampling or don't obtain it at all. Consider the problem facing the analyst wishing to map trends in newspaper treatment of the war in Vietnam. Although the subject matter and time period are quite restricted, the volume of relevant material which might be examined is enormous, running into hundreds of newspapers, tens of thousands of issues, and millions of pages. Unless it were feasible to examine only a small portion of it, the projected study would no doubt be dropped.

The initial impetus for sampling may be the very practical requirement of reducing the volume of data to manageable proportions, but sampling is not merely a process of data reduction. It would be unusual indeed to find an analyst satisfied with confining his conclusions to the sample of documents he examined. Content analysis findings are usually discussed, implicitly or explicitly, as being relevant to some larger body of documents than those being coded. The interests of an analyst who examines editorials appearing in every tenth issue of *Jen-min Jih-pao* are surely not limited to those newspapers. It would be hard for us to conceive of a research question in which "every tenth issue" were to represent all members of a theoretically meaningful class of documents, but we might well be prepared to accept them as a representative sample from which valid conclusions about all issues of the newspaper can be drawn. The findings might, for example, be used to make inferences about all *Jen-min Jih-pao* editorials, or perhaps about a larger universe—party newspapers in China. Or, the analyst may even use his results as an index of elite attitudes in China. These research goals present different problems of inference, but in each instance the initial requirement of validity is that the sample be representative of the universe about which generalizations are made. An adequate sampling design is a necessary but not a sufficient condition for validity.

Decisions at any step in the research process are not independent of those made at earlier stages. Thus once the research problem has been defined, the sampling design has been partly determined. The investigator studying social values in post-World War II American literature has already limited his data according to time, source, and, in a rather general way, type of document. He is still faced with a number of further sampling decisions if he is to reduce his data to manageable proportions. What does he mean by the term "literature?" Should he examine mass (best sellers, book club selections) or quality (those with good reviews or National Book Award winners) books, or a combination of both types? Should his sample include novels, drama, short stories, poetry? Should each work be considered in its entirety, or is it feasible to sample pages or chapters? Such choices are not merely a matter of convenience or economy; they are likely to affect the results and they determine the kinds of generalizations that may be drawn from them. Social values found in books distributed by the Literary Guild are likely to differ significantly from those found in plays winning the Drama Critics Award.

The first step in sampling is to list all members of the class of documents about which generalizations are to be made. The analyst of American daily newspapers may, for example, define his universe as the newspapers catalogued in *Editor and Publisher Yearbook*. In a small group experiment the investigator may also be able to list the entire universe of relevant messages of communication without undue difficulty. Analysis of a random sample drawn from such lists permits precise statements to be made about the universe within specified confidence limits.

In practice, however, it is not always possible to prepare such a list. The inability of a psychologist working with personal documents (e.g., diaries, letters, and the like) to do so is clear. Perhaps less evident is the resulting inference problem. Of what universe of communicators are the letters of a single individual such as Jenny Gove Masterson a sample (Baldwin, 1942; Paige, 1966)? This is, of course, an instance of the problem of generalizing from a single case. But the problem is not limited to the case study. What range of generalization is possible from the extensive research on suicide notes? Given the fact that not all suicides leave notes, are findings based on those that do applicable to all persons who commit suicide, or only to that much smaller group of suicides who write farewell messages? Is there reason to suspect that members of the latter group differ in some theoretically significant way from those who do not leave a final note?

Similarly, in historical and political research one rarely has access to more than the written documents; oral communication represents an inaccessible, and generally unknown, proportion of the whole. Misfiling or destruction of documents, and bias or carelessness by those commissioned to collect and publish the documents, may further complicate matters. Or, consider the problems of working with Congressional documents. Senators and Representatives may amend their speeches before they are published in the *Congressional Record;* witnesses before committees may exercise the privilege of deleting statements for reasons of national security; and the records of entire hearings held behind closed doors may not be published. In each case the same question arises: how can we generalize from a known sample to an unknown—*and perhaps qualitatively different*—population? Note that in none of these instances does the analyst's problem arise from an insufficient *quantity* of documentation; indeed, he may have far more data than he can manage to code. Rather, the difficulty stems from doubts, which can never be wholly disspelled, that the missing data may be *qualitatively* different, in terms of the problems at hand, from the available documents.*

Once the universe of relevant communication has been defined, a single-stage sampling design may suffice. More often, a multistage sample is

---

* This is, of course, not the only point at which the analyst may be unable to satisfy the requirements of an "ideal" research design. Identifying such difficulties should serve not to deter or discourage research under less than ideal circumstances, but rather, to stimulate the analyst to consider ways to enhance the quality of his inferences. See, for example, the "multiple operations" philosophy of social research advocated by Webb *et al.* (1966).

required. This may involve as many as three steps: selecting *sources* of communication, *sampling* documents, and sampling *within documents.*

Selecting *communication sources* is the first sampling decision. Which newspapers, magazines, books, novelists, political leaders, poets, or propagandists will be selected as representative of the universe to which one wants to generalize? The analyst may draw a random sample—i.e., a sample in which every source has had an equal chance of being selected—by one of several standard methods, including a table of random numbers. This procedure is applicable when every source can be considered equally important for purposes of the study. If this assumption is not warranted, a purposive sample may be drawn to reflect qualitative or quantitative aspects of the sources which are deemed important. Analyses employing editorials as data have focused on "prestige" newspapers and journals because they were felt to represent most adequately the views of political elites (Lasswell, Lerner, and Pool, 1952; Angell, Dunham, and Singer, 1964). In studies of decision-makers' attitudes during international crises, sources were selected on the basis of role, thus heads of state, heads of government, and foreign ministers were selected, but ambassadors were excluded (North *et al.,* 1963; Holsti, North, and Brody, 1968).

There may be no obvious criteria by which to select the "most important" sources for a specific study. One method of meeting the objection that such choices are arbitrary is to use the pooled judgments of experts. In studies of psychological research (Allport and Bruner, 1940), and of newspaper coverage of the 1960 election (Stempel, 1961), sources rated most important by professional psychologists and journalists, respectively, were included. Whatever the advantages of this type of sample, it must be borne in mind that it is by definition not representative of the larger universe from which it was drawn. We would not, for example, have much confidence in conclusions about the general quality of political reporting by American newspapers if only the *New York Times, Washington Post,* and *Wall Street Journal* were analyzed.

For some purposes quantitative criteria may be deemed more important than qualitative ones for selecting sources. Kayser (1953) analyzed the largest circulation newspaper in each of 15 countries, Schneider and Dornbusch (1958) examined only that sample of inspirational literature which appeared on best-seller lists, and McGranahan and Wayne (1948) confined their study of German drama to the most widely attended plays. Other criteria which have been used to select a sample of communication sources include editorial position (Hage, 1959), geographical location (Willey, 1926; Taeuber, 1932), and time of issue (Danielson and Adams, 1961).

Stratified sampling is often used in studies of the mass media to permit dissimilar subclasses of a larger class of sources to be treated differently.

The universe is first divided into subgroups (strata) according to certain criteria. A random sample of items is then drawn from each stratum. Consider a hypothetical study designed to compare the views of Democratic and Republican Senators toward the danger of Nazi aggression in 1937 and 1938. The 75th Congress included 76 Democrats, 16 Republicans, and four members of other parties. A random sample of 12 senators might be expected to yield about 10 Democrats and only two Republicans. Because such a disparity could present problems of comparison, stratified sampling might be used. Two lists of senators (one of Democrats and the other of Republicans) could be drawn up, and a random sample of six could then be drawn from each list. This procedure might be useful for the purposes of our hypothetical study, but note that the sample of 12 is *not* representative of the entire Senate because Republicans are heavily overrepresented. It could not, therefore, be used to make generalizations about attitudes of the Senate as a whole.

A technique which permits stratification on the basis of circulation and geographical location has been developed (Maccoby, Sabghir, and Cushing, 1950). All dailies in the United States were originally listed in descending order of circulation within each of the nine census districts. The sampling rate was obtained by dividing the number of newspapers desired for the study into the total newspaper circulation, providing "circulation units." Each newspaper in which the nth circulation unit appeared was chosen (with the first paper selected from a table of random numbers) to yield a true probability sample of *circulation units* in the universe. Note that this will *not* yield the same result as a random sample of newspapers because the sampling unit is the reader rather than the newspaper. Another successful stratified sampling design for newspapers is described in Coats and Mulkey (1950).

Owing to the nature of the problem, it may not be necessary to sample communication sources. In a study of Nazi propaganda broadcasts during World War II the nature of the inquiry defined the single relevant source. Sampling may still be used, however. Rather than analyzing every broadcast, the analyst may wish to *sample documents;* here "document" refers to every item comprising the universe of items produced by the communication source. Thus he might examine only a subset consisting of every third broadcast.

Sampling of documents is often required when the first stage of the sampling design does not reduce the volume of data to manageable proportions. In our hypothetical study of newspaper treatment of the war in Vietnam, the first stage of the sampling design may have reduced sources to a dozen American newspapers. As a second step we would probably want to further reduce our data, perhaps by randomly drawing every nth issue of each newspaper.

Even after selecting documents, the investigator may wish to reduce his data further by some sort of *sampling within documents*. He may, for example, restrict his study to 30 pages drawn at random from a book (Harvey, 1953), to only the front page of a newspaper (Kingsbury *et al.*, 1937), or to every second story in a magazine (Berelson and Salter, 1946). The problem is the same as for other sampling decisions: does the selected sample accurately represent the attributes of content relevant to the study? The front page of newspapers may be a valid sample for some purposes, but probably not if one wants to measure community stratification by analyzing social news.

Each of these three types of sampling may be used alone or they may be used in various combinations as required by the research problem. Just as we could not specify the best coding system without reference to a specific problem, so it is impossible to identify a single sampling procedure for all content analysis research. Sampling decisions will vary according to the type of documents and the analyst's purpose. Moreover, the choice between sampling designs—each of which carries with it certain assumptions—may significantly affect the results. This point is well summarized by Kaplan:

*As with measurement where there are many different scales that might be used, each having its own properties, sampling is not a simple uniform procedure but one which varies from problem to problem in a way that permits and even demands correspondingly different mathematical treatment.**

How large should the sample be to permit generalization within specified confidence limits? The necessary sample size may vary depending upon the kinds of questions being asked of the data, the degree of precision with which they must be answered, and the nature of the data. Sampling always introduces an element of uncertainty or "sampling error" into the results. Error is not used here in the usual sense of a mistake; rather, it refers to variations between samples drawn from the same universe of data. We would not expect to get five heads and five tails every time we toss a coin—even a perfectly fair one—10 times; nor should we expect 10 samples of documents drawn from the same universe to be identical with each other and for each of them to be a perfect small-scale representation of the entire group of documents from which they were drawn. In general sampling error can be reduced by increasing the size of

* From *The Conduct of Inquiry: Methodology for Behavioral Science* by Abraham Kaplan, published by Chandler Publishing Company, San Francisco. Copyright 1964 by Chandler Publishing Company. Reprinted by Permission.

the sample* or by using better instruments of measurement, e.g., more precisely defined categories.

No single answer to the question of sample size can cover every inquiry, but some guidelines applicable to newspaper research are available from experimental studies. Four methods of sampling newspaper headlines in *Pravda* were compared with data for the entire month (Mintz, 1949). The results revealed that every-fifth-day samples (fifth, tenth, fifteenth, twentieth, twenty-fifth, and thirtieth day of each month) and odd-day samples did not differ significantly from the figures for the entire month. On the other hand, weekly samples and every-tenth-day samples (fifth, fifteenth, and twenty-fifth day of each month) were inferior. These findings were supported by another study, in which every-sixth-day samples provided sufficiently accurate results for most research purposes (Davis and Turner, 1951). Stempel (1952) drew samples of 6, 12, 18, 24, and 48 issues of a newspaper and compared the average content for a single subject matter category against the average for the entire year. The data indicated that each of the five sample sizes was adequate, and that increasing the sample size beyond 12 did not produce significantly more accurate results.

The uncertainty introduced into research by sampling error is random error in which, over the long run, deviations from the true score can be expected to cancel each other out. The larger the sample, the more certain can the investigator be that this cancelling out process is in fact operating. Thus, he can control the degree of uncertainty in his findings.

The much more serious threat to validity is bias, or systematic error, in the sampling design. Systematic error means that scores are consistently biased in one direction, and instead of errors cancelling each other out to produce a good representation of the universe from which the sample was drawn, as in the case of random error, they accumulate in the direction of the bias. Or, to state this somewhat differently: when only random error is present, increasing the sample size enhances our confidence in making valid inferences from the sample; when systematic error is present, the larger our sample, the more confidently will we make *invalid* inferences. Thus, in preparing a sampling design the analyst must ensure that his sample of documents, whatever its size, is free of idiosyncrasies which may bias his findings. Some types of content may be subject to seasonal variations; news about Congress is generally heavier during the first half of the year than during the second, but the reverse is usually true about news of the United Nations General Assembly; and political rhetoric in the

---

* However, sampling error is *inversely proportional to the square root* of the sample size. Hence, to reduce sampling error by half, one must increase the sample by a factor of four.

United States during the autumn of even-numbered years is likely to vary in style and content from that of other periods owing to national electoral campaigns.

Unless taken into account in the sampling design, such variations can render invalid an otherwise well designed, well executed project. A study of marriage announcements in the *New York Times,* based on Sunday issues of the newspaper appearing in June during the years 1932 to 1942, revealed no announcement of a marriage in a Jewish synagogue (Hatch and Hatch, 1947). A critic later pointed out that June almost invariably falls within a period during which tradition prohibits Jewish marriages (Cahnman, 1948). Because the religion of brides and grooms represented only a small part of the data reported in the study, this sampling bias may not initially appear overly damaging. But suppose that there is a relationship between religion on the one hand, and education, occupation, listing in the *Social Register,* and club affiliation (other variables in the study), on the other? Should this be the case, a systematic bias with respect to one variable—religion—may result in a sample which is also unrepresentative in other ways. If, for example, the educational level of Jewish brides and grooms is higher than average, or if there are proportionately fewer of them listed in the *Social Register,* then a sample from which they are systematically excluded is likely to have a lower mean level of education and a higher proportion of those listed in the *Social Register* than the population it is intended to represent.

There are also regular variations within the week which may affect the content of mass media; e.g., a study of Monday newspapers for financial news or news regarding governmental agencies would result in serious underestimation of coverage. Several methods of accounting for variations within the week can be used. Every-nth-day samples will ensure an equal distribution of days within the week if two conditions are met: n must not equal seven; and the number of weeks studied must be divisible by n. Jones and Carter (1959) have developed a "constructed week" procedure in which the period under study is divided into seven strata or subpopulations; all Mondays are grouped together, as are all Tuesdays, and so on. A random sample of n issues is then taken from each stratum. Such methods may be used to guard against cyclical variations in the mass media, but these are by no means the only idiosyncrasies in documentary data which may render invalid an otherwise well-designed sampling design.

Another consideration in sampling is that of efficiency. Which method of sampling will yield satisfactory results at least cost? Again, no single answer covers every situation. A case in point is the "cluster" design, in which the analyst selects units containing more than one item; the unit identifies a cluster consisting of all items appearing in it. For example, rather than listing all *articles* and drawing a sample from them, the investigator may sample *issues* of the magazine and analyze all articles which appear within the selected issues. Because it costs less to list all issues than all articles with each issue, research expenses are reduced. However, lower costs must be weighed against other factors. An experiment with content data revealed that, depending on the data, cluster sampling frequently leads to overestimating levels of significance (Backman, 1956).

Finally, it should be borne in mind that technical competence in sampling procedures is rarely the most important asset the investigator brings to his research. Professional advice of a sampling expert is usually available, but it will only be useful if sought before rather than after the sample has been drawn. The analyst must, however, be able to give an unambiguous answer to the question, "What is the purpose of my study?" He must also know his data well enough to recognize any idiosyncrasies which may ruin an otherwise sound sampling design. He cannot expect the expert on sampling to be of assistance in these matters.

RELIABILITY

If research is to satisfy the requirement of objectivity, measures and procedures must be reliable; i.e., repeated measures with the same instrument on a given sample of data should yield similar results. Reliability is a function of coders' skill, insight, and experience, clarity of categories and coding rules which guide their use; and the degree of ambiguity in the data. Because the nature of the data is usually beyond the investigator's control, opportunities for enhancing reliability are generally limited to improving coders, categories, or both.

Unless an objective instrument such as a computer is used for coding, the analyst must rely upon pooled judgments of coders. *Individual reliability* reflects the extent of agreement between coders. Even if they possess skills necessary to make the judgmental tasks required of them, training is usually necessary to ensure that coders are relying upon the same aspects of their experience in their decisions. Experimental studies have demonstrated that training prior to coding can significantly increase the level of intercoder agreement (Kaplan and Goldsen, 1949; Woodward and Franzen, 1948). However, another study revealed that nondirected discussion of categories and coding rules failed to result in significantly higher agreement, in part because discussions tended to focus on the utility of categories rather than on the ways in which they should be applied to the data (Spiegelman, Terwilliger, and Fearing, 1953b).

Before the actual coding begins, the investigator may want to run experiments to identify judges consistently deviating from the group. This can be done by tabulating the percentage of agreement between every pair of judges. It may be necessary to eliminate dissenting coders, but such a step should be taken with some caution, and only after efforts to identify the reasons for the deviation. The single "bad" coder may in fact be sensitive to important elements in the data to which the others are oblivious.

Category reliability depends upon the analyst's ability to formulate categories "for which the empirical evidence is clear enough so that competent judges will agree to a sufficiently high degree on which items of a certain population belong in the category and which do not" (Schutz, 1958, p. 512). When pretesting reveals poor agreement among coders, the analyst should be alert to the possibility that the source of disagreement lies in the categories rather than in the judges. Especially if coder training fails to resolve the problem, there is good reason to suspect that the categories are ambiguously defined, inappropriate to the data, or in some other way deficient. The hypothesis that untrained coders are more likely to agree if categories are defined clearly than are well-trained coders working with ambiguous categories was confirmed in an experimental study. For both symbol coding and theme analysis, variance between categories was significant, but that between coders was not (Stempel, 1955).

In coding content data, the judges must first decide on the boundaries of units coded—sometimes called the process of *unitizing*. If the unit is a symbol, paragraph, or an item, unitizing presents relatively few difficulties because the data provide coders with certain physical guides—the symbol is bounded by spaces, the paragraph is set off by indentation, and so on. Thematic analysis presents the most serious problem because the theme is not a "natural unit" for which physical guides exist. Many sentences contain more than one theme, and identifying proper boundaries between them is a judgmental process for which it may be difficult to formulate rules that cover every type of theme that may occur in the text.

After identifying boundaries of the content unit, the judge must decide the category into which the unit is to be placed. Assuming that coders are well trained, reliability of classification is largely a function of category definition and the types and numbers of discriminations to be made. Pretesting categories on a sample of the material to be coded will enable the investigator to determine which categories require further clarification. Guetzkow (1950) has derived reliability estimates for both unitizing and categorizing operations which permit the investigator to determine how large a sample of the data needs to be cross-checked to ensure any desired level of accuracy.

The content analysis literature contains a number of approaches which may be used to resolve problems of reliability attributable to categories. The analyst may define his categories rigidly and exhaustively, attempting to reduce coding from a judgmental task to a clerical one. An experiment has demonstrated that coding symbols according to general rules yields significantly less reliable results than when every member of a category is specified (Geller, Kaplan, and Lasswell, 1942a). Inasmuch as few categories lend themselves to exhaustive definition, however, this solution is rarely applicable for research employing units larger than the word or symbol. The investigator contemplating a study using words or symbols as units may want to consider one of the many available computer methods of analysis,* thereby eliminating for all practical purposes the problem of reliability.

Second, requiring judges to make fine discriminations between subcategories often results in a high incidence of disagreement. Aggregating subcategories may increase reliability, but this approach is applicable only if the fine distinctions are not of major theoretical significance.

A third approach to the problem of low reliability is the introduction of additional judges to broaden the base of consensus. The logic of this procedure is summarized by Block (1961, p.38):

At the same time, because our chosen score is an average, simple psychometric logic argues quite convincingly that the consensus will cumulate validity disproportionately more rapidly than it will cumulate error. Idiosyncrasies of observers, inattentions, and other observer flaws can be expected, in the main, to cancel each other and let through the stubborn truth. The expectation of higher validity in the consensus is supported empirically almost universally in the research instances where the matter has been investigated.

A composite reliability coefficient may be computed by the following formula, in which N denotes the number of judges.

$$\text{Composite reliability} = \frac{N\,(\text{average inter-judge agreement})}{1 + [(N-1)\,(\text{average inter-judge agreement})]}$$

Consider a case in which agreement between four judges, A, B, C, and D, is as follows:†

	A	B	C
D	0.71	0.66	0.68
C	0.70	0.69	
B	0.64		

The average inter-judge agreement is 0.68, and the composite reliability score is $4(0.68)/[1 + 3(0.68)]$, or 0.90. The expedient of introducing additional judges may be necessary for the most difficult

---

* Some of these are described in Chapter 7.

† Alternative methods of computing agreement between judges are discussed below.

judgmental tasks, e.g., scaling the intensity of the themes (North *et al.*, 1963), but it also adds considerably to research costs and it should not be considered as a substitute for precise coding rules.

A solution more generally applicable to decisions of categorization—but not to unitizing or scaling for intensity—consists of defining the task as a series of dichotomous decisions; i.e., coding is broken down into a sequence of judgments, each of which requires the coder to make a choice between only two alternatives (Schutz, 1958). A hypothetical study of Congressional attitudes toward various forms of foreign aid can be used to illustrate this technique. Let us assume that content units were to be placed into one of five categories: loans, economic grants, military grants to allies, military grants to India, and military grants to all other neutral nations. One source of difficulty in this classification scheme is that the categories are at different levels of generality. For example, the distinction between economic and military grants depends on a prior decision of a more general nature, the choice between loans and grants. Arrangements of these categories into a series of dichotomous decisions can be illustrated schematically:

Decision 1.   Loans _____ Grants
   Decision 2.   Economic ____⌐ Military
      Decision 3.   Allied nations ___⌐ Neutral nations
         Decision 4.   India ____ ____ ⌐ Other nations

Note that for purposes of this study, not all logically possible categories are used; e.g., once a statement is classified as an assertion about foreign loans, no further discriminations about its nature or recipient are required. Using an analogous set of categories, Schutz (1958, p. 507) found that inter-judge agreement was raised from 61% using traditional methods of judgment to not less than 90% when the dichotomous decision method was employed. Tables of confidence limits have been developed from which one can determine, knowing the number of judges and the number of judgments they are required to make, the percentage of agreement necessary for acceptance at the 0.01 and 0.05 levels (Schutz, 1952).

There are several advantages associated with the dichotomous decision technique. It permits coders to focus on a single decision at a time and to review the criteria for choice at each step. It has been demonstrated that with traditional methods, increasing the number of categories within the category set decreases reliability (Janis, Fadner, and Janowitz, 1943). Thus the dichotomous decision method should be particularly useful when many categories are necessary.

Coding problems may also arise when the process of categorization consists of several judgments, but one decision is logically prior to another because it is relevant to a larger class, as in the example cited above. The

TABLE 6-1

Comparison of two coders

Theme	Coder A Document			Coder B Document		
	I	II	III	I	II	III
1	$X+$	$X-$	$Y-$	$X+$	$X+$	$Y-$
2	$Y-$	$Y-$	$X+$	$Y+$	$Y+$	$Y+$
3	$X+$	$Y+$	$Y+$	$X+$	$Y-$	$X+$
4	$X+$	$Y-$	$Y-$	$X+$	$Y-$	$X-$
5	$Y-$	$X+$	$X+$	$Y-$	$X-$	$X+$
6	$Y+$	$X+$	$X-$	$Y-$	$X+$	$X-$
7	$Y-$	$X+$	$X+$	$Y-$	$X+$	$X+$
8	$Y-$	$X+$	$X-$	$Y-$	$X+$	$Y-$
Totals						
$X+$	3	4	3	3	4	3
$X-$	0	1	2	0	1	2
$Y+$	1	1	1	1	1	1
$Y-$	4	2	2	4	2	2

dichotomous decision method ensures that choices coders are asked to make follow a logical sequence. Finally, the method permits one to determine precisely where agreement between judges is breaking down, information which is useful in redefining categories. Suppose that coding with categories in the example above resulted in a disappointing level of inter-coder agreement. With traditional coding methods it might be difficult, short of extensive discussions with each coder, to locate the source of disagreement. When using the dichotomous decision method, however, we might discover that there was near unanimity on Decisions 1 and 2, but that agreement broke down in deciding which were allied and neutral nations. Armed with this information we can resolve the issue by developing more precise operational definitions of allied and neutral.

Inter-coder agreement can be computed by a variety of methods. It should initially be noted that identical frequency tabulations do *not* necessarily indicate a high level of agreement. Consider a hypothetical example drawn from our illustrative case study of American presidential campaign speeches. Two coders are given 24 themes from three documents and asked to tally the number of favorable (+) and unfavorable (−) references to welfare legislation (X) and interventionist foreign policies (Y), as in Table 6-1. If we examined only the totals we would mistakenly conclude that there had been perfect agreement between coders. It would not be apparent that the coders had in fact disagreed on 10 of the 24 themes. In some cases the same theme was placed in different categories and in others there was agreement on the substantive category but disagreement in rating the themes as favorable or unfavorable.

A widely used coefficient of reliability is the ratio of coding agreements to the total number of coding decisions:

$$C.R. = \frac{2M}{N_1 + N_2} .$$

In this formula M is the number of coding decisions on which the two judges are in agreement, and N_1 and N_2 refer to the number of coding decisions made by judges 1 and 2, respectively. In our example each coder identified and categorized 24 themes, but they were in agreement on only 14 of them. According to the formula, C.R. = 2(14)/24 + 24, or 0.58. This formula has been criticized, however, because it does not take into account the extent of inter-coder agreement which may result from chance (Bennett, Alpert, and Goldstein, 1954). By chance alone, agreement should increase as the number of categories decreases.

Scott (1955) subsequently developed an index of reliability (*pi*) which corrects not only for the number of categories in the category set, but also for the probable frequency with which each is used.. Originally developed for coding data into nominal categories, Scott's formula may also be used with ordinal, interval, or ratio scales. Scott's *pi* is computed as follows:

$$pi = \frac{\% \text{ observed agreement} - \% \text{ expected agreement}}{1 - \% \text{ expected agreement}} .$$

To use this formula it is first necessary to determine the percentage of expected agreement by chance. This is done by finding the proportion of items falling into each category of a category set, and summing the square of those proportions. Consider again the example in which themes relating to interventionist foreign policies and welfare programs in three documents were scored as favorable or unfavorable:

Category	Frequency	Proportion of all themes
X+	10	0.42
X−	3	0.13
Y+	3	0.13
Y−	8	0.33

The expected agreement is

$$(0.42)^2 + (0.13)^2 + (0.13)^2 + (0.33)^2 = 0.32.$$

That is, even if they assign content units to categories randomly, two coders should agree on about 32% of the items. Recalling that in our

TABLE 6-2

Possible patterns of agreement among five coders

Pattern of agreement	Rank-order	Number of agreements	% agreements out of total possible
5 (complete agreement)	1	10	100
4, 1	2	6	60
3, 2	3	4	40
3, 1, 1	4	3	30
2, 2, 1	5	2	20
2, 1, 1, 1	6	1	10
1, 1, 1, 1, 1 (No agreement)	7	0	0

example the observed level of agreement was 0.58, we can now compute *pi*:

$$pi = \frac{0.58 - 0.32}{1 - 0.32} = 0.38.$$

For a more extensive illustration of Scott's *pi* as applied to content analysis data, see Angell, Dunham, and Singer (1964).

Another method of computing and reporting the overall reliability of any category set with a single figure has been developed by Spiegelman, Terwilliger, and Fearing (1953b). The technique involves ranking the patterns of agreement among judges on each item. For example, with five judges seven patterns are possible, as shown in Table 6-2.

The reliability of any category set can be reported as the mean rank order of all items. In our example, scores would range from 1.0 (complete agreement on all items) to 7.0 (no agreement on any items). Alternatively, reliability may be reported as the number of agreements between pairs of judges out of the total possible, computed by the formula $N(N-1)/2$. With five judges, there are $5(4)/2$, or 10 pairs. Thus when the pattern of agreement is 3-2, there are $3(2)/2 + 2(1)/2 = 4$ agreements, or 40% of the total possible.

Other methods of computing agreement applicable to content analysis are described in Kaplan and Goldsen (1949), Robinson (1957), and Stempel (1955), but Scott's formula, which produces a conservative estimate of reliability, appears to be the most useful.

Although individual and category reliability have been discussed separately, this distinction is a somewhat artificial one. Indeed, the investigator may find that it is not always readily apparent to which factor low reliability should be attributed. The "random-systematic-error coefficient" is a measure which can be used to determine the nature and source of disagreement in coding. Interpretation of the RSE coefficient is based on the finding that "errors resulting from a defective code (e.g., an ambiguous code) seem generally to be scattered about the range of possible disagreements, while errors originating in the coders tend to fall into systematic patterns" (Funkhouser and Parker, 1968, p. 123). Calculation of RSE coefficients can be programmed into the same computer routines that calculate Scott's *pi* for the overall test of reliability.

Defining an *acceptable level of reliability* is one of the many problems in content analysis for which there is no single solution. The question, which can only be answered within the context of a given research problem, sometimes poses real dilemmas for the investigator. That high reliability can be achieved for simple forms of content analysis, in which coding is essentially a mechanical task, is amply documented in the literature. Conversely, as categories and units of analysis become more complex, they may yield results that are both more useful and less reliable. Reliability *is* a necessary condition for valid inquiry but, paradoxically, the cost of some steps taken to increase reliability may be a *reduction* in validity. Recall the study of colonial newspapers which was intended to map trends in the growth of national consciousness among the 13 American colonies (Merritt, 1966). The method of measuring such sentiments—counting the frequency of American place names—yielded an exceptionally high coefficient of reliability. But what was actually being measured is open to question. Coding more appropriate units, perhaps themes expressing a sense of community, would no doubt have resulted in a somewhat less impressive level of reliability, but it might also have enhanced the validity of inferences drawn from the findings. Thus, in formulating research design the analyst may be forced to strike some balance between reliability and relevance of categories and units; the coefficient of reliability cannot be the sole criterion for making such decisions.

VALIDITY

Validity is usually defined as the extent to which an instrument is measuring what it is intended to measure. This is not, of course, the first time we have encountered the problem of validity. The quantitative-qualitative and manifest-latent debates discussed in Chapter 1 are in fact disagreements about the validity of alternative approaches to content data. The importance of research designs was emphasized in Chapter 2 because valid inference depends upon careful planning of the comparisons to be made with content data. Choice of categories and content units similarly enhance or diminish the likelihood of valid inferences; unless they are appropriate indices of the events, attitudes or behaviors the analyst wants to measure, inferences drawn from the findings will not be valid. The validity of any study is also inextricably interrelated with its sampling design and reliability. If the analyst studying the proportion of international news in American daily newspapers examines only issues of the *New York Times,* well-constructed categories or precise measurement will not ensure the validity of his findings. Even if the universe from which the sample was drawn were expanded to make it more representative, low reliability on categorizing international news would render the results suspect. Adequate sampling and reliability are necessary, but not sufficient, conditions for validity. In summary, then, valid inference is the goal of all inquiry, but it does not exist independently of other aspects of the research process.

The meaning of validity may differ from study to study, depending on the investigator's purposes. The American Psychological Association Committee on Psychological Tests has distinguished between *content validity, predictive validity, concurrent validity,* and *construct validity.* The distinction between them can be illustrated by an example. Documents may be analyzed by means of a measure such as the type-token ratio, the number of different words in message samples of a given length. Results may be used as a direct measure of the author's vocabulary; in this case the analyst is concerned with content validity. The same measure might also be used to predict subjects' success in college, to distinguish schizophrenics from normal persons, or to explain the writer's general intellectual capacity. For these purposes the investigator would be interested in the predictive validity, concurrent validity, and construct validity, respectively, of his measure (*Technical Recommendations,* 1954, p. 13).

Content validity, also sometimes referred to as *face validity,* has most frequently been relied upon by content analysts. If the purpose of the research is a purely descriptive one, content validity is normally sufficient. Content validity is usually established through the informed judgment of the investigator. Are the results plausible? Are they consistent with other information about the phenomena being studied? Consider a hypothetical analysis of Chinese and Soviet elite pronouncements during the 1960's which revealed that each nation's leaders viewed the other in an increasingly favorable light. Such a finding is so at odds with evidence of decreased Sino-Soviet trade and aid, increased frequency of border incidents, and other indications of mutual hostility as to render the analysis suspect. At minimum one would want to ask a series of questions about the research process that led to such a conclusion: Was the sample of documents analyzed representative of statements by leaders in the two nations? Were the categories adequate for the purposes of the study? Was the coding reliable?

Predictive validity is concerned with the ability of an instrument to predict events for which evidence is not at present available to the analyst. He may use his data to predict the occurrence of future events. An example of predictive validity has been cited in a study of Knut Hamsun's novels; the inference that Hamsun was a latent fascist was later validated by his collaboration with the Nazis (Lowenthal, 1949).

Predictive validity can also be illustrated by a study of reports written by successful and unsuccessful volunteers for field work in Africa to test the hypothesis that, "The products of consciousness of people engaged in successful and meaningful action will show a better integration of subjective and objective elements than the products of unsuccessful agents" (Ramallo, 1966, pp. 536-537). Volunteers for "Operation Crossroads Africa" were asked to write three reports about their work, the first one a fictional report before departure from the United States, the second and third during their stay in Africa. Reports by volunteers rated as failures and successes by their field supervisors were analyzed. Predicted differences between the groups were found in both field reports but not in the simulated reports.

Numerous other examples of predictive validity in the content analysis literature exists in the area of propaganda analysis. Access to Nazi documents following World War II permitted those engaged in predicting aspects of Axis behavior to assess the accuracy of their inferences (George, 1959a, pp. 253-284; Berelson and De Grazia, 1947).

Predictive validity is not limited to future events. It may also be established when research findings are used to predict past events for which evidence is not currently available. In their study of suicide notes, Ogilvie, Stone, and Shneidman (1966) began with 66 notes (33 genuine and 33 simulated) which were paired according to age, race, religion, and age of the authors. The first 15 pairs were used to discover a combination of three content attributes which discriminated between the real and simulated notes: references to concrete things, persons, and places; use of the word "love"; and references to processes of thought and decision. The first and second characteristics occurred with higher frequency in the genuine notes, and the third was found more often in the simulated ones. These criteria were then applied to the remaining 18 pairs of messages by an analyst who was not familiar with their identity. Successful identification of the genuine notes in 17 of 18 cases, a highly improbable occurrence by chance, can be interpreted as an instance of predictive validity even though the predicted events (suicides) occurred many years prior to the research.

Concurrent validity is also established by prediction to an external criterion. If a measure is able to distinguish sources with known differences, as the type-token ratio has done with schizophrenic and normal patients, the validity of the measure for that purpose is confirmed.

As in the case of predictive validity, an important element in concurrent validity is the external criterion with which content data are being compared. If the criterion itself is not a valid measure of the phenomena to be explained, little is gained by demonstrating that content data are significantly related to it. The authors of a simplified readability formula found that results with their test were significantly correlated with those derived by the Flesch method (Farr, Jenkins, and Patterson, 1951). To the extent that the latter is a true measure of readability, the validity of the Farr formula was established. But it has been demonstrated that the applicability of the Flesch method is limited to certain types of writing (Taylor, 1953); thus, unless established by other methods, the validity of the Farr formula is similarly limited.

Efforts to establish concurrent validity can be illustrated by an experiment undertaken in conjunction with research on the crisis leading to World War I (Holsti and North, 1966). Documents written by top-ranking foreign policy officials were analyzed and trends in such variables as hostility were plotted on a day-to-day basis. Although coding was completed with satisfactory reliability, a number of questions about validity of the results remained. Not the least of these derived from the sampling problem inherent in the use of historical materials. Although all available diplomatic documents were analyzed, they represented an unknown sample of the larger universe of political communication which would include face-to-face discussions, telephone conversations, Cabinet meetings, and the like.

Direct and systematic methods of validation—e.g., interviewing or observing decision-makers during the crisis—could not be used because the events under analysis took place over a half century ago. Alternatively, one could search for eyewitness reports which might tend to confirm inferences drawn from the content analysis data. Such reports, drawn from diaries and memoirs of those who took part in the 1914 decisions, were in fact consistent with the content data. An analysis of the Kaiser's messages and the marginal comments he wrote on many other documents indicated that he was under considerable stress during the final days prior to the outbreak of war. This inference received support from the observations of those who saw him frequently. Admiral Tirpitz wrote of the Kaiser during the critical phase of the crisis: "I have never seen a more tragic, more ravaged face than that of our Emperor during those days." But at best, such eyewitness evidence is anecdotal and unsystematic; at times it may even be highly suspect, as in the case of memoirs written years after the actual events. Thus, while it would have been desirable to have direct,

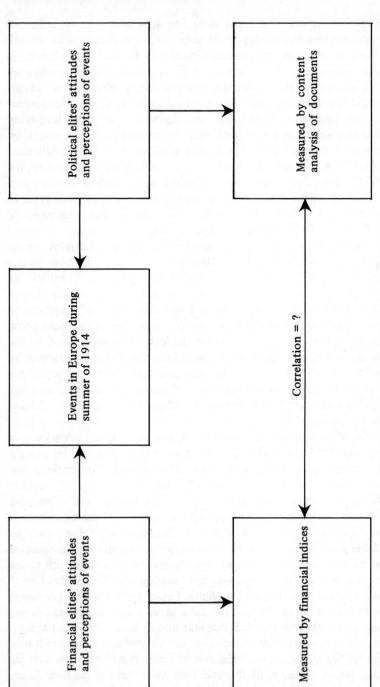

Fig. 6-1 Design to test the validity of content analysis data.

systematic, and reliable evidence regarding the attitudes, perceptions, and values of decision-makers in the various capitals of Europe during the summer of 1914, such data were not available.

It was therefore decided to adopt an indirect approach to validation by comparing the content analysis data with a series of indices which met several criteria. They had to be available in quantitative form in sources of unquestioned authenticity. They had to be reported on a daily basis, hence, such otherwise useful data as trade statistics, which are usually reported annually, quarterly, or monthly, were of little use. And most importantly, they had to be indices whose sensitivity to changes in the international political climate could be demonstrated. Figures on the flow of gold, the price of securities, commodity futures, exchange rates, interest rates, and marine insurance rates, collected from sources quite separate from the diplomatic documents which had been subjected to content analysis, satisfied the first two requirements. We shall return to the third one later.

The logic of the experiment, summarized in Fig. 6-1, is as follows. Elites for whom international events are salient include not only political decision-makers. Members of the financial community must also be sensitive to international developments because virtually all forms of investments will be affected by them. The attitudes of political leaders were measured by content analysis of documents; at issue was the validity of the findings. The attitudes of financial elites were measured directly with a high degree of precision and reliability by changes in various financial indices. If there were a high correlation between the financial and content data, confidence in the validity of the latter would be enhanced. Were such a relationship not found to exist, the value of content analysis data would have been open to serious question. Results of this series of experiments revealed strong correlations (generally in the order of 0.90 or higher) between the content and financial data.

Before concluding the experiment one further step was required; it was necessary to determine whether the financial indices were in fact valid criteria for the purposes at hand. That is, if they were to serve as criteria with which to validate the content data, it was necessary to determine if they varied systematically with changes in international tensions. This last step was accomplished in various ways. Further analysis revealed that the gold leaving London was destined for the European nations most deeply involved in the crisis, in response to emergency measures taken by their central banks. Security prices of prospective belligerents were compared with those of traditionally neutral nations (Switzerland, Sweden); whereas the former fell precipitously each time war seemed closer at hand, the latter remained steady throughout the crisis. These and other tests confirmed that the financial indices were indeed sensitive to international developments.

Construct validity is concerned not only with validating the measure, but also the theory underlying the measure. It is not enough to establish that variable X is a good predictor of variable Y, or that it is capable of discriminating between individuals type A and type B. It also involves explaining *why* variable X has these properties. Construct validity may be established by several methods; that most frequently discussed in the literature involves interrelating the construct within a "nomological network" of external variables from many different sources (Cronbach and Meehl, 1955, p. 290; see also Janis, 1949, pp. 78-79; *Technical Recommendations,* 1954; and Kerlinger, 1964, pp. 448-454).

One requirement of construct validity is that hypotheses derived from the theory should yield similar results in different settings, i.e., the results should be generalizable rather than specific to a single situation. An effort in this direction is Zinnes' (1966) study of hostility in international communication. A series of hypotheses derived from a theory relating alliance structure, hostile communication, perceptions of the international environment, and aggressive conduct were initially tested and supported in an analysis of documents written by top-level decision-makers during the weeks prior to the outbreak of World War I. The same hypotheses were retested using as data the messages exchanged by high school students acting in the roles of foreign policy leaders during a series of "Inter-Nation Simulations." The results were, on the whole, strikingly similar to those found in the 1914 study; thus this experiment can be interpreted as one step in the direction of establishing construct validity.

An example of a concept for which the evidence of construct validity appears quite substantial is that of "need achievement." A number of studies have established an impressive network of evidence supporting the validity of both the measure and its underlying theory. That need achievement can successfully differentiate between groups known to differ in regard to relevant characteristics, as predicted by the theory, has been demonstrated in a study of various Indian tribes (McClelland and Friedman, 1952) and nations (McClelland, 1961). Need achievement, as measured by content analysis of diverse literary products, has also been shown to correlate with broad patterns of culture change in settings as different as ancient Greece and the United States. Finally, the concept has been found to correlate significantly with such external measures of entrepreneurial achievement as trade and issuance of patents (McClelland, 1958; deCharms and Moeller, 1962).

These, then, are some of the problems which content analysts share with all scientists. The published literature reveals considerable unevenness in dealing with them; e.g., in regard to reliability, Berelson (1952, p. 172) noted that:

Whatever the actual state of reliability in content analysis, the published record is less than satisfactory. Only about 15-20% of the studies report the reliability of the analysis contained in them. In addition, about five reliability experiments are reported in the literature.

The more recent record is considerably better. It reveals that, on the whole, content analysts share the general concern within the social sciences for problems of inference, of which sampling, reliability, and validity are an integral part. At the same time, it is clear that progress has been far from even. For example, one has little difficulty finding either experimental studies or imaginative examples of sampling the printed mass media. On the other hand, given the tendency of analysts to draw inferences about the causes of communication from their data, less than a commensurate share of attention has been paid to problems of validity.

7   Computers in Content Analysis

The most vivid impression in the mind of the reader may be that content analysis involves a certain amount of drudgery; nothing could be closer to the truth. Content analysis usually requires skilled and sensitive coders, the very persons who soon become bored and frustrated by the tedious and repetitive nature of the task. Manual methods of content analysis may also suffer in varying degrees from other limitations. Some methods are expensive and time-consuming. Moreover, many techniques lack flexibility and possess only limited ability to deal with complex units. These problems lend considerable support for Berelson's (1952, p. 198) warning that "unless there is a sensible, or clever, or sound, or revealing, or unusual, or important notion underlying the analysis, it is not worth going through the rigor of the procedure, especially when it is so arduous and so costly of effort."

A significant effort to deal with these problems has been the development of computer programs to handle a variety of operations involved in textual analysis. This chapter examines a number of general topics which have emerged from the introduction of computers into content analysis. We initially consider the classes of research problems for which computers are most and least likely to prove useful. This is followed by a survey of some existing programs and the types of investigations in which they have been used. A broad overview of the burgeoning literature necessarily precludes detailed description of each system. To offset in part the inevitable sketchiness of the survey, one computer program is examined in detail, with a discussion of its purposes, dictionary, data input requirements, and data output format. The chapter concludes with an assessment of the implications, both positive and negative, of computers in content analysis.

A number of problems associated with manual coding can be minimized or overcome by use of computers, but computers are not currently able to undertake all of the repetitive and routine chores associated with content analysis. Nor is use of computers warranted for every type of research.

What, then, can computers do, and what can they not do? The most general answer is that they can do any task for which the analyst can prepare unambiguous instructions. It is a truism that a computer cannot appreciate good poetry, but if the investigator were able to specify all the necessary and sufficient conditions for a good poem, then the computer could be used to judge poetry according to those criteria. More specifically, we can identify certain classes of research problems for which computers are likely to be of significant assistance.

First, computers are likely to be especially useful when the unit of analysis is the word or symbol, and inferences are to be based on the frequency with which they appear. This is a chore that computers do well at almost unbelievable speed, and many versions of word count programs are available. Although counting words is not a complex task, we might bear in mind the "important empirical principle" discovered by Mosteller and Wallace (1964, p. 7) in their study of the *Federalist Papers:* "people cannot count, at least not very high." Perhaps an equally important point is that the time an investigator spends on such tedious and unrewarding tasks can be put to better use on other aspects of research.

Second, when the technique of analysis is a complex one the ability of computers to deal with a large number of variables simultaneously may prove very useful. Consider the case of an analyst who is working with several dozen categories, each of which is operationally defined by a large number of content units. Because the capacity of even a well-trained human coder for committing to memory such instructions is limited, reliability is likely to suffer. Many forms of contingency analysis, in which inferences are based on the co-occurrence of two or more concepts in a sentence or any other specified unit of text, are also of such complexity that computers can perform the necessary coding tasks with significantly higher reliability than human judges.

Third, when there is strong reason to suspect beforehand that completion of the research will require many different analyses, having the data on IBM cards for machine analysis will probably save many hours—if not months—of labor. In some types of exploratory studies the analyst may be able to state his goals unambiguously, but he may not be certain which of several possible operations on his data will best enable him to achieve his purposes. This type of research should not be confused with "fishing expeditions" in which the goals of inquiry are little more than a hope that some interesting findings will emerge. The need to test alternative research strategies frequently occurs in authorship studies. Mosteller and Wallace, for example, could state their problem clearly: which of two authors wrote certain political articles? Finding the appropriate indicators to distinguish the style of Madison from that of Hamilton was the necessary first step in the analysis, one which required going through the data several times.

Fourth, if the data are to be reused for a series of investigations, the initial costs of preparing the data, when spread over several studies, may render computer analysis far less costly than any manual technique. This may be a particularly appropriate manner of calculating research costs when the data in question are very basic documents. For example, all American major party platforms since 1844 were initially analyzed by computer to test several hypotheses relating to concerns for economic values (Namenwirth, in press). They are being re-examined in a broader analysis of other politically relevant values (Namenwirth and Lasswell, forthcoming). It seems unlikely that even the latter study will exhaust all questions for which political scientists, historians, sociologists, and others might analyze party platforms.* When viewed in this light, the initial costs of data preparation for computer analysis seem small indeed.

These are some types of research problems for which computer analysis may be quite appropriate, but there are also a great many others for which manual techniques are likely to prove superior on several counts.

First, for the "one shot" study, in which a single analysis of rather specialized documents will suffice, computer analysis may be prohibitively expensive. Pending the availability of optical scanners capable of transforming the printed page into machine readable form directly, the text must be punched onto IBM cards, a cost of no small magnitude if the data are extensive. If the analyst must prepare a "dictionary"† for his variables, rather than borrowing one of those already available, research costs are further increased. In short, overhead costs that could be justified for an inquiry in which data and dictionaries are to be used many times may simply be too high when viewed from the perspective of a single study.

Second, computer analysis is usually impractical when the volume of data is large, but only a limited amount of information from each document is required. A case in point is an analysis of French and Chinese documents for themes relating to alliances, such as "Praise (or condemnation) of NATO," and "Praise (or condemnation) of the USSR" (Holsti and

---

* This does not, of course, imply that computer content analysis represents the only or even the best way to analyze party platforms. For an interesting example of manual techniques applied to platforms, see Benson (1961). But even the investigator who uses manual techniques might find it useful to have such documents available at a central archive in card form for supplementary analyses.

† Dictionaries for computer analysis are discussed as part of the General Inquirer programs below.

Sullivan, in press). Over 600 documents totalling some 3000 printed pages were examined. To have keypunched this volume of documentation for the limited purposes at hand clearly would not have been justified.

Third, when the research problem calls for use of space or time measures, simpler instruments such as the ruler will yield sufficiently precise answers at far lower cost. Thus media inventories and related inquiries will rarely warrant the use of computers. The same suggestion usually applies when the entire item (speech, article, book, and the like) serves as the recording unit. In both instances, however, computers may be very useful in the final stages of research for purely numerical and statistical operations (cross tabulations, correlational analyses, and the like).

Fourth, the case for or against use of computers for thematic analysis is less clearcut. Thematic analysis usually requires not only specifying the occurrence or co-occurrence of certain words, but also the relationship between them. At present there are two approaches to the problem, both of which involve a combination of manual and computer effort. (For an exception to this point, see the "need achievement" scoring system, described later in this chapter, in which coding is done entirely by computer.) One solution is to specify relationships between parts of themes by some form of syntax coding prior to keypunching,* but the added research costs may be considerable. Alternatively, the analyst may use the computer to retrieve and print out all themes in which certain words occur, and then sort them out manually. Consider a research problem intended to compare Chinese and Soviet assessments of nuclear war in terms of: likely causes of nuclear war, duration, the role of conventional forces in such a war, extent of destruction, and long-range political consequences. All sentences in which the term "nuclear war" and its synonyms are found could be retrieved by computer and then further categorized by hand. Whether either of these approaches to thematic analysis is more satisfactory than doing all the coding manually will depend on the nature of the inquiry.

At present, most computer content analysis programs fall into one of two categories. Those of the first type are essentially word count programs, the output consisting of the frequency with which each word in the text appears. The second type of computer program is characterized by a dictionary system in which text words are looked up in the dictionary and automatically coded with information representing the investigator's frame of reference and assumptions. The coded text may then be manipulated, categorized, tallied, and retrieved according to the analyst's data requirements.

---

* For a further elaboration of this point, see the program described in greater detail below.

WORD COUNT PROGRAMS

Word or symbol counting is one of the most widely used forms of content analysis. Although considerably less complex than some other methods, notably theme analysis, symbol counting can nevertheless present serious problems of reliability. Evidence from the RADIR studies of political symbols indicates that when the number of categories is large, even if they are defined rigidly and exhaustively, reliability may prove disappointingly low; inter-coder agreement on inclusion and exclusion of symbols ranged between 66% and 70% (Lasswell, Lerner, and Pool, 1952, p. 62). This is one of the operations for which computers are ideally suited. Computers will perform frequency counts at high speeds with perfect reliability, assuming that there are no keypunching errors in the IBM cards. Moreover, computers can locate, tally, and manipulate all symbols, not only those believed, *a priori,* to be of interest or significance. Thus examination of the output may well reveal the appearance of theoretically important symbols which might not have been considered in the original research design.

There has long been a strong tendency for those analyzing psychotherapeutic interviews and related materials to base their inferences on word frequencies and contingencies.* Thus it is not surprising that substantial contributions to computer-based word count programs have emerged from research of this type.

A program for building specialized dictionaries within the vocabulary usage of individual patients has been developed. The computer prints out, in rank order of frequency, the patient's entire vocabulary, as well as tabulating a type-token ratio (Starkweather and Decker, 1964; Starkweather, in press).

A word count program which automatically codes the entire language into 114 categories has been developed for investigating the language content of individual speakers. This approach to content analysis has been used to test rival explanations—those of Sigmund Freud and Macalpine and Hunter, two English psychoanalysts—of Daniel Paul Schreber's delusions, and to map the cognitive development of children from content analyses of stories they tell (Laffal, in press).

Perhaps the most elaborate program of this type is the WORDS system developed for investigating content changes across time, speakers, and circumstances in psychotherapeutic interviews (Iker and Harway, in press, see also Harway and Iker, 1964; 1966; Iker and Harway, 1965). WORDS is actually a package of 40 integrated programs for various types of data sorting, editing, and statistical analysis. For example, raw text can be

---

* See, for example, the research reviewed in Chapter 4 and the extended bibliographic essays by Auld and Murray (1955) and Marsden (1965).

converted into factor scores through a sequence of five steps:

1. Articles, prepositions, and conjunctions are deleted.
2. Certain words that mean little outside of their context are deleted.
3. Certain words are deleted according to a combination of word/speech rules; e.g., *kind* as an adjective is kept, but as a noun it is deleted.
4. A synonymization routine subsumes closely related high frequency words under a single generic word.
5. Frequencies of the remaining words are computed, the incidence of each of the 215 most frequently appearing words within a segment of text is correlated with every other word, and the resulting matrix is factor analyzed.

This system has been used on over 400 continuous psychotherapeutic interviews.

One of the standard readability formulas has been adapted for computer analysis. Despite difficulties in programming—e.g., in defining rules of identification of monosyllables—the program operates at better than 99% reliability. At the same time, desire for greater efficiency led the investigators to develop a new readability formula more suitable to the capabilities of the machine (Danielson and Bryan, 1963). A method of computing various scores from the Cloze readability formula has also been developed. Scores are tabulated for relative entropy, type-token ratios, and noun/verb ratios (Carstenson and Stolz, 1964).

Several computer-based approaches to literary research have been developed. The Verbally Indexed Associations (VIA) program indexes text, groups content words in text together by root, and counts occurrences of words within root groups (Sedelow and Sedelow, in press). This program has been used to analyze various kinds of literature, including Shakespeare's *Hamlet.*

A combination word count and information retrieval system produces concordances of poetry (Painter, 1960; Sebeok and Zeps, 1961). Such programs have been used to analyze the complete works of Matthew Arnold and Yeats (Parrish, 1959; Parrish and Painter, 1963). The program first produces an index of all words appearing in the text in order of frequency. On the concordance pages, the line in which each word appears is followed by the page number in the standard edition of the poet's collected works, the abbreviated title of the poem, and the line number within the poem. An example* is given on the following page.

YOUTHFUL		
DEAD HER PRINCELY YOUTHFUL		
HUSBAND	14 CHURCH BROU I	49
LAY BEFORE HIS YOUTHFUL		
WIFE	14 CHURCH BROU I	50
PASSING ALL HER YOUTHFUL		
HOUR	131 TRISTAM 1	39
BUT THE BRILLIANT YOUTHFUL		
KNIGHT	134 TRISTAM 1	127
CHATTING WITH HER YOUTHFUL		
KNIGHT	134 TRISTAM 1	214
OF HIS TIMID YOUTHFUL BRIDE	137 TRISTAM 1	269

Such information retrieval programs do not produce content analyses, but their output may serve as the basis for subsequent analysis. They have also proved useful in the preliminary stages of developing dictionaries for computer programs of the "General Inquirer" type.

One limitation of word count studies is the problem of context, which may lend a given word a considerably different meaning. This problem is partially solved in a program which searches the text for concepts of importance to the investigator and prints them out together with up to 120 words appearing before and after each key concept. The program may be operated with two search options: exact matching of key and content words, or the matching of initial letters in the key and content words (Danielson and Jackson, 1963).

"GENERAL INQUIRER" PROGRAMS

Probably the computer content analysis programs currently in widest use are those which have been developed as part of the "General Inquirer" system, "a set of computer procedures for processing 'natural text' . . . that locates, counts, and tabulates text characteristics" (Stone, 1964). Originally developed at the Laboratory for Social Relations at Harvard University for studying psychological and sociological materials (Stone *et al.*, 1962; Dunphy, Stone and Smith, 1965), this system now encompasses a family of dictionaries, data preparation systems, and data analysis programs being used in nearly all social sciences (Stone *et al.*, 1966; 1968).

Dictionaries

The core of each General Inquirer system of content analysis is a dictionary in which each entry word is defined with one or more "tags" representing categories in the investigator's theory. A dictionary entry may also specify that the computer check whether specified neighboring words are present in the text; the tags assigned then depend on the idiom found. The dictionary provides the vital link between the theoretical formulation of the research problem and the mechanics of analysis. The necessity for developing rigorous rules concerning "tagging" of words, by forcing unstated assumptions into the open for critical scrutiny, is an important check on many theoretical aspects of a research project—unambiguous definition of categories, precise delineation of the boundaries between concepts, and internal logic of the research design.

Entry words may be listed in the dictionary in root form, without frequently appearing endings such as *e, s, es, ed, ing, ion,* and *ly.* If a word in the text with such an ending is not found in the dictionary, the computer will automatically remove the ending and look up the word root. A single dictionary entry *(attack)* can pick up all forms *(attack, attacks, attacked, attacking)* appearing in the text. One study of a half million words of text drawn from a wide variety of sources revealed that 500 word roots accounted for 80% of the text, excluding proper nouns. One thousand and five thousand word lists picked up 87.1% and 97.7% of the text, respectively (Stone *et al.,* 1966, pp. 164-165.). Thus even a dictionary of moderate size is likely to be effective for most types of text. But the analyst need not settle for a less than comprehensive dictionary. Words appearing in the text but not in the dictionary are printed out separately on a "leftover" list, and may be added to the dictionary later if deemed important. Thus with a second pass through the data one can eliminate error resulting from omission, but not, of course, error from poorly defined or inappropriate categories.

More than a dozen General Inquirer dictionaries are currently in operation. The Harvard Third Psychosociological Dictionary* of 3500 entries uses 83 tag categories, all but three of which consist of at least 20 words. Two sets of tags are incorporated into the dictionary. Each word is assigned a single "first-order" tag which represents the common or manifest meaning of the word. These are discrete, independent variables and can be treated as such statistically. Fifty-five first-order tags are grouped under 13 major headings: *persons* (self, selves, others); *roles* (male role, female role, neuter role, job role); *collectivities* (small group, large group); *cultural objects* (food, clothing, tools); *cultural settings* (social place); *cultural patterns* (ideal value, deviation values, action norms, message form, thought form, nonspecific object); *natural realm* (body part, natural object, natural world); *emotions* (arousal, urge, affection, anger, pleasure, distress); *thought* (sense, think, if, equal, not, cause);

---

* This is the second revision of the original Harvard dictionary. Its authors are presently preparing a third revision which will incorporate results of their "disambiguation" project (described below).

evaluation (good, bad, ought); *social-emotional actions* (approach, guide, control, attack, avoid, follow, communicate); *instrumental actions* (attempt, work, move, get, possess, expel); and *qualifiers* (time reference, space reference, quantity reference, quality reference).

Entry words may also be assigned "second-order" tags which represent their connotative meanings. The second-order tags are not independent variables. The meaning of an entry word may be defined by one or more of the 28 second-order tags: *institutional context* (academic, artistic, community, economic, family, legal, medical, military, political, recreational, religious, technological); *status connotations* (higher status, lower status, peer status); and *psychological themes* (overstate, understate, strong, weak, accept, reject, male theme, female theme, sex theme, ascend, authority, danger, death). For example, *teacher* is tagged with three meanings: job role, higher status, and academic—one first-order tag followed by two second-order tags.

The Harvard dictionary has been used in a number of different applications, including an examination of self-analytic small groups (Dunphy, 1966), a case study of the "Letters from Jenny" (Paige, 1966), comparative analyses of presidential nomination acceptance speeches (Smith, Stone, and Glenn, 1966), writings of popular and unpopular students (Goldberg, 1966), projected autobiographies by Radcliffe and Egyptian students (Dahlberg and Stone, 1966), reports written by successful and unsuccessful volunteers for field work in Africa (Ramallo, 1966), and real and simulated suicide notes (Ogilvie, Stone, and Shneidman, 1966).

A dictionary based on the semantic differential has been developed for analysis of political documents (Holsti, 1964). Nearly 4000 words are tagged along three dimensions, positive-negative, strong-weak, and active-passive. At present this is the only dictionary which is coded for intensity as well as for meaning.* This version of the General Inquirer has been used to develop and test hypotheses relating to decision-making in crisis (Holsti, Brody, and North, 1965), cohesion within the Soviet bloc (Holsti, 1965a; Hopmann, 1967; Hopmann, forthcoming), and attitudinal components of neutralism (Choucri, 1967, 1968a, 1968b).

The Santa Fe Third Anthropological Dictionary, written by Colby (1966c) for cross-cultural comparison of folktales and projective test materials, incorporates 99 tag categories, including a number of value categories developed by Clyde Kluckhohn. Initial studies with the dictionary have included analyses of folktales from five cultures (Kwakiutl, Egyptian, Eskimo, Indian, and Chinese), and TAT protocols of

---

* The program with which this dictionary operates is described in considerable detail below.

Navajos and Zunis (Colby, Collier, and Postal, 1963; Colby and Menchik, 1964; Colby, 1966a).

Psathas (in press) has developed a version of the General Inquirer system for in-process analysis of conversation between two or more persons communicating via computer, and more specifically, for therapist-patient interactions. Content classification and statistical analyses are produced as the conversation proceeds. Three dictionaries are included in the program. The first is an interpersonal identification dictionary to identify persons; the Therapist Tactics Dictionary classifies the therapist's statements according to a theory of therapeutic strategies, the general content dictionary is applied to the statements of both participants.

Eight value categories developed by Lasswell and Kaplan (1950) define the tag categories in a political dictionary written at Yale (Peterson and Brewer, n.d.). The value dictionary is being used to analyze platforms of major parties from 1844 through 1964. An initial study tested alternative hypotheses relating values to social change by examining concerns for economic values in 62 platforms. A comparison of the content data with economic indices such as unemployment figures revealed that social changes tend to cause rather than to follow changes in values (Namenwirth, in press).

A number of special purpose dictionaries have also been prepared. An "alcohol" dictionary of 95 separate tags has been constructed for testing hypotheses relating themes to cultural uses of alcohol. This dictionary of about 3600 entry words and 99 tags has been used to analyze a worldwide sample of folktale collections (Kalin, Davis, and McClelland, 1966). A set of dictionaries has been developed to analyze themes, images, and evaluations associated with both products and corporate images. Some 2500 entries are classified into 70 tag categories, such as product properties, institutional references, and product areas (Stone, Dunphy, and Bernstein, 1965). The "need achievement" dictionary (D. M. Ogilvie and Louise Woodhead, Harvard) follows the rules developed by McClelland for manual scoring of achievement imagery in projective test materials. The dictionary classifies about 1200 entries into 25 tag categories. Thirty-eight tag concepts suggested by the theoretical work of Talcott Parsons are used to classify about 2400 entries in a political dictionary developed for analyzing lobbying behavior (McPherson, 1964). In the WAI dictionary, developed for analyzing multiple open-ended responses to the question "Who am I?" 3000 entry words are used to define 30 tag categories (McLaughlin, 1966). A dictionary for studying survey responses, based on the Harvard dictionary but incorporating adjustments for language used by middle and lower class subjects, has been written by B. Frisbie (University of Chicago). The Icarus dictionary classifies about 2500 words into 74 categories, including some from the Harvard Psychosociological Dictionary. It has been used to study the Icarian themes in folktales from primitive societies, relating them to patterns of family decision-making (Ogilvie, in press). Finally, dictionaries have been prepared to score "need affiliation" (J. Williamson, Harvard), modes of reaction to psilocybin (Tara Dinkel, Chicago), newspaper editorials (Namenwirth and Brewer, 1966), humorous texts in the Mayan Indian language, Tzotzil (V. R. Bricker), plot structures in Ge mythology (P. Maranda, Harvard), and case discussions by panels representing various professions (T. Burns and R. Johnson, Edinburgh).

One of the many advantages of the General Inquirer system is that the dictionaries are basically interchangeable; thus the investigator may run his data on another dictionary tagged for different variables. For example, presidential nomination acceptance speeches were analyzed on several different dictionaries (Smith, Stone, and Glenn, 1966). In interpreting the results it is, of course, important to be cognizant of the theoretical assumptions underlying the dictionary, including the premise that it will be used with populations similar to those for which it was constructed.

Data Preparation

The text to be analyzed is punched on IBM cards with as little or as much preediting as required by the analyst's problem. Most investigations use text directly transcribed onto IBM cards without any coding. Minimal coding normally involves the separation of complex sentences into one or more themes or "thought sequences," and identification of indefinite terms such as pronouns.

To answer some research questions on the basis of communication content, it may not be enough to know that X, Y, or both X and Y occur in a sentence; it may be more important to know the perceived relationship between X and Y. Consider the following three sentences:

This Soviet action is a deliberately provocative and unjustified threat to Czechoslovakian security.

This Czechoslovakian action is a deliberately provocative and unjustified threat to Soviet security.

This deliberately provocative unjustified action is a threat to Soviet and Czechoslovakian security.

Each one contains exactly the same words but their meaning is clearly different. Neither word frequency nor contingency analysis can distinguish between these three sentences. To do so requires some form of theme analysis which, in turn, necessitates some prior coding of data. More elaborate coding systems include the identification of syntactical position of key *words* in the text, and the addition of certain other codes for the theme as a whole (Stone *et al.,* 1962; Holsti, 1964). For example, these sentences might be coded as follows:*

CD This Soviet/3 action/3 is a deliberately/3 provocative/3 and unjustified/3 threat/4 to Czechoslovakian/7 security/7

CD This Czechoslovakian/3 action/3 is a deliberately/3 provocative/3 and unjustified/3 threat/4 to Soviet/7 security/7

CD This deliberately/3 provocative/3 unjustified/3 action/3 is a threat/4 to Soviet/7 and Czechoslovakian security/7

These codes identify the subject-verb-object (3-4-7) relationship, links between modifiers and referents, time (C = current), and mode of expression (D = indicative). While such operations add to the time and effort required for data preparation, they also permit use of more elaborate analysis programs to yield data in the form required by some research designs. As automated language processing routines and syntax identification programs become available, it will be possible to forego most, if not all, precoding. A realistic appraisal of present achievements and future prospects along these lines has been prepared by Simmons (1966).

Data Analysis Programs

The General Inquirer system includes a broad range of programs for analyzing text. A *text and tag list* program prints out the text and tags assigned by sentence in the form of a bilingual book. A *tag tally* program counts words in the text which have been defined by tags in the dictionary. In addition to raw scores, an index based on the ratio of occurrence of tag words to total words in the document is computed. For rapid visual interpretation of results, tag tallies can be printed in graph form. A separate list of all text words not found in the dictionary is also printed out.

A *question and search* program retrieves, tallies, and prints out all sentences meeting any desired specifications. The analyst may wish to search the text for all sentences containing a certain *text word* or *cluster of words*—e.g., all sentences in which "Soviet Union" occurs as the subject and which also contain the words "nuclear" and "weapons." Questions may also retrieve themes in terms of *tags,* with or without specification of intensity or syntax position. The *theme codes,* if used, may also serve as the basis for retrieval. Any of the question specifications may be used singly or in any desired combination, and up to 100 retrieval questions can be processed at once.

---

* The coding system used in these examples is described in more detail in a later section of this chapter.

Users of content analysis often require psychological indexes that will discriminate between two sources. The General Inquirer program has been combined with the Hunt-Hovland "Concept Learner" to produce a program for identifying discriminate functions. The strategy on which the program is based is to search the text for a single concept, or a combination of concepts, which discriminate sentences in document A from those in document B. Failing this, the program will continue the process of subdivision until a subgroup is found where a test does apply or one of the document sources runs out of sentences (Stone and Hunt, 1963; Hunt, Kreuter, and Stone, 1965).

Another variation of the General Inquirer approach to content analysis involves efforts to duplicate manual scoring methods by constructing rules that enable the computer to analyze its own tag applications. The computer is also programmed to make decisions about the nature of a document on the basis of tag profiles. The following document was scored by the Woodhead-Ogilvie need achievement scoring system:

SENTENCE 1	(TAGS APPLIED)
THE STUDENT IS *DREAMING* ABOUT *BECOMING* A *GREAT INVENTOR.*	*NEED TO-BE* ADJECTIVE-POSITIVE *ROLE-POSITIVE* SENTENCE SUMMARY= ACHIEVEMENT IMAGERY.
SENTENCE 2	
AFTER *YEARS* OF *LABOR* THE CRUCIAL MOMENT ARRIVES.	TIME VERB-POSITIVE SENTENCE SUMMARY = UNRELATED IMAGERY
SENTENCE 3	
HE *HOPES* EVERYTHING WILL *PAN OUT PROPERLY.*	NEED *VERB-POSITIVE ADVERB-POSITIVE* SENTENCE SUMMARY = ACHIEVEMENT IMAGERY
SENTENCE 4	
BUT THE *INVENTION* WILL BE A *FAILURE.*	VALUES-POSITIVE *FAILURE* SENTENCE SUMMARY = UNRELATED IMAGERY
SENTENCE 5	
HE WILL DIE *DISCOURAGED.*	*AFFECT-NEGATIVE* SENTENCE SUMMARY = ACHIEVEMENT IMAGERY
SUMMARY	THIS DOCUMENT CONTAINS ACHIEVE-MENT IMAGERY

Tags correspond to the underlined sentence words. Underlined tag words indicate that a prespecified achievement related sequence has been matched. For a document to be scored "Achievement Imagery" it must contain at least one sentence that meets the criteria of one or more of the prespecified rules within the program. For example, sentence 1 contains the sequence: NEED TO-BE ROLE-POSITIVE. This matches an achievement imagery rule. A more complex rule is matched in sentence 5. This rule states that when AFFECT is evident check the preceding sentence for mention of SUCCESS or FAILURE. If either of these tags are located, the sentence containing reference to AFFECT is scored achievement imagery. The computer scoring method correlates well with manual coding.

Computers and the Problem of Homographs

The inability of computers to make routine judgments for which they are not programmed creates a difficult problem in the case of homographs, words with different meaning but identical spelling. Consider, for example, some of the ways in which the word *bear* might appear.

The circus bear performed a high wire act.

The Russian bear has always coveted an outlet to the Mediterranean.

The 1929 crash was the start of a long and severe bear market.

It's time to bear down and finish this job.

Bear in mind that this is important.

Your data bear out my contention.

This farm should bear several thousand bushels of wheat.

Bear with me just a little while longer.

I'm a bear before the first cup of coffee in the morning.

The brave bear up under the most adverse conditions.

When you reach that intersection, bear off to the right.

The villains plan to bear off with the child.

Admittedly, this is an extreme example, but it is by no means unique.

When reasonably well-trained persons are engaged in reading and coding text, homographs generally present few difficulties because the context provides sufficient cues for making reliable decisions. A human coder may occasionally miss a sentence in which *bear* appears, but in the other cases he would have little difficulty deciding whether it is a reference to an animal, grouchy person, stock markets, yield, and so on. The computer, on the other hand, is more reliable in locating every reference to *bear*, but it runs into difficulty because the contextual clues which normally alert any coder to the proper word sense mean nothing to the computer unless it is programmed to take them into account. The problem is especially acute for English words because their meaning is often dependent on context.

The usual solution to the problem of homographs has been to define dictionary entries according to the word sense which is likely to occur most frequently. For a study of Joel Chandler Harris' "Uncle Remus" stories, *bear* would probably be defined as an animal, but presumably some other definition would be more appropriate for an analysis of Shakespeare's sonnets. Nevertheless, faulty codes are almost certain to occur, and the only method for eliminating them is to retrieve each sentence or theme by computer and recode the errors by hand.

A more satisfactory solution which makes fuller use of the computer's capabilities is emerging from the "disambiguation" project undertaken by the original developers of the General Inquirer programs (Stone *et al.*, in press). The goal is to develop a set of grammatical and contextual rules by which a computer can be programmed to make reliable decisions about the proper meaning for 1000 homographs. A Key Word in Context (KWIC)* program was used to locate every word in 56 samples of text totalling over a half million words. This served not only to identify words with different senses, but also to locate them in enough context to permit development of rules for distinguishing one meaning from another. For example, 151 occurrences of the word *matter* were found to have six different senses. Six rules for disambiguation include searching a specified amount of preceding or following text for the presence or absence of certain attributes such as the words *it, no,* or *for that.* If the first rule fails, the computer goes on to the following ones until a rule is satisfied. Only three of 151 occurrences of *matter* were not properly identified (Stone *et al.*, in press).†

When this project is completed, one of the recurrent criticisms (e.g., Kadushin, Lovett, and Merriman, 1968) of computer-based content analysis will have lost much of its force. There are also some preliminary indications that the results are yielding a theoretical payoff by stimulating a reconsideration of content categories in General Inquirer dictionaries.

COMPUTER CONTENT ANALYSIS: AN EXAMPLE

By this time it should be apparent that computer content analysis is not *a* system. Rather, there are *many* techniques which have been developed for a wide variety of purposes. A comprehensive description of all programs is not possible within a single volume, let alone one chapter. It would, in any case, rapidly become outdated because of continuing developments taking place in a field that is still in its infancy. It may, however, be useful to examine in detail one program with potential applicability to several

---

* These programs are described in many sources, including IBM (1962) and Janda (1965, pp. 187-200).
† Another effort at identifying word senses is described in Laffal (in press).

disciplines, in order to impart a general sense of how computers may be used in content analysis.* The description that follows will describe the *purposes* for which the program might be used, *dictionaries, data preparation,* and *data output.*

Among the basic problems for which content analysis has been used is that of inferring authors' attitudes from the messages they produce. Usually attitudes have been classified into a category set consisting of pro, con, and neutral. Bases for classification of attitudes—i.e., the "context units" which have been considered in judging whether an attitude is favorable, unfavorable, or neutral—have sometimes been the sentence or theme. Often, however, analysts have found that coding each small unit of a document is too costly, and they have instead relied upon a single overall judgment of attitudes expressed in the entire book, speech, editorial, diary, etc. Even such apparently simple coding operations have sometimes produced problems of reliability.

Other research projects may require more precise and complex techniques of content analysis. In the first place, giving the entire document a single rating for each attitude object may result in the loss of certain nuances. It has been demonstrated that the choice of context units affects the results of content analysis; the larger the context unit which is coded, the less likely are neutral attitudes to be recorded (Geller, Kaplan, and Lasswell, 1942b). Moreover, it may sometimes be important to take into consideration not only the direction but also the intensity of expressed attitudes. Finally, some analysts may require a technique which distinguishes between various components of attitudes. For example, Parsons, Shils, and Olds (1952, p. 57) pointed out that social objects may be significant as *complexes of qualities* or *complexes of performance.* In the former case the object is considered in terms of its attributes, of *what it is,* whereas in the latter case the object is viewed in terms of *what it does.* Attitudes about qualities and performances may, but need not, be congruent. A study of John Foster Dulles' attitudes revealed that when the Soviet Union was perceived to be acting most aggressively toward the West, his assessment of Soviet attributes was a negative one. That is, his views of Soviet qualities and performance were congruent. But when Dulles regarded Soviet policy as more accommodating and less hostile, there was no corresponding reassessment of Soviet qualities (Holsti, 1967). Because the existence of discrepancies between components of attitudes is often of interest, a technique of content analysis capable of distinguishing between the

---

* This section is adapted from a paper prepared for the National Conference on Content Analysis in 1967, the proceedings of which are to be published in 1969 (Gerbner *et al.,* in press). For detailed description and operating instructions of many other programs in the General Inquirer family, the reader should consult Stone *et al.* (1966), and a companion *User's Manual for the General Inquirer* (1968) by the same authors.

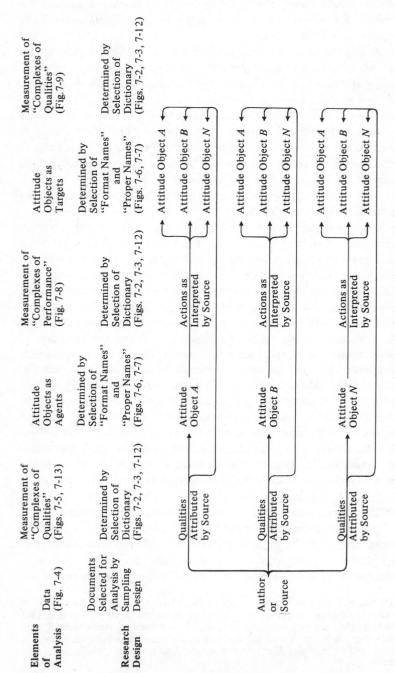

Fig. 7-1 Design of measurements by computer content analysis program.

subject's assessment of qualities and performance may sometimes be needed.

One method of content analysis which meets these requirements is "evaluative assertion analysis," described in Chapter 5, in which the first step in coding is reduction of the entire text into simple assertions of two classes which correspond to assessments of "complexes of qualities" and "complexes of performance." The content analysis program described here represents the most recent in a series of efforts to provide a computer-based analog to evaluative assertion analysis.* The substantive impetus for this effort has been an interest in the attitudes and beliefs of political elites, and more specifically, in those of foreign policy decision-makers. But the problem of measuring attitudes is of interest not only to students of international relations, and the flexibility of the present program is such that it can be used with any variables, attitude objects, and class of documents. A schematic representation of the type of research design for which this program was developed is presented in Fig. 7-1.

Dictionaries

Each version of computer content analysis which has emerged from the General Inquirer system has at its core a dictionary in which entry words are defined with one or more tags representing categories in the investigator's theory. The dictionary based on the semantic differential which was developed for the earlier General Inquirer program (Holsti, 1964) remains the primary instrument in the present program. Each entry word in the dictionary is defined or tagged along three dimensions: positive-negative, strong-weak, and active-passive.

The three scales correspond to the *evaluative, potency,* and *activity* dimensions which have often been found to be primary in cognition irrespective of culture (Osgood, Suci, and Tannenbaum, 1957; Osgood, 1962). The dictionary thus reflects the assumption that when human beings perceive themselves, other persons, events, or any attitude object, the most relevant discriminations are made in terms of these dimensions. Entry words are also assigned one of three intensity ratings for each tag:

Positive affect	3	2	1	0	−1	−2	−3	Negative affect
Strong	3	2	1	0	−1	−2	−3	Weak
Active	3	2	1	0	−1	−2	−3	Passive

←   Increasing intensity   →

---

* This program exists in both a BALGOL version for operation on IBM 7090 or 7094 computers and a FORTRAN IV version for the IBM 360 system.

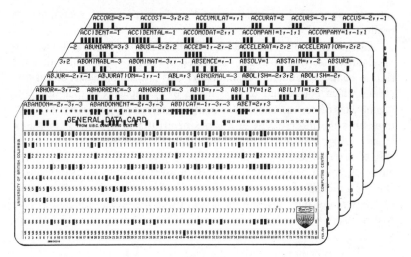

Figure 7-2

A zero intensity indicates that the word receives no score for that dimension. Thus, an entry word may have as many as three definitions (e.g., penetration = negative 1, strong 3, active 2), or as few as one (e.g., illicit = negative 1). Many high frequency words such as articles, conjunctions, and most prepositions receive no tags.

Entry words are listed in the dictionary in root form, with the endings *e, es, s, ed,* and *ing,* but not *ion* or *ly,* removed. If a word in the text with any of these endings is not found in the dictionary, the computer will automatically remove the ending and look up the word root. Numbers and their positions are used to designate tag categories and intensity levels (Fig. 7-2). The first position following the equal sign represents the affect dimension, the second is the potency dimension, and the third is the activity dimension. Numbers which appear in these positions refer to points within each scale. For example, the dictionary includes Accost = −3, 2, 2, indicating that the term is defined as *negative* (intensity 3), *strong* (intensity 2), and *active* (intensity 2). Extra commas are used to denote the absence of a tag, i.e., the zero point on any of the scales. Thus, the double commas between 2 and 3 in the definition of ABET mean that it is scored zero along the potency dimension.

This program may be used with any dictionary adhering to the format specified in Fig. 7-2. Tags for entry words are identified by a set of numbers ranging from +3 to −3 in three positions, defining a maximum of 18 variables. These may be used to designate six points on each of three scales, as in the semantic differential dictionary, or they may be used to define 18 separate variables. For example, a small supplementary dictionary for four variables—conflict, cooperation, economic develop-

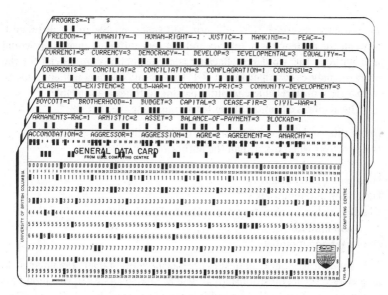

Figure 7-3

ment, and ideal values—was prepared to examine certain United Nations documents. It is punched in the format shown in Fig. 7-3. Because the data tables can accommodate only 18 tag categories, dictionaries with more variables must be divided into sets of 18 or less and used in separate runs through the data. Thus, should the analyst wish to use the Harvard Third Psychosociological Dictionary (Stone *et al.*, 1966, pp. 170-186) with this program, he would need to divide it into four dictionaries of 18 tags each and a fifth one with the remaining 11 categories.

Data Preparation

Inferences about attitudes cannot be made solely from frequency or contingency analysis. Consider the following sentence:

During the years since my last report, the wealthy nuclear powers have not provided enough vital economic aid to the many poor, underdeveloped, noncommitted nations.

Poor and *nuclear powers* both occur in the sentence, but we would surely be misled if we therefore inferred that the author of the document believed that these nations are poor. Nor does an analysis that informs us only that *noncommitted nations, aid,* and *nuclear powers* appear in this sentence tell us what the author believes about the relationship between these two groups of countries. The same information would be produced were the subject (nuclear powers) and object (noncommitted nations) in the sentence reversed. It would not, moreover, enable us to distinguish between the sentence as it appears and the very different meaning it would have without the word *not*. Because such distinctions are crucial for the types of analyses described in Fig. 7-1, some syntax coding will continue to be necessary until reliable computer parsing routines are available.

The symbols currently in use for subscripting the text are:*

The author of document (appears on ID card only)	/1
The perceiver when other than the author of the document	/2
The agent and modifiers	/3
The action and modifiers	/4
The direct object (when target is indirect object) and modifiers	/5
The target and modifiers	/7

The numerical codes indicate the agent-action-target (analogous to subject-verb-object) relationship, as well as linking all descriptive modifiers to the proper terms. The subscript system described here is flexible, and these numbers may be used to designate other types of relationships. But for reasons that will be made clearer when we turn to data output format, *this program will not operate on uncoded text.*

The entire theme may also be coded for certain essential information which cannot be effectively transmitted through word subscripting alone. Unlike the required syntax marks, data to be analyzed with this program may, but need not, be theme coded.

Three theme codes are currently being used:

1. *The time element*
   C — Current
   P — Past
   F — Future

2. *The mode of expression*
   D — Indicative
   N — Normative
   M — Comparative
   V — Imperative
   B — Probability
   T — Interrogative
   X — Aspiration

3. *Conditional statements*
   A — Antecedent (if . . .)
   S — Subsequent (then . . .)

---

* Alternative syntax coding schemes are described in Stone *et al.* (1962) and Miller (1967).

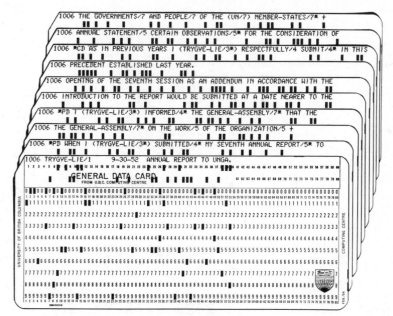

Figure 7-4

These codes, which are preceded by a star, are inserted into the text as the first word of each theme. The entire text is punched on IBM cards in the format shown in Fig. 7-4.

Output Format: "Complexes of Qualities"

As indicated in Fig. 7-1, the data output format in this program is designed to measure attitudes about both "complexes of qualities" and "complexes of performance" from the content of communications. A's assertions about B's qualities may take a variety of forms. For example, each of the following assertions by A contain information about A's assessment of B. This is found in the modifying words coded with the same numbers as that used for B.

THE AGGRESSIVE/3 POLICIES/3 OF B/3 ENDANGER/4
THE PEACE/7.
(Description of B as an agent of action)

OUR/3 GOALS/3 ARE TO SUPPORT/4 OUR BRAVE/7 AND
STURDY/7 ALLY/7 B/7.
(Description of B as the target of action)

B/3 IS/4 A STRUGGLING/3 UNDERDEVELOPED/3 NATION/3.
(Predicate adjective and predicate noun).

NUMBER OF WORDS IN TEXT- 5877

1009 HAMMARSKJOLD/1   1955   UNGAR REPORT   UNGA.

EVALUATIVE PERCEPTION ......AGENT

	U.N.	U.S.	USSR	WEST	EAST	N.A.	M.N.	BIGPOW	CRISIS	OTHER	TOTAL
POSITIVE AFFECT	78.000 .013	.000 .000	.000 .000	4.000 .001	.000 .000	17.000 .003	20.000 .003	.000 .000	3.000 .001	21.000 .004	143.000 .024
NEGATIVE AFFECT	1.000 .000	.000 .000	.000 .000	.000 .000	.000 .000	3.000 .001	7.000 .001	.000 .000	2.000 .000	20.000 .003	33.000 .006
STRONG	113.000 .019	.000 .000	.000 .000	3.000 .001	1.000 .000	15.000 .003	21.000 .004	.000 .000	.000 .000	57.000 .010	210.000 .036
WEAK	3.000 .001	.000 .000	.000 .000	.000 .000	.000 .000	.000 .000	.000 .000	.000 .000	.000 .000	10.000 .002	13.000 .002
ACTIVE	86.000 .015	.000 .000	.000 .000	2.000 .000	.000 .000	6.000 .001	9.000 .002	.000 .000	.000 .000	24.000 .004	127.000 .022
PASSIVE	25.000 .004	.000 .000	.000 .000	1.000 .000	.000 .000	.000 .000	2.000 .000	.000 .000	.000 .000	11.000 .002	39.000 .007

Figure 7-5 (a)

FREQUENCY TABLE	U.N.	U.S.	USSR	WEST	EAST	N.A.	M.N.	BIGPOW	CRISIS	OTHER	TOTAL
POSITIVE 1	26	0	0	2	0	5	2	0	0	9	44
POSITIVE 2	17	0	0	1	0	3	9	0	0	6	36
POSITIVE 3	6	0	0	0	0	2	0	0	1	0	9
NEGATIVE 1	1	0	0	0	0	3	2	0	0	4	10
NEGATIVE 2	0	0	0	0	0	0	1	0	1	5	7
NEGATIVE 3	0	0	0	0	0	0	1	0	0	2	3
STRONG . 1	20	0	0	1	1	4	1	0	0	10	37
STRONG . 2	39	0	0	1	0	4	7	0	0	16	67
STRONG . 3	5	0	0	0	0	1	2	0	0	5	13
WEAK ... 1	1	0	0	0	0	0	0	0	1	2	4
WEAK ... 2	1	0	0	0	0	0	0	0	0	4	5
WEAK ... 3	0	0	0	0	0	0	0	0	0	0	0
ACTIVE . 1	24	0	0	0	0	2	2	0	0	4	32
ACTIVE . 2	25	0	0	1	0	2	2	0	0	4	34
ACTIVE . 3	4	0	0	0	0	0	1	0	0	4	9
PASSIVE 1	9	0	0	1	0	0	2	0	0	1	13
PASSIVE 2	5	0	0	0	0	0	0	0	0	2	7
PASSIVE 3	2	0	0	0	0	0	0	0	0	2	4

Figure 7-5 (b)

In each case the numerical codes serve to link attitude object B with the qualities attributed to it by the source. The program may also be used to analyze what A says regarding B's performance toward $A, B, C, \ldots, N$. Scores are based on words and phrases with the /4 syntax code in sentences in which B is the agent of action and $A, B, C, \ldots, N$ are the targets.

The tables produced by this program are intended to answer questions about both "qualities" and "performance" exhaustively for any specified attitude objects, be they nations, institutions, groups, persons, concepts, programs, ideologies, or whatever, which might appear in the data. The first pair of tables presents scores on the perceived qualities of attitude objects when they appear as agents in the sentence (Fig. 7-5). The top of the first table includes identification information for the document and a tally of the number of words it contains. Row headings identify the dictionary variables (or tags) and column headings are the attitude objects designated by the investigator. Our example includes variables in the semantic differential dictionary and nine attitude objects—the United Nations, United States, USSR, West, East, nonaligned nations, U.N. member nations, big powers, and crisis—relevant to a study of the United Nations Secretary General's attitudes. The initial figure in each cell represents a weighted (frequency $\times$ intensity) total for the designated relationship. Thus the 78.00 in the upper left-hand cell indicates a weighted score for the U.N. on the variable positive affect, and the number immediately underneath is the weighted score divided by the number of words in the text $(78.00/5877 = 0.013)$.

The combination of frequencies and intensities resulting in a score of 78.00 is not revealed in Fig. 7-5a. It might have been based on 78 references scored "positive affect-intensity one" in the dictionary $(78 \times 1 = 78)$, 20 references scored positive-three and 18 positive-one $[(20 \times 3) + (18 \times 1) = 78]$, or any other combination of frequency and intensity totalling 78. A glance at the corresponding cell in the immediately following table (Fig. 7-5b) reveals that the weighted score was based on 49 assertions about the United Nations as the agent, 26 of which were scored positive 1, 17 as positive 2, and six as positive 3 $[(26 \times 1) + (17 \times 2) + (6 \times 3) = 78]$. Because some statistical tests cannot be used with weighted data such as appear in Fig. 7-5a, the frequency distributions provided in the table that follows are often useful for statistical purposes.

Any single pass through the data will accommodate analysis of up to 12 attitude objects. The next column—"others"—records scores for all other attitude objects which appear in the document. These will be identified in the leftover list which appears with each set of tables. Figures in the right-hand column "total"—represent the total score for each row.

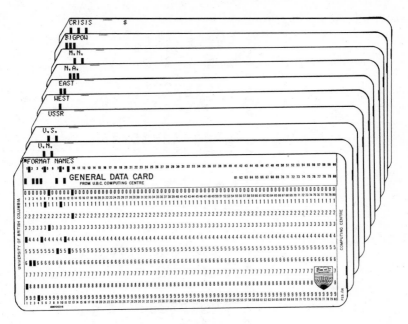

Figure 7-6

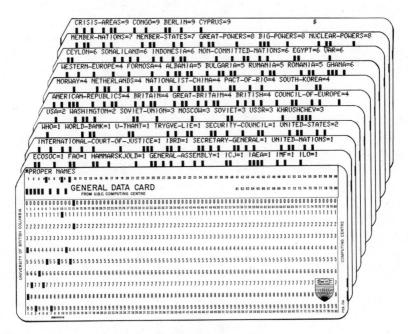

Figure 7-7

EVALUATIVE PERCEPTION .....TARGET

	U.N.	U.S.	USSR	WEST	EAST	N.A.	M.N.	BIGPOW	CRISIS	OTHER	TOTAL
POSITIVE AFFECT	34.000 .006	.000	.000	.000	.000	6.000 .001	4.000 .001	.000	.000	47.000 .008	91.000 .015
NEGATIVE AFFECT	16.000 .003	.000	.000	.000	.000	4.000 .001	4.000 .001	.000	.000	23.000 .004	47.000 .008
STRONG	56.000 .010	.000	.000	.000	.000	17.000 .003	8.000 .001	.000	.000	66.000 .011	147.000 .025
WEAK	10.000 .002	.000	.000	.000	.000	.000	.000	.000	.000	20.000 .003	30.000 .005
ACTIVE	36.000 .006	.000	.000	.000	.000	9.000 .002	4.000 .001	.000	.000	43.000 .007	92.000 .016
PASSIVE	11.000 .002	.000	.000	.000	.000	4.000 .001	2.000 .000	.000	.000	18.000 .003	35.000 .006

Figure 7-8 (a)

FREQUENCY TABLE	U.N.	U.S.	USSR	WEST	EAST	N.A.	M.N.	BIGPOW	CRISIS	OTHER	TOTAL
POSITIVE 1	13	0	0	0	0	2	1	0	0	13	29
POSITIVE 2	6	0	0	0	0	2	0	0	0	11	19
POSITIVE 3	3	0	0	0	0	0	1	0	0	4	8
NEGATIVE 1	5	0	0	0	0	4	1	0	0	9	19
NEGATIVE 2	4	0	0	0	0	0	0	0	0	4	8
NEGATIVE 3	1	0	0	0	0	0	1	0	0	2	4
STRONG . 1	9	0	0	0	0	2	1	0	0	12	24
STRONG . 2	13	0	0	0	0	3	2	0	0	12	30
STRONG . 3	7	0	0	0	0	3	1	0	0	10	21
WEAK ... 1	2	0	0	0	0	0	0	0	0	4	6
WEAK ... 2	4	0	0	0	0	0	0	0	0	5	9
WEAK ... 3	0	0	0	0	0	0	0	0	0	2	2
ACTIVE . 1	6	0	0	0	0	3	1	0	0	13	23
ACTIVE . 2	12	0	0	0	0	3	0	0	0	12	27
ACTIVE . 3	2	0	0	0	0	0	1	0	0	2	5
PASSIVE 1	1	0	0	0	0	0	0	0	0	3	4
PASSIVE 2	5	0	0	0	0	2	1	0	0	3	11
PASSIVE 3	0	0	0	0	0	0	0	0	0	3	3

Figure 7-8 (b)

Column headings are controlled by two sets of cards. "Format Names" cards designate the titles at the head of each column and the order in which they are to appear. Each name or appropriate six-digit abbreviation should end on column 6 for proper alignment of the columns in the tables. The last card is punched with a dollar sign in column 15. The "Format Names" cards used to produce the tables in the example above appear in Fig. 7-6.

A set of "Proper Names" cards (Fig. 7-7) is used to identify the text words which are to be classified under each column heading. For example, in Fig. 7-5 the column "United Nations" was defined by a series of terms designating persons and agencies associated with the U.N.* The United Nations appears in column 1 of each table because it was placed first in the deck of "Format Names" cards; thus each of these terms was punched with =1: ECOSOC = 1, FAO = 1, HAMMARSKJOLD = 1, and so on. The same procedure is followed for all terms which are to be scored under each column heading.†

The second and third sets of tables produced for each document are similar in format to those described above, but they compute scores for perceived qualities of attitude objects in themes in which they appear as *direct objects* and *targets* of action. Consider again the example cited earlier:

DURING THE YEAR SINCE MY LAST REPORT, THE WEALTHY/3 NUCLEAR-POWERS/3 HAVE NOT/4 PROVIDED/4 ENOUGH/4 VITAL/5 ECONOMIC/5 AID/5 TO THE MANY/7 POOR/7, UNDERDEVELOPED/7, NON-COMMITTED-NATIONS/7.

The first pair of tables prints out scores for the subject of the sentence—nuclear powers—based on dictionary tags of the words used to describe it; the second pair of tables presents scores for the direct object based on the described attributes of foreign aid; and the third pair of tables indicates the author's attitudes toward the target of action, noncommitted nations. An example of the latter type of table is given in Fig. 7-8. The mechanics of scoring are the same as for the tables in Fig. 7-5.

Output Format: "Complexes of Performance"

To answer questions about "complexes of performance" we need to determine how the source perceives A's (or B's . . . N's) actions toward A, $B, . . . , N$. This program produces a complete set of tables measuring the

---

* Fig. 7-7 includes only a small sample, for purposes of illustration, of the "Proper Names" that were actually used to produce the tables in Figs. 7-5, 7-8, and 7-9.

† Note that punching of entries on "Proper Names" cards begins in column 2.

perceived relationship between every pair of attitude objects. Thus for each of the nine attitude objects for which Format Names and Proper Names cards were prepared in our example, the program computes and prints out a pair of tables scoring its actions in terms of the dictionary variables. In our illustrative document, the first pair of tables reveals the author's assessment of United Nations actions toward all targets (Fig. 7-9). A similar pair of tables is produced for the United States, USSR, West, East, nonaligned nations, U.N. member nations, big powers, and crisis areas. The basic table format and the method of computation are, with two important exceptions, identical with those described for earlier tables.

The first exception concerns the use of negatives. Clearly it is important to distinguish between two sentences such as: "The nuclear powers have provided economic aid to the noncommitted nations," and "The nuclear powers have *not* provided economic aid to the non-committed nations." When any action is modified by terms of negation— *no, never, not,* and the like—it is automatically given a reverse score. In the example above the term "provide" is tagged in the dictionary as "positive 1, strong 2, active 1." In the second sentence it is preceded by a negation, causing the program to score the action of the nuclear powers toward noncommitted nations as "negative 1, weak 2, passive 1."

A second feature of the tables for action relationships is that the mode of expression may result in a somewhat reduced intensity score. The mode of expression is indicated by a single letter code preceding each theme. The codes and the intensity weights assigned to each shown in Table 7-1 are currently being used.

Consider our previous example, which might also have appeared as:

The nuclear powers hope to provide economic aid to the non-committed nations.

The nuclear powers may provide economic aid to the non-committed nations.

TABLE 7-1

Codes and intensity weights

Code	Mode of expression	Weight
X	Aspiration	0.4
B	Probability	0.5
N	Normative	0.6
V	Imperative	0.7
D	Indicative	1.0
M	Comparative	1.0
T	Interrogative	1.0

ACTION PERCEPTIONS

AGENT--   U.N.

	U.N.	U.S.	TARGET NATIONS USSR	WEST	EAST	N.A.	M.N.	BIGPOW	CRISIS	OTHER	TOTAL
POSITIVE AFFECT	9.900	.000	.000	.000	.000	6.000	1.500	.000	2.400	15.000	34.800
	.002	.000	.000	.000	.000	.001	.000	.000	.000	.003	.006
NEGATIVE AFFECT	.700	.000	.000	.000	.000	3.000	3.000	.000	.000	10.000	16.700
	.000	.000	.000	.000	.000	.001	.001	.000	.000	.002	.003
STRONG	25.400	.000	.000	.000	1.000	5.700	2.500	.000	5.300	44.900	84.800
	.004	.000	.000	.000	.000	.001	.001	.000	.001	.008	.014
WEAK	.000	.000	.000	.000	.000	1.000	9.000	.000	.000	.000	10.000
	.000	.000	.000	.000	.000	.000	.002	.000	.000	.000	.002
ACTIVE	18.700	.000	.000	.000	1.000	2.400	3.000	.000	4.200	29.000	58.300
	.003	.000	.000	.000	.000	.000	.001	.000	.001	.005	.010
PASSIVE	3.300	.000	.000	.000	1.000	6.000	9.000	.000	1.200	5.000	25.500
	.001	.000	.000	.000	.000	.001	.002	.000	.000	.001	.004

Figure 7-9 (a)

FREQUENCY TABLE	U.N.	U.S.	USSR	WEST	EAST	N.A.	M.N.	BIGPOW	CRISIS	OTHER	TOTAL
POSITIVE 1	4	0	0	0	0	1	2	0	1	4	12
POSITIVE 2	3	0	0	0	0	1	0	0	1	4	9
POSITIVE 3	1	0	0	0	0	1	0	0	1	1	4
NEGATIVE 1	1	0	0	0	0	1	3	0	0	2	7
NEGATIVE 2	0	0	0	0	0	1	0	0	0	1	2
NEGATIVE 3	0	0	0	0	0	0	0	0	0	2	2
STRONG . 1	6	0	0	0	1	1	3	0	1	6	18
STRONG . 2	6	0	0	0	0	1	0	0	2	13	22
STRONG . 3	3	0	0	0	0	1	0	0	1	7	12
WEAK ... 1	0	0	0	0	0	1	0	0	0	0	1
WEAK ... 2	0	0	0	0	0	0	0	0	0	0	0
WEAK ... 3	0	0	0	0	0	0	3	0	0	0	3
ACTIVE . 1	2	0	0	0	1	1	1	0	0	14	19
ACTIVE . 2	9	0	0	0	0	1	1	0	3	9	23
ACTIVE . 3	0	0	0	0	0	0	0	0	0	1	1
PASSIVE 1	3	0	0	0	1	2	0	0	1	1	8
PASSIVE 2	1	0	0	0	0	2	2	0	1	2	8
PASSIVE 3	0	0	0	0	0	0	2	0	0	0	2

Figure 7-9 (b)

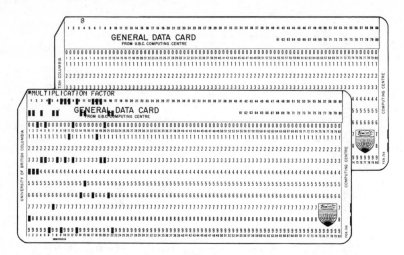

Figure 7-10

When stated in these forms, the automatic intensity reduction feature of the program will multiply the score for the action term—*provide* (positive 1, strong 2, active 1)—by the indicated weights. Hence, in the sentence above stating aspiration, multiplication by 0.4 will result in a score of nuclear powers' action toward noncommitted nations of positive 0.4, strong 0.8, active 0.4.

The intensity reduction feature of the program is optional. The analyst who does not wish to employ theme codes may still use the program. In that case, all actions are scored at full dictionary value. The assigned weights for various modes of expression are, of course, arbitrary and may be easily changed. If the intensity reduction feature is used, two cards (Fig. 7-10) are submitted with the data to identify the column on the data cards in which the theme code for modes of expression appears. The number 8 in column 5 of the second card indicates that the various theme codes for mode of expression appear in column 8 of the data cards.

If codes for mode of expression are used, some apparent discrepancies between the tables providing weighted (intensity X frequency) and simple frequency scores will appear. In Fig. 7-9a United Nations actions toward crisis areas received a score for "strong" of 5.3, which is somewhat less than that indicated in the accompanying (Fig. 7-9b) frequency table: $(1 \times 1) + (2 \times 2) + (1 \times 3) = 8$. This indicates that several of the action scores received less than a full value owing to their mode of expression.

Tables can be produced at any designated interval between or within documents. Each segment of text for which tables are to be produced is preceded by a "New Text" card. Scores will be computed for all subsequent text until a "Tag Tally" card is inserted, at which point the

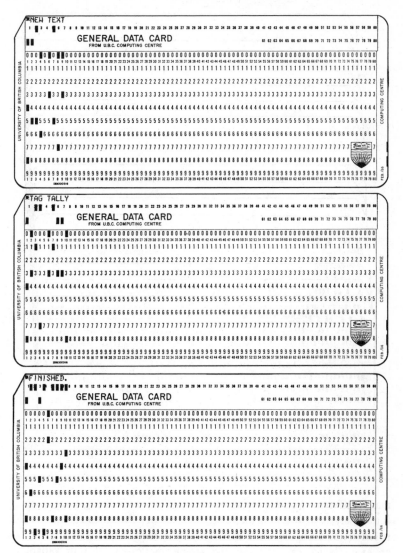

Figure 7-11

program prints out tables for the text between these two cards. This procedure is followed through to the end of the data, which is marked by a "Finished" card. The format of these cards is indicated in Fig. 7-11.

Should the analyst wish to use variables other than those in the semantic differential dictionary, he may do so without recoding or in any other way changing his data. Once the data have been punched in the format described earlier, they may be reanalyzed as often and with as

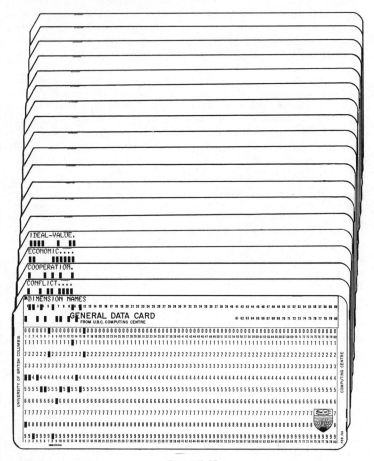

Figure 7-12

many different dictionaries as necessary. Only two changes are required for reanalysis with a new dictionary. A deck of "Dimension Names" cards is submitted along with the dictionary entry words and tag definitions. As an example we can consider the sample dictionary of four variables— conflict, cooperation, economic development, and ideal values—illustrated in Fig. 7-3. The corresponding Dimension Names cards appear in Fig. 7-12. Variable names are punched in columns 1 to 12 and a dollar sign is punched in column 15 of the final card. When the variable name requires less than 12 spaces, periods are punched after the end of the word through column 12. If the dictionary includes fewer than 18 variables, as is the case in our example, blank cards are inserted to bring the total number of cards to 18.

1009 HAMMARSKJOLD/1   1955   UNGAR REPORT   UNGA.

NUMBER OF WORDS IN TEXT- 5886

EVALUATIVE PERCEPTION ......AGENT

	U.N.	U.S.	USSR	WEST	EAST	N.A.	M.N.	BIGPOW	CRISIS	OTHER	TOTAL
(1)+(2)+(3)...	97.000	.000	.000	5.000	.000	17.000	10.000	.000	.000	81.000	210.000
	.016	.000	.000	.001	.000	.003	.002	.000	.000	.014	.036
(-1)..........	3.000	.000	.000	1.000	.000	1.000	1.000	.000	1.000	1.000	8.000
	.001	.000	.000	.000	.000	.000	.000	.000	.000	.000	.001
	.000	.000	.000	.000	.000	.000	.000	.000	.000	.000	.000
	.000	.000	.000	.000	.000	.000	.000	.000	.000	.000	.000
	.000	.000	.000	.000	.000	.000	.000	.000	.000	.000	.000
	.000	.000	.000	.000	.000	.000	.000	.000	.000	.000	.000
	.000	.000	.000	.000	.000	.000	.000	.000	.000	.000	.000
	.000	.000	.000	.000	.000	.000	.000	.000	.000	.000	.000
	.000	.000	.000	.000	.000	.000	.000	.000	.000	.000	.000
	.000	.000	.000	.000	.000	.000	.000	.000	.000	.000	.000
	.000	.000	.000	.000	.000	.000	.000	.000	.000	.000	.000

Figure 7-13 (a)

FREQUENCY TABLE

	U.N.	U.S.	USSR	WEST	EAST	N.A.	M.N.	BIGPOW	CRISIS	OTHER	TOTAL
CONFLICT....	0	0	0	0	0	3	2	0	0	10	15
COOPERATION	14	0	0	1	0	1	4	0	0	13	33
ECONOMIC....	23	0	0	1	0	4	0	0	0	15	43
IDEAL-VALUE	3	0	0	1	0	1	1	1	1	1	8
	0	0	0	0	0	0	0	0	0	0	0
	0	0	0	0	0	0	0	0	0	0	0
	0	0	0	0	0	0	0	0	0	0	0
	0	0	0	0	0	0	0	0	0	0	0

Figure 7-13 (b)

Except for the variable names at the beginning of each row, tables produced with any dictionary are similar to those described earlier. Interpretation of the tables however, will vary according to the nature of the dictionary. Figure 7-13b, in which simple frequencies appear, presents no problem. But the table in Fig. 7-13a, which computes a weighted score (frequency X intensity) when used with the semantic differential dictionary, produces meaningless scores in the present example. That is, with the semantic differential dictionary the first three variables (positive 1, positive 2, and positive 3) represent points of differing intensity on a single scale. Hence, the weighted scores may be a useful summary score of attitudes on that scale. In the dictionary used in Fig. 7-13, however, the first three variables (conflict, cooperation, and economic development) clearly do not represent different points on a single scale. Thus, the weighted scores in Fig. 7-13a should be disregarded. In summary, then, the simple frequency tables produced by this program can always be used, irrespective of the dictionary, but the weighted scores will be meaningful only with dictionaries in which tag definitions include intensity scores.

Leftover List

Preceding the tables for each document is a series of messages listing potential deficiencies in the data or dictionary. The appearance of single words on the list reveals that they are not listed in the dictionary. In Fig. 7-14, *events, fore, concepts, static,* and so on are words which occurred in the text but are not in the dictionary. A rapid glance through this list reveals which words, if any, should be tagged and added to the dictionary for future passes through the data. Because mispunched or misspelled words will also appear on this leftover list, it also provides a rapid check for the adequacy of keypunching.

The messages also reveal coding irregularities such as occurred in themes 2, 8, and 14. The analyst can readily turn to these themes in his data to determine whether the problem is one which makes a substantive difference. Such irregularities do not stop the program from operating, nor do they prevent tables from being prepared.

The leftover list also discloses the attitude objects that appear in the document, but for which Format Names and Proper Names cards were not provided. A typical message is that reading "Nations assumed other," indicating that any references to unspecified nations were scored in the "others" column of the tables. This feature can be particularly useful for large-scale analyses in which the investigator may not be certain that a given pass through the data has exhausted the information of interest to him. A glance through these messages reveals whether further runs incorporating attitude objects that appear as "others" with some frequency in the text are warranted. For example, were repeated messages

LEFTOVERS--

    EVENTS
    FORE
    CONCEPTS
UN IMPROPERLY TAGGED 7 IN THEME 1
    CERTAIN
NATIONS ASSUMED 'OTHER'
ORGANIZATION IMPROPERLY TAGGED 7 IN THEME 2
    STATIC
    MACHINERY
    IDEOLOGIES
    VIEW
    IDEOLOGIES
NATIONS ASSUMED 'OTHER'
    INSTRUMENT
NATIONS ASSUMED 'OTHER'
    SHOULD   -
RECONCILIATION ASSUMED 'OTHER'
NATIONS ASSUMED 'OTHER'
    SHOULD
    EXECUTIVE
    UNTAKEN
MEMBERS IMPROPERLY TAGGED 7 IN THEME 8
    FORESTALLING
    DIPLOMATIC
    POLITICAL
    SPIRIT
    OBJECTIVITY
    IMPLEMENTATION
    LATTER
CONCEPT ASSUMED 'OTHER'
    POINT
CONCEPT ASSUMED 'OTHER'
CONCEPT ASSUMED 'OTHER'
CONCEPT ASSUMED 'OTHER'
    POINT
CONCEPT ASSUMED 'OTHER'
    ENVISAGING
    INCREASINGLY
    FORMS
    INTERNATIONAL
CONCEPT ASSUMED 'OTHER'
    ORGANS
UN IMPROPERLY TAGGED 7 IN THEME 14
    CONCEPT
HISTORY ASSUMED 'OTHER'
    POLICIES
    PAST
    CONCEPT
    POINT
    FUTURE
WORLD ASSUMED 'OTHER'
    IS
    INTERNATIONAL
INTERDEPENDENCE ASSUMED 'OTHER'
NATIONS ASSUMED 'OTHER'
CONCEPT ASSUMED 'OTHER'
    PHILOSOPHY

Figure 7-14

about "interdependence" to appear, as in the fourth line from the bottom of Fig. 7-14, the analyst might decide to rerun all or parts of his data to pick up these references if he deemed them to be theoretically significant.

The sequence in which various cards are assembled for running is summarized in Fig. 7-15.

In concluding it should be stated once again that this is neither a general purpose program applicable to all content analysis problems, nor is it the perfect computer analog of evaluative assertion analysis. Ideally such a program should provide precise measurement of attitudes with flexibility and speed at minimal cost. It is apparent that the present program does not meet all of these specifications equally well.

If there are no coding or punching errors, this program does provide precise and reliable (but not, of course, necessarily valid) measures of attitudes. The leftover list can be an invaluable tool for virtually eliminating both coding and punching errors.

The requirement of flexibility is also reasonably well achieved within the broad framework of analyses for which the program was developed. It can operate with a variety of dictionaries, and it may be used to measure the author's views toward any attitude object. This is not to say, however, that the program will necessarily prove useful in all content analysis research involving attitude measurement. The analyst requiring only a rough index of attitude change in a large volume of documentation will no doubt find the added cost of whatever precision is gained with this program superfluous and prohibitively expensive. Other research designs may require data in a format quite different from that provided here. Hence, as with any content analysis scheme, it is important for the analyst to determine whether the output of this program satisfies the requirements of his research design before coding and punching his text.

Finally, the program achieves the goal of high speed and low cost if we consider *only* the costs of computer time. It is impossible to state precisely the running speed of this program, as it will vary depending on dictionary length, the number of tables to be produced, the number of objects for which attitudes are to be scored, and many other factors. A reasonable estimate might be based on a recent run in which the semantic differential dictionary was used to assess attitudes toward 10 attitude objects. Sixteen documents totalling 92,000 words were processed in 17 minutes, an average of over 5300 words per minute. The program produced 13 pairs of tables (one for frequencies, one for frequency X intensity) for each document, for a total of 416 tables. In turn, each pair of tables listed scores for 180 cells (6 tags X 3 intensities X 10 attitude objects). These figures exclude scores computed for "others," attitude objects not included in the Format Names. To accomplish the same result with the "sentence retrieval" program would have required 2340 separate ques-

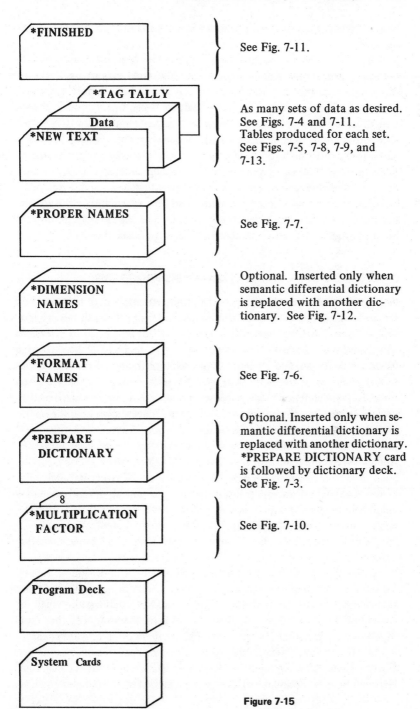

*FINISHED — See Fig. 7-11.

*TAG TALLY / **Data** / ***NEW TEXT** — As many sets of data as desired. See Figs. 7-4 and 7-11. Tables produced for each set. See Figs. 7-5, 7-8, 7-9, and 7-13.

*PROPER NAMES — See Fig. 7-7.

*DIMENSION NAMES — Optional. Inserted only when semantic differential dictionary is replaced with another dictionary. See Fig. 7-12.

*FORMAT NAMES — See Fig. 7-6.

*PREPARE DICTIONARY — Optional. Inserted only when semantic differential dictionary is replaced with another dictionary. *PREPARE DICTIONARY card is followed by dictionary deck. See Fig. 7-3.

8 / ***MULTIPLICATION FACTOR** — See Fig. 7-10.

Program Deck

System Cards

Figure 7-15

tions, which could have been processed in a minimum of 23 passes through the data.

But any realistic assessment of speed and cost must also include necessary precomputer data preparation. The most serious drawback of the program is that the text must be coded manually before computer processing. The coding itself is easily learned, it can be accomplished with a high degree of reliability, and, because it requires syntactical rather than substantive judgments, it neither locks the analyst into a single theoretical framework, nor does it "contaminate" the data for other types of analyses. Nevertheless, coding is time-consuming—although far less so than that required by many forms of manual content analysis—and it represents the highest cost factor in any research using this program. For this reason, the investigator contemplating its use should make certain that, in terms of his research interests, its advantages outweigh the costs of coding.

OTHER COMPUTER CONTENT ANALYSIS PROGRAMS

One by-product of recent interest in machine translation of text has been computer programs for syntactical, as distinct from semantic, discriminations. These may be used for a variety of content analysis problems concerning the question "how it is said?" e.g., analysis of literary style (Sedelow, Sedelow, and Ruggles, 1964). One difficulty of these programs is that there may be more than one possible translation from a given sentence. This defect for the purpose of translation can be turned into an advantage for the content analyst. Two studies have shown how the ability of the computer, unencumbered by any preconceptions or "cognitive set," may be used to produce all possible interpretations of legal literature. Allen (1963) and Langevin and Owens (1963) analyzed sections of the Nuclear Test Ban Treaty to determine the degree of structural ambiguity in its text. While not all solutions were meaningful, several sentences yielded more than one reasonable, and substantively significant, interpretation. Such programs appear to have wide potential application, not only for legal analysis but also in many other aspects of communication research.

Content analysis by computer is still in its infancy and it appears certain that the various programs described here will be modified, if not superseded, in the near future. Five periodical publications may be consulted by the reader wishing to inform himself of the rapid developments which are likely to take place: *Behavioral Science* (quarterly, Mental Health Research Institute, University of Michigan), *Current Research and Development in Scientific Documentation* (semiannual, National Science Foundation), *Computer Newsletter* (occasional, Michigan

State University), *Computers and the Humanities* (quarterly, Queen's College), and *Computer Studies in the Humanities and Verbal Behavior* (quarterly, Universities of Colorado, Kansas, and North Carolina). .

IMPLICATIONS OF COMPUTERS IN CONTENT ANALYSIS

As stated in the preface, the major themes this book has tried to develop are the *opportunities* for studying human affairs through the rich and pervasive evidence available in communication materials, and the *dangers* that await the unimaginative or uncritical user.   It therefore seems appropriate to conclude both this chapter and the book by examining the opportunities and dangers in the use of computers for content analysis. All too often discussion of this question is dominated by enthusiasts ready to tackle any problem with computers, but without much concern for the purpose of their research, and by critics (e.g., Barzun, 1965) whose definition of "trivial" includes any study in which computers may play a role.

The most apparent characteristic of computers, the ability to analyze text reliably at almost unbelievable speed, requires no further elaboration. Less obvious, but perhaps of greater importance, are the following points.

First, it is perhaps ironic that the severest limitation of computers—their tolerance for ambiguity is nil—actually contributes to the quality of inference by forcing greater rigor, discipline, and clarity into the planning of research. The investigator using computers for content analysis is forced to make every step of his research design explicit. A dictionary requires an unambiguous definition of each variable, and each step in data analysis by computer must be specified with precision. Every analyst approaches his data with a set of assumptions and a theory, however crude or implicit. Computers, on the other hand, have no hidden assumptions, and they can do only what they are specifically told.

Thus, in a very real sense the most valuable contribution of computers in content analysis research is made long before the first data tape is mounted on a computer or the first printout is produced. The need to state one's problem with the clarity required by computers can have far reaching consequences, even to the point of requiring the analyst to confront the questions, "What am I doing, and why?" The experience of a literary scholar is illuminating:

. . . *communicating with computer technicians, who never in my experience claim to understand the technicalities of* my *discipline, can be exciting and self-illuminating. Let me cite a specific example. I went to the University of Wisconsin's Computing Center and said, "I want to use your machines to analyze fictional prose style." The immediate answer I got was, "Fine, we think we can help you; but first you'll have to tell us what you mean by style." That conversation took place many months ago, and I'm still trying to find out what I do mean by style. In the Computing Center I've been forced to recognize how little I know about my own subject, and I've been forced to criticize assumptions I had used unthinkingly for years. Furthermore, I have had to estimate the value of my own work in terms of the general progress of literary studies.* *

It is not wholly facetious to suggest that all content analysis should be designed *as if* it were to be done by computer. At minimum, making premises and rules of inference explicit permits informed communication and evaluation of results.

Second, when data are punched on IBM cards they are amenable to reanalysis as often and for as many different purposes as desired. Traditional methods of content analysis rarely permit the degree of flexibility necessary to exhaust the potential information in one's data. Even the most meticulously coded data can rarely be used later for answering research questions that were not incorporated in the original design. In conventional content analysis research the analyst almost of necessity instructs coders to prepare the data to yield answers only for the initial theoretical problems. When content analysis is done manually, if a new hypothesis suggests itself after the data have been coded, the investigator often must choose between recoding the data and dropping the new idea because he is "locked in" by his research design. Data on IBM cards, on the other hand, may be rerun to test hypotheses that had not even been considered at the time of data preparation. The investigator's theory and assumptions are built into the dictionary, not into the data, and the dictionary can be expanded in response to new questions. For example, a set of documents was originally prepared to analyze Sino-Soviet-American interaction during a number of recent crisis periods. Later the same materials were rerun for the purpose of testing a quite different hypothesis about the effects of East-West conflict on relations between Moscow and Peking.

Third, use of computers enables the analyst to undertake very complex data manipulations, such as contingency analyses involving numerous variables, which often cannot be done reliably or economically by hand. It is also possible to combine content and complex statistical analyses, e.g., factor analysis, into a single integrated set of programs. When computers are used, the problem of scoring reliability is completely

---

* Karl Kroeber, Computers and Research in Literary Analysis, from Edmund A. Bowles, Editor, *Computers in Humanistic Research: Readings and Perspectives* © 1967, pp. 135-136. Reprinted by permission of Prentice-Hall, Inc. Englewood Cliffs, New Jersey.

resolved; this does not mean, of course, that the investigator can assume the validity of his results.

The availability of computer assistance will also facilitate (but certainly not make inevitable) research of wide scope—both across time and space—on problems of critical importance. Content analysts have often been criticized for bypassing research questions of this type (e.g., Stephenson, 1963). Such studies are not, of course, impossible to design and execute by manual techniques. But we should not casually dismiss the lesson of the RADIR research on political symbols in the early 1950's. The enormous labors associated with analyzing documentation running into millions of words proved a deterrent to further studies of a similar scope. Well before the computer era the authors of the RADIR studies foresaw the need for computer asistance in large-scale content analysis research (Lasswell, Lerner, and Pool, 1952, p. 63):

> *Perhaps the evolution of modern computing machinery may prove to be the key to the tremendously complex problems involved in the statistical analysis of language . . . . The advantage of a sufficiently flexible mechanical system would have been that we could have gone back to the original data at will. With the system actually used, tabulation was so laborious that, once the summary tables by periods were made up, it was almost never possible to go back for another look at them.*

Put most simply, it's easier to "think big" when doing so doesn't condemn the investigator (or his graduate assistants) to years of thought-numbing drudgery.

Fourth, documents punched on IBM cards can readily be reproduced and exchanged between scholars. There already exist several examples of such exchanges, both within and between disciplines. The folktales collected by Colby for anthropological investigations, for instance, were made available to a psychologist who used them for a cross-cultural study of the Icarus complex (Ogilvie, in press). At the time of this writing, General Inquirer users alone have prepared over 50 different studies, comprising over six million words on IBM cards, and this total is but a fraction of the total text in machine readable form. As a result, serious discussion and planning for central data archives to replace informal data sharing are taking place in various social and humanistic disciplines.

Fifth, computers can free the scholar from many of the most laborious chores associated with content analysis research. The computer, like any tool properly used, can enhance the creativity of the scholar by freeing more of his time for those indispensable ingredients of significant research—the original idea, the creative hunch, the insight which is necessary to make "facts" meaningful.

Despite this optimistic appraisal of the implications of computers, it may be well to conclude on a more cautious note. Just as all research does not lend itself to content analysis, not all content analysis should be done by computer. It is important to remain aware of the dangers in what Kaplan (1964, p. 28) called the "law of the instrument," exemplified by the child who, when given a hammer, suddenly discovers that everything needs pounding. Man and computer each have unique capabilities which are required in different combinations, depending upon the nature of the inquiry. Well-designed research will divide the labor in a way that permits each to do the tasks best suited to those capabilities. For some research, computer assistance is necessary, but it can never be sufficient.

Nor should the limitations of computers be overlooked. Bad data on IBM cards, magnetic tape, or printout are still bad data. The epithet GIGO—Garbage In, Garbage Out—should not be dismissed as merely the slogan of those too reactionary or unsophisticated to appreciate the wonders of the computer era. Perhaps the single greatest danger in the use of computers is that a misplaced faith may lull us into accepting the validity of findings without a critical consideration of the steps preceding and following machine processing. Computers cannot save a sloppy research design nor will they transform a trivial research problem into an important one. There is no guarantee that they will not be used to inundate us with studies of great precision and little importance. The machine output only reflects the skill and insight—or lack thereof—with which the investigator constructed his dictionary and formulated his research design.

Some years ago Bernard Berelson (1954, p. 518) wrote, "Content analysis, as a method, has no magical qualities—you rarely get out of it more than you put in, and sometimes you get less. In the last analysis, there is no substitute for a good idea." Development of computer content analysis programs detracts nothing from the wisdom of that assertion.

References

In the references below, * indicates that the selection includes a useful special bibliography, and † indicates that the selection includes a useful general bibliography.

Abcarian, G. E., and S. M. Stanage (1965). Alienation and the radical right. *Journal of Politics,* **27,** 776-796.

Abu-Lughod, I. (1962). International news in the Arabic press: a comparative content analysis. *Publ. Opin. Quart.,* **26,** 600-612.

Albig, W. (1938). The content of radio programs–1925-1935. *Social Forces,* **16,** 338-349.

Albrecht, M. C. (1956). Does literature reflect common values? *Amer. Sociol. Rev.,* **21,** 272-279.

*Allen, L. E. (1963). Automation: substitute and supplement in legal practice. *Amer. Behav. Scientist,* **7,** 39-44.

*Allport, G. W. (1942). *The use of personal documents in psychological science.* Social Science Research Council. Bulletin No. 49.

_____ (1946). Letters from Jenny. *J. Abnorm. Soc. Psychol.,* **41,** 315-350, 449-480.

Allport, G. W., and J. Bruner (1940). Fifty years of change in American psychology. *Psychol. Bull.,* **37,** 757-776.

Allport, G. W., J. S. Bruner, and E. M. Jandorf (1953). Personality under social catastrophe: ninety life-histories of the Nazi revolution. In C. Kluckhohn and H. A. Murray (Eds.), *Personality in nature, society and culture.* 2nd ed. London: Jonathan Cape. pp. 436-455.

Almond, G. A. (1954). *The appeals of communism.* Princeton: Princeton University Press.

Andrews, T. G., and Gertrude Muhlhan (1943). Analysis of congruent idea patterns as a study in personality. *Char. and Pers.,* **12,** 101-110.

Angell, R. C., Vera S. Dunham, and J. D. Singer (1964). Social values and foreign policy attitudes of Soviet and American elites. *J. Confl. Resol.,* **8,** 330-491.

Armour, Anne (1964). A Balgol program for quantitative format in automated content analysis. Stanford University. (Mimeo).

Arnheim, R. (1944). The world of the daytime serial. In P. F. Lazarsfeld and F. N. Stanton (Eds.), *Radio research: 1942-1943.* New York: Duell, Sloan, and Pearce. pp. 34-85.

Arnold, Magda B. (1962). *Story sequence analysis: a new method of measuring motivation and predicting achievement.* New York: Columbia University Press.

Aronson, E. (1958). The need for achievement as measured by graphic expression. In J. W. Atkinson (Ed.), *Motives in fantasy, action and society.* Princeton: Van Nostrand. pp. 249-265.

Ash, P. (1948). The periodical press and the Taft-Hartley Act. *Publ. Opin. Quart.,* **12,** 266-271.

Asheim, L. (1950). From book to film. In B. Berelson and M. Janowitz (Eds.), *Reader in public opinion and communication.* Glencoe, Ill.: Free Press. pp. 299-306.

*Auld, P., Jr., and E. J. Murray (1955). Content analysis studies of psychotherapy. *Psychol. Bull.,* **52,** 377-395.

Backman, C. W. (1956). Sampling mass media content: the use of the cluster design. *Amer. Sociol. Rev.,* **21,** 729-733.

Badri, M. B., and W. Dennis (1964). Human-figure drawings in relation to modernization in Sudan. *J. Psychol.,* **58,** 421-425.

Bagdikian, B. H. (1959). The newsmagazines. *The New Republic,* **16,** Feb. 2, 11-16; Feb. 16, 9-14; Feb. 23, 9-15.

Baldwin, A. L. (1942). Personality structure analysis: a statistical method for investigating the single personality. *J. Abnorm. Soc. Psychol.,* **37,** 163-183.

Bales, R. F. (1950). *Interaction process analysis.* Reading, Mass: Addison-Wesley.

Bandura, A., D. H. Lipsher, and Paula E. Miller (1960). Psychotherapists' approach-avoidance reactions to patients' expressions of hostility. *J. Consul. Psychol.,* **24,** 1-8.

†Barcus, F. E. (1959). Communications content: analysis of the research, 1900-1958. Unpublished doctor's dissertation, University of Illinois.

————— (1961). A content analysis of trends in Sunday comics, 1900-1959. *Journalism Quart.,* **38,** 171-180.

Barghoorn, F. C. (1964). *Soviet foreign propaganda.* Princeton: Princeton University Press.

Barzun, J. (1965). A panel discussion. In *Computers for the Humanities?* New Haven: Yale University Press. pp. 145-150.

Batlin, R. (1954). San Francisco newspapers' campaign coverage: 1896, 1952. *Journalism Quart.,* **31,** 297-303.

Bauer, R. A. (1964). The obstinate audience: the influence process from the point of view of social communication. *Amer. Psychologist,* **19,** 319-328.

Becker, H. P. (1930). Distribution of space in the American Journal of Sociology, 1895-1927. *Amer. J. Sociol.,* **36,** 461-466.

──────── (1932). Space apportioned forty-eight topics in the American Journal of Sociology, 1895-1930. *Amer. J. Sociol.,* **38,** 71-78.

Bennett, E. M., R. Alpert, and A. C. Goldstein (1954). Communications through limited response questioning. *Publ. Opin. Quart.,* **18,** 303-308.

Benson, L. (1961). *The concept of Jacksonian democracy.* Princeton: Princeton University Press.

†Berelson, B. (1952). *Content analysis in communication research.* Glencoe, Ill.: Free Press.

†──────── (1954). Content analysis. In G. Lindzey (Ed.), *Handbook of social psychology.* Reading, Mass: Addison-Wesley. pp. 488-518.

Berelson, B., and S. De Grazia (1947). Detecting collaboration in propaganda. *Publ. Opin. Quart.,* **9,** 244-253.

Berelson, B., and Patricia J. Salter (1946). Majority and minority Americans: an analysis of magazine fiction. *Publ. Opin. Quart.,* **10,** 168-190.

Berkman, D. (1963). Advertising in Ebony and Life: Negro aspirations vs. reality. *Journalism Quart.,* **40,** 53-64.

Bernstein, M. H. (1953). Political ideas of selected American business journals. *Publ. Opin. Quart.,* **17,** 258-267.

Berreman, J. V. M. (1940). Factors affecting the sale of modern books of fiction: a study of social psychology. Unpublished doctor's dissertation, Stanford University.

Block, J. (1961). *The Q-sort method in personality assessment and psychiatric research.* Springfield, Ill.: Charles C. Thomas.

Blumberg, N. B. (1954). *One party press? Coverage of the 1952 presidential campaign in 35 daily newspapers.* Lincoln: University of Nebraska Press.

Boder, D. P. (1940). The adjective-verb quotient: a contribution to the psychology of language. *Psychol. Record,* **3,** 310-343.

Breed, W. (1958). Comparative newspaper handling of the Emmett Till case. *Journalism Quart.,* **35,** 291-298.

Brinegar, C. (1963). Mark Twain and the Quintus Curtius Snodgrass letters: a statistical test of authorship. *J. Amer. Statist. Assoc.,* **58,** 85-96.

Brinton, J., and W. A. Danielson (1958). A factor analysis of language elements affecting readability. *Journalism Quart.,* **35,** 420-426.

Brody, R. A. (1963). Some systemic effects of the spread of nuclear weapons technology: a study through simulation of a multi-nuclear future. *J. Confl. Resol.,* **7**, 663-753.

Brooks, M. R. (1959). *The Negro press re-examined.* Houston: Christopher.

Broom, L., and Shirley Reece (1955). Political and racial interest: a study in content analysis. *Publ. Opin. Quart.,* **19**, 5-19.

Brown, W. B. (1960). *The people's choice.* Baton Rouge: Louisiana State University Press.

Bruner, J. S. (1941). The dimensions of propaganda: German shortwave broadcasts to America. *J. Abnorm. Soc. Psychol.,* **41**, 311-337.

Budd, R. W. (1964). U.S. news in the press down under. *Publ. Opin. Quart.,* **28**, 39-56.

Budlong, D. H. (1952). Analysis of radio programs by four commentators. *Journalism Quart.,* **29**, 458-459.

Bush, C. R. (1960). A system of categories for general news content. *Journalism Quart.,* **37**, 206-210.

Cahnman, W. J. (1948). A note on marriage announcement in the New York Times. *Amer. Sociol. Rev.,* **13**, 96-97.

Campbell, D. T., and J. C. Stanley (1963). *Experimental and quasi-experimental designs for research.* Chicago: Rand-McNally.

Cannell, C. F., and J. C. MacDonald (1956). The impact of health news on attitudes and behavior. *Journalism Quart.,* **33**, 315-323.

Carstenson, F. W., and W. S. Stolz (1964). Cloze procedure analysis programs. *Computer Newsletter,* **3**, 5-6.

Carter, R. E., Jr. (1957). Segregation and the news: a regional content study. *Journalism Quart.,* **34**, 3-18.

† Cartwright, D. P. (1953). Analysis of qualitative material. In L. Festinger and D. Katz (Eds.), *Research methods in the behavioral sciences.* New York: Holt, Rinehart, and Winston. pp. 421-470.

Choucri, Nazli (1967). Nonalignment in international politics: an analysis of attitudes and behavior. Doctoral dissertation, Stanford University.

————(1968a). *The nonalignment of Afro-Asian states: policy, perceptions, and behavior.* Paper read at annual meeting of the Canadian Political Science Association.

———— (1968b). *The perceptual base of nonalignment.* Queen's University. (Mimeo.).

Christenson, R. M. (1964). Report on the Reader's Digest. *Columbia Journalism Rev.,* **3**, 30-36.

Coats, W. J., and S. W. Mulkey (1950). A study in newspaper sampling. *Publ. Opin. Quart.,* **14**, 533-546.

Cochran, T. C. (1953). *Railroad leaders, 1845-1890: the business of mind in action.* Cambridge: Harvard University Press.

Cohen, B. D. (1957). *The political process and foreign policy: the making of the Japanese peace settlement.* Princeton: Princeton University Press.

Colby, B. N. (1966a). The analysis of culture content and the patterning of narrative concern in texts. *Amer. Anthropologist,* **68**, 374-388.

————— (1966b). Cultural patterns in narrative. *Science,* **151**, 793-798.

————— (1966c). Development and application of an anthropological dictionary. In P. J. Stone, D. C. Dunphy, M. S. Smith, and D. M. Ogilvie, *The General Inquirer: a computer approach to content analysis in the behavioral sciences.* Cambridge: M.I.T. press. pp. 603-615.

Colby, B. N., G. A. Collier, and Susan K. Postal (1963). Comparison of themes in folktales by the General Inquirer system. *J. Amer. Folklore,* **76**, 318-323.

Colby, B. N., and M. D. Menchik (1964). A study of Thematic Apperception Tests with the General Inquirer system. *El Palacio,* **71**, 29-36.

Coleman, E. B. (1962). Improving comprehensibility by shortening sentences. *J. Appl. Psychol.,* **44**, 131-134.

Content analysis—a new evidentiary technique (1948). *Univ. Chicago Law Rev.,* **15**, 910-925.

Cony, E. R. (1953). Conflict-cooperation of five American dailies. *Journalism Quart.,* **30**, 15-22.

Cornwell, E. E., Jr. (1959). Presidential news: the expanding public image. *Journalism Quart.,* **36**, 275-283.

Craddick, R. A. (1961). Size of Santa Claus drawings as a function of time before and after Christmas. *J. Psychol. Studies,* **12**, 121-125.

————— (1962). Size of witch drawings as a function of time before, on, and after Halloween. *Amer. Psychologist,* **17**, 307.

*Cronbach, L., and P. Meehl (1955). construct validity of psychological tests. *Psychol. Bull.,* **52**, 281-302.

Dahlberg, Frances M., and P. J. Stone (1966). Cross-cultural contrasts in interpersonal structuring. In P. J. Stone, D. C. Dunphy, M. S. Smith, and D. M. Ogilvie, *The General Inquirer: a computer approach to content analysis in the behavioral sciences.* Cambridge: M.I.T. Press. pp. 589-602.

Dale, E. (1935). *The content of motion pictures.* New York: Macmillan.

Dale, E., and Jeanne S. Chall (1948). A formula for predicting readability. *Educ. Res. Bull.,* **27**, 11-20, 37-54.

Danielson, W. A., and J. B. Adams (1961). Completeness of press coverage of the 1960 campaign. *Journalism Quart.,* **38**, 441-452.

Danielson, W. A., and S. D. Bryan (1963). Computer automation of two readability formulas. *Journalism Quart.,* **40**, 201-206.

Danielson, W. A., and H. Jackson (1963). A computer program for scanning tapes for key concepts and their immediate contexts. *Computer Newsletter,* **1**, 1-2.

Davis, F. J., and L. W. Turner (1951). Sampling efficiency in quantitative newspaper content analysis. *Publ. Opin. Quart.*, 15, 762-763.

Davison, W. P. (1947). An analysis of the Soviet-controlled Berlin press. *Publ. Opin. Quart.*, 11, 40-57.

deCharms, R., and G. H. Moeller (1962). Values expressed in American children's readers: 1900-1950. *J. Abnorm. Soc. Psychol.*, 64, 136-142.

De Fleur, M. L. (1962). Mass communication and the study of rumor. *Sociol. Inquiry*, 32, 51-70.

———— (1964). Occupational roles as portrayed on television. *Publ. Opin. Quart.*, 28, 57-74.

Deutsch, F. (1947). Artistic expression and neurotic illness. *Amer. Imago*, 4, 64-102.

Dibble, V. R. (1963). Four types of inference from documents to events. *History and Theory*, 3, 203-221.

Dollard, J., and O. H. Mowrer (1947). A method of measuring tension in written documents. *J. Abnorm. Soc. Psychol.*, 42, 3-32.

Dornbusch, S. M., and Lauren C. Hickman (1959). Other-directedness in consumer-goods advertising: a test of Riesman's historical theory. *Social Forces*, 38, 99-102.

Dovring, Karin (1954). Quantitative semantics in 18th century Sweden. *Publ. Opin. Quart.*, 18, 389-394.

———— (1959). *Road of propaganda: the semantics of biased communication.* New York: Philosophical Library.

Dunphy, D. C. (1964). Content analysis—development and critical issues. Cambridge: Harvard University. (Mimeo)

———— (1966). Social change in self-analytic groups. In P. J. Stone, D. C. Dunphy, M. S. Smith, and D. M. Ogilvie, *The General Inquirer: a computer approach to content analysis in the behavioral sciences.* Cambridge: M.I.T. Press. pp. 287-340.

Dunphy, D. C., P. F. Stone, and M. S. Smith (1965). The general inquirer: further developments in a computer system for content analysis of verbal data in the social sciences. *Behav. Sci.*, 10, 468-480.

Eckhardt, W. (1965). War propaganda, welfare values and political ideologies. *J. Confl. Resol.*, 9, 345-358.

Eckhardt, W. and R. K. White (1967). A test of the mirror-image hypothesis: Kennedy and Khrushchev. *J. Confl. Resol.*, 11, 325-332.

Ehrle, R. A., and B. G. Johnson (1961). Psychologists and cartoonists. *Amer. Psychologist*, 16, 693-695.

*Ekman, P. (1965). Communication through nonverbal behavior: a source of information about an interpersonal relationship. In S. S. Tomkins and C. E. Izard (Eds.), *Affect, cognition and personality.* New York: Springer.

Elizur, A. (1949). A content analysis of the Rorschach with regard to anxiety and hostility. *Rorschach Res. Exch.*, 13, 247-284.

Ellegård, A. (1962). *A statistical method for determining authorship.* Göteborg, Sweden: Acta Universitatis Gothoburgensis.

Ellison, J. W. (1965). Computers and the Testaments. In *Computers for the humanities.* New Haven: Yale University Press. pp. 64-74.

Ellsworth, J. W. (1965). Rationality and campaigning: a content analysis of the 1960 presidential campaign debates. *Western Political Quart.,* **18,** 794-802.

———— (1967). Policy and ideology in the campaigns of 1960 and 1964: a content analysis. Southern Illinois University. (Mimeo)

† Eto, S., and T. Okabe (1965). Content analysis of statements in regard to Japan made by the People's Republic of China. *Developing Economies,* **3,** 49-72.

Exline, R. V., and Barbara H. Long (1965). An application of psychological scaling methods to content analysis: the use of empirically derived criterion weights to improve intercoder reliability. *J. Appl. Psychol.,* **49,** 142-149.

Fagen, R. R. (1967). The Cuban revolution: enemies and friends. In D. J. Finlay, O. R. Holsti, and R. R. Fagen, *Enemies in politics.* Chicago: Rand-McNally. pp. 184-231.

Fairbanks, H. (1944). Studies in language behavior: II. The quantitative differentiation of samples of spoken language. *Psychol. Monogr.,* **56,** 13-38.

Farr, J. N., J. J. Jenkins, and D. G. Patterson (1951). Simplification of the Flesch reading ease formula. *J. Appl. Psychol.,* **35,** 333-337.

Fillenbaum, S., and L. V. Jones (1962). An application of 'Cloze' technique to the study of aphasic speech. *J. Abnorm. Soc. Psychol.,* **65,** 183-189.

Flesch, R. (1943). *Marks of readable style.* New York: Teachers College, Columbia University.

———— (1948). A new readability yardstick. *J. Appl. Psychol.,* **32,** 221-233.

Foster, H. S. (1935). How America became belligerent: a quantitative study of war news. *Amer. J. Sociol.,* **40,** 464-475.

———— (1937). Charting America's news of the world war. *Foreign Affairs,* **15,** 311-319.

Foster, H. S., and C. J. Friedrich (1937). Letters to the editor as a means of measuring the effectiveness of propaganda. *Amer. Polit. Sci. Rev.,* **31,** 71-79.

Funkhouser, G. R., and E. B. Parker (1968). Analyzing coding reliability: the random-systematic-error coefficient. *Publ. Opin. Quart.,* **23,** 122-128.

Galtung, J., and Mari Holmboe Ruge (1965). The structure of foreign news: the presentation of the Congo, Cuba and Cyprus crises in four Norwegian newspapers. *J. Peace Res.,* **1,** 64-91.

Gardiner, L. W. (1962). A content analysis of Japanese and American television. *J. Broadcasting*, **6**, 45-52.

Garver, R. A. (1961). Polite propaganda: "USSR" and "American Illustrated." *Journalism Quart.*, **38**, 480-484.

Geller, A., D. Kaplan, and H. D. Lasswell (1942a). *The differential use of flexible and rigid procedures of content analysis.* Washington, D.C.: Library of Congress, Experimental Division for Study of War-Time Communications, Document No. 12.

———— (1942b). An experimental comparison of four ways of coding editorial content. *Journalism Quart.*, **19**, 362-370.

George, A. L. (1959a). *Propaganda analysis.* Evanston, Ill.: Row, Peterson.

———— (1959b). Quantitative and qualitative approaches to content analysis. In I. de S. Pool (Ed.), *Trends in content analysis.* Urbana: University of Illinois Press. pp. 7-32.

Gerbner, G. (1964). Ideological perspectives and political tendencies in news reporting. *Journalism Quart.*, **41**, 495-508.

†Gerbner, G., O. R. Holsti, K. Krippendorff, W. J. Paisley, and P. J. Stone, Eds. (in press). *The analysis of communication content: developments in scientific theories and computer techniques.* New York: Wiley.

Gerbner, G., and P. H. Tannenbaum (1960). Regulation of mental illness content in motion pictures and television. *Gazette*, **6**, 365-385.

Gillespie, J. M., and G. W. Allport (1955). *Youth's outlook on the future.* Garden City, N.Y.: Doubleday.

Gillie, P. A. (1957). A simplified formula for measuring abstraction in writing. *J. Appl. Psychol.*, **41**, 214-217.

Ginglinger, Genevieve (1955). Basic values in Reader's Digest, Selection and Constellation. *Journalism Quart.*, **32**, 56-61.

Gleser, Goldine C., L. A. Gottschalk, and Kayla J. Springer (1961). An anxiety scale applicable to verbal samples. *Arch. Gen. Psychiat.*, **5**, 593-605.

Goldberg, Janice B. (1966). Computer analysis of sentence completions. *J. Proj. Tech. Pers. Assess.*, **30**, 37-45.

Gordon, D. A. (1952). Methodology in the study of art evaluation. *J. Aesthet.*, **10**, 338-352.

*Gottschalk, L. A., Ed. (1961). *Comparative psycholinguistic analysis of two psychotherapeutic interviews.* New York: International University Press.

Gottschalk, L. A., and Goldine C. Gleser (1960). An analysis of the verbal content of suicide notes. *Brit. J. Med. Psychol.*, **33**, 195-204.

Gottschalk, L. A., Goldine C. Gleser, E. B. Magliocco, and T. D'Zmura (1961). Further studies on the speech patterns of schizophrenic patients: measuring inter-individual differences in relative degree of personal disorganization and social alienation. *J. Nerv. Ment. Dis.*, **132**, 101-113.

Gottschalk, L. A., Goldine C. Gleser, and Kayla J. Springer (1963). Three hostility scales applicable to verbal samples. *Arch. Gen. Psychiat.,* **9,** 254-279.

Gray, W. (1959). *Historian's handbook: a key to the study and writing of history.* Boston: Houghton Mifflin.

Gray, W. S., and Bernice E. Leary (1935). *What makes a book readable.* Chicago: University of Chicago Press.

Guetzkow, H. (1950). Unitizing and categorizing problems in coding qualitative data. *J. Clin. Psychol.,* **6,** 47-58.

Haas, M. (1966). Aggregate analysis. *World Politics,* **19,** 106-121.

Hafner, A. J., and A. M. Kaplan (1960). Hostility content analysis of the Rorschach and TAT. *J. Proj. Tech.,* **24,** 137-143.

Hage, G. S. (1959). Anti-intellectualism in press comment, 1828 and 1952. *Journalism Quart.,* **36,** 439-446.

Haigh, G. (1949). Defensive behavior in client-centered therapy. *J. Consul. Psychol.,* **13,** 181-189.

Hall, C. (in press). Content analysis of dreams: categories, units, and norms. In G. Gerbner, O. R. Holsti, K. Krippendorff, W. J. Paisley, and P. J. Stone (Eds.), *The analysis of communication content: developments in scientific theories and computer techniques.* New York: Wiley.

Hall, C. S., and R. L. Van de Castle (1966). *The content analysis of dreams.* New York: Appleton-Century-Crofts.

Hamilton, T. (1942). Social optimism and pessimism in American Protestantism. *Publ. Opin. Quart.,* **6,** 280-283.

Hart, J. A. (1961). The flow of international news into Ohio. *Journalism Quart.,* **38,** 541-543.

———— (1965). Election campaign coverage in English and U.S. daily newspapers. *Journalism Quart.,* **42,** 213-218.

————(1966). Foreign news in U.S. and English daily newspapers: a comparison. *Journalism Quart.,* **42,** 213-218.

Harvey, J. (1953). The content characteristics of best-selling novels. *Publ. Opin. Quart.,* **17,** 91-114.

Harway, N. I., and H. P. Iker (1964). Computer analysis of content in psychotherapy. *Psychol. Reports,* **14,** 720-722.

————(1966). Objective content analysis of psychotherapy by computer. In K. Enslein (Ed.), *Data acquisition and processing in biology and medicine.* Vol. 4, New York: Pergamon Press. pp. 139-151.

Haskins, J. B. (1960). Validation of the abstraction index as a tool for counter-effects analysis and content analysis. *J. Appl. Psychol.,* **44,** 102-106.

Hatch, D. L., and Mary Hatch (1947). Criteria of social status as derived from marriage announcements in the New York Times. *Amer. Sociol. Rev.,* **12,** 396-403.

Hays, D. G. (in press). Linguistic foundations for a theory of content analysis. In G. Gerbner, O. R. Holsti, K. Krippendorff, W. J. Paisley, and P. J. Stone (Eds.), *The analysis of communication content: developments in scientific theories and computer techniques.* New York: Wiley.

Hayworth, D. (1930). An analysis of speeches in the presidential campaigns from 1884-1920. *Quart. J. Speech,* **16,** 35-42.

Head, S. W. (1954). Content analysis of television drama programs. *Quart. Film, Radio and Television,* **9,** 175-194.

Herma, H., H. Kris, and J. Shor (1943). Freud's theory of the dream in American textbooks. *J. Abnorm. Soc. Psychol.,* **38,** 319-334.

Hermann, C. F., and Margaret G. Hermann (1967). An attempt to simulate the outbreak of World War I. *Amer. Polit. Sci. Rev.,* **61,** 400-416.

Holsti, O. R. (1962). The belief system and national images: John Foster Dulles and the Soviet Union. Unpublished doctor's dissertation, Stanford University.

―――――――(1964). An adaptation of the 'General Inquirer' for the systematic analysis of political documents. *Behav. Sci.,* **9,** 382-388.

†―――――― (1965a). East-West conflict and Sino-Soviet relations. *J. Appl. Behav. Sci.,* **7,** 115-130.

―――――― (1965b). The 1914 case. *Amer. Polit. Sci. Rev.,* **59,** 365-378.

†―――――― (1967). Cognitive dynamics and images of the enemy. In D. J. Finlay, O. R. Holsti, and R. R. Fagen, *Enemies in politics.* Chicago: Rand-McNally. pp. 25-96.

―――――― (in press). Time, alternatives, and communication: the 1914 and Cuban missile crises. In C. F. Hermann (Ed.), *Contemporary research in international crises.* New York: Free Press.

Holsti, O. R., R. A. Brody, and R. C. North (1965). Measuring affect and action in international reaction models: empirical materials from the 1962 Cuban crisis. *Peace Res. Soc. Papers,* **2,** 170-190.

Holsti, O. R., and R. C. North (1965). History of human conflict. In E. B. McNeil (Ed.), *Social science and human conflict.* Englewood Cliffs, N.J.: Prentice-Hall. pp. 155-171.

―――――― (1966). Perceptions of hostility and economic variables. In R. Merritt and S. Rokkan (Eds.), *Comparing nations.* New Haven: Yale University Press. pp. 169-190.

Holsti, O. R., R. C. North, and R. A. Brody (1968). Perception and action in the 1914 crisis. In J. D. Singer (Ed.), *Quantitative international politics: insights and evidence.* New York: Free Press. pp. 123-158.

Holsti, O. R., and J. D. Sullivan (in press). National-international linkages: France and China as non-conforming alliance members. In J. N. Rosenau (Ed.), *Politics in a shrinking world: essays on the linkages between national and international systems.* New York: Free Press.

Honigfeld, G., A. Platz, and R. D. Gillis (1964). Verbal style and personality authoritarianism. *J. Communic.*, **14**, 215-218.

Hopmann, P. T. (1967). International conflict and cohesion in the communist system. *Int. Stud. Quart.*, **11**, 212-236.

———(forthcoming). International conflict and cohesion in international political coalitions: NATO and the communist system during the postwar years. Doctoral dissertation, Stanford University.

Horton, D. (1957). The dialogue of courtship in popular songs. *Amer. J. Sociol.*, **62**, 569-578.

Hovland, C. I., I. L. Janis, and H. H. Kelley (1953). *Communication and persuasion.* New Haven: Yale University Press.

Hughes, F. (1950). *Prejudice and the press.* New York: Devin-Adair.

Hunt, E. B., J. Kreuter, and P. J. Stone (1965). *Experiments in induction.* New York: Academic Press.

Iker, H. P., and N. I. Harway (1965). A computer approach toward the analysis of content. *Behav. Sci.*, **10**, 173-182.

——— (in press). A computer systems approach toward the recognition and analysis of content. In G. Gerbner, O. R. Holsti, K. Krippendorff, W. J. Paisley, and P. J. Stone (Eds.), *The analysis of communication content: developments in scientific theories and computer techniques.* New York: Wiley.

Inkeles, A. (1952). Soviet reactions to the Voice of America. *Publ. Opin. Quart.*, **16**, 612-617.

Inkeles, A., and H. Geiger (1952). Critical letters to the editors of the Soviet press. I. Areas and modes of complaint. *Amer. Sociol. Rev.*, **17**, 694-703.

——— (1953). Critical letters to the editors of the Soviet press: II. Social characteristics and interrelations of critics and the criticized. *Amer. Sociol. Rev.*, **18**, 12-22.

International Business Machines Corporation (1962). *Keyword-in-context (KWIC) indexing.* Publication E20-8091-0. White Plains, N. Y. IBM Technical Publications Department.

Jacob, P. E. (1942). Atrocity propaganda. In H. L. Childs and J. B. Whiton (Eds.), *Propaganda by short wave.* Princeton: Princeton University Press. pp. 211-259.

Jaffe, J. (1963). Electronic computers in psychoanalytic research. In J. H. Masserman (Ed.), *Violence and war, with clinical studies.* New York: Grune & Stratton, pp. 160-170.

*———(1964). Computer analysis of verbal behavior in psychiatric interviews. In D. M. Rioch and E. A. Weinstein (Eds.), *Disorders of communication.* Research Publications of the Association for Research on Nervous and Mental Disorders, No. 42. pp. 389-399.

*——— (1966). The study of language in psychiatry: psycholinguistics and computational linguistics. In S. Arieti (Ed.), *American handbook of psychiatry.* Vol. 3. New York: Basic Books. pp. 689-704.

†Janda, K. (1965). *Data processing: applications to political research.* Evanston, Ill.: Northwestern University Press.

Janes, R. W. (1958). A technique for describing community structure through newspaper analysis. *Social Forces,* 37, 102-109.

Janis, I. L. (1943). Meaning and the study of symbolic behavior. *Psychiatry,* 6, 425-439.

_____ (1949). The problem of validating content analysis. In H. D. Lasswell, N. Leites, R. Fadner, J. M. Goldsen, A. Gray, I. L. Janis, A. Kaplan, D. Kaplan, A. Mintz, I. De Sola Pool, and S. Yakobson, *The language of politics: studies in quantitative semantics.* New York: George Stewart. pp. 55-82.

Janis, I. L., and R. Fadner (1949). The coefficient of imbalance. In H. D. Lasswell, N. Leites, R. Fadner, J. M. Goldsen, A. Gray, I. L. Janis, A. Kaplan, D. Kaplan, A. Mintz, I. De Sola Pool, and S. Yakobson, *The language of politics: studies in quantitative semantics.* New York: George Stewart. pp. 155-169.

Janis, I., R. H. Fadner, and M. Janowitz (1943). The reliability of a content analysis technique. *Publ. Opin. Quart.,* 7, 293-296.

*Janis, I. L., C. I. Hovland, P. B. Field, Harriet Linton, Elaine Graham, A. R. Cohen, D. Rife, R. P. Abelson, G. S. Lesser, and B. T. King, (1959). *Personality and persuasibility.* New Haven: Yale University Press.

Janowitz, M. (1944). The technique of propaganda for reaction: Gerald L. Smith's radio speeches. *Publ. Opin. Quart.,* 8, 84-93.

Johns-Heine, P., and H. H. Gerth (1949). Values in mass periodical fiction, 1921-1940. *Publ. Opin. Quart.,* 13, 105-113.

Johnson, W. (1944). Studies in language behavior: I. A program of research. *Psychol. Monogr.,* 56, No. 2, whole No. 255, 1-15.

Jones, Dorothy B. (1942). Quantitative analysis of motion picture content. *Publ. Opin. Quart.,* 6, 411-428.

Jones, R., and R. Carter (1959). Some procedures for estimating 'news hole' in content analysis. *Publ. Opin. Quart.,* 23, 399-403.

Josselson, H. H. (1953). *The Russian word count.* Detroit: Wayne State University Press.

Kadushin, C., J. Lovett, and J. D. Merriman (1968). Literary analysis with the aid of the computer: a review symposium. *Computers and the Humanities,* 2, 177-202.

Kalin, R., W. N. Davis, and D. C. McClelland (1966). The relationship between use of alcohol and thematic content of folktales in primitive societies. In P. J. Stone, D. C. Dunphy, M. S. Smith, and D. M. Ogilvie, *The General Inquirer: a computer approach to content analysis in the behavioral sciences.* Cambridge: M.I.T. Press. pp. 569-588.

Kanzer, M. (1948). Dostoyevsky's matricidal impulses. *Psychoanal. Rev.,* 35, 115-125.

Kaplan, A. (1943). Content analysis and the theory of signs. *Philos. Sci.,* **10,** 230-247.

————— (1964). *The conduct of inquiry.* San Francisco: Chandler.

Kaplan, A., and J. M. Goldsen (1949). The reliability of content analysis categories. In H. D. Lasswell, N. Leites, R. Fadner, J. M. Goldsen, A. Gray, I. L. Janis, A. Kaplan, D. Kaplan, A. Mintz, I. De Sola Pool, and S. Yakobson, *The language of politics: studies in quantitative semantics.* New York: George Stewart. pp. 83-112.

Kauffman, P. E., and V. C. Raimy (1949). Two methods of assessing therapeutic progress. *J. Abnorm. Soc. Psychol.,* **44,** 379-385.

Kayser, J. (1953). *One week's news: comparative study of seventeen major dailies for a seven-day period.* Paris: Paul Dupont, for UNESCO.

Kearl, B. (1948). A closer look at readability formulas. *Journalism Quart.,* **25,** 344-348.

Kerlinger, F. N. (1964). *Foundations of behavioral research: educational and psychological inquiry.* New York: Holt, Rinehart, and Winston.

Kim, K. W. (1965). The limits of behavioral explanation in politics. *Canadian J. Econ. Polit. Sci.,* **31,** 315-327.

Kingsbury, Susan M., H. Hart, and Associates (1937). *Newspapers and the news.* New York: Putnam.

Klapper, J. (1960). *The effects of mass communication.* Glencoe, Ill.: Free Press.

Klapper, J., and C. Glock (1949). Trial by newspaper. *Sci. Amer.,* **180** (Feb. 1949), 16-21.

Klein, M. W., and N. Maccoby (1954). Newspaper objectivity in the 1952 campaign. *Journalism Quart.,* **31,** 285-296.

Knepprath, H. E. (1962). The elements of persuasion in the nationally broadcast speeches of Eisenhower and Stevenson during the 1956 presidential campaign. Unpublished doctor's dissertation, University of Wisconsin.

Kobre, S. (1953). How Florida dailies handled the 1952 presidential campaign. *Journalism Quart.,* **30,** 163-169.

Kracauer, S. (1952). The challenge of qualitative content analysis. *Publ. Opin. Quart.,* **16,** 631-642.

Krippendorff, K. (1966). Content analysis: history and critical issues. Unpublished doctor's dissertation, University of Pennsylvania.

Kris, E., and N. Leites (1953). Trends in twentieth century propaganda. In B. Berelson and M. Janowitz (Eds.), *Public opinion and communication.* Glencoe, Ill.: Free Press. pp. 278-288.

Kroeber, K. (1967). Computers and research in literary analysis. In E. A. Bowles (Ed.), *Computers in humanistic research.* Englewood Cliffs, N.J.: Prentice-Hall. pp. 135-142.

Kuhn, A. (1963). *The study of society: a unified approach.* Homewood, Ill.: Dorsey.

Laffal, J. (1965). *Pathological and normal language.* New York: Atherton.

————(in press). Contextual similarities as a basis for inference. In G. Gerbner, O. R. Holsti, K. Krippendorff, W. J. Paisley, and P. J. Stone (Eds.), *The analysis of communication content: developments in scientific theories and computer techniques.* New York: Wiley.

Lane, R. E. (1951). Government regulation and the business mind. *Amer. Sociol. Rev.,* 16, 163-173.

Lang, Gladys E., and K. Lang (1955). The inferential structure of political communications: a study in unwitting bias. *Publ. Opin. Quart.,* 19, 168-183.

Langevin, R. A., and M. Owens (1963). Application of automatic syntactic analysis to the Nuclear Test Ban Treaty. Burlington, Mass.: Technical Operations Research. (Mimeo)

Larson, O. N., L. N. Gray, and J. G. Fortis (1963). Goals and goal-achievement methods in television content: models for anomie? *Sociol. Inquiry,* 33, 180-196.

La Rue, J. (1967). Two problems in musical analysis: the computer lends a hand. In E. A. Bowles (Ed.), *Computers in humanistic research.* Englewood Cliffs, N.J.: Prentice-Hall. pp. 194-203.

Lasswell, H. D. (1927). *Propaganda technique in the world war.* New York: Knopf.

———— (1935). *World politics and personal insecurity.* New York: McGraw-Hill.

———— (1938). A provisional classification of symbol data. *Psychiatry,* 1, 197-204.

———— (1941). The world attention survey. *Publ. Opin. Quart.,* 5, 456-462.

———— (1942). Communications research and politics. In D. Waples (Ed.), *Print, radio, and film in a democracy.* Chicago: University of Chicago Press. pp. 101-117.

†———— (1946). Describing the content of communication. In B. L. Smith, H. D. Lasswell, and R. D. Casey (Eds.), *Propaganda, communication and public opinion.* Princeton: Princeton University Press. pp. 74-94.

———— (1949). Detection: propaganda detection and the courts. In H. D. Lasswell, N. Leites, R. Fadner, J. M. Goldsen, A. Gray, I. L. Janis, A. Kaplan, D. Kaplan, A. Mintz, I. De Sola Pool, S. Yakobson, *The language of politics: studies in quantitative semantics.* New York: George Stewart. pp. 173-232.

Lasswell, H. D., and Dorothy Blumenstock (1939). *World revolutionary propaganda: a Chicago study.* New York: Knopf.

Lasswell, H. D., and A. Kaplan (1950). *Power and society*. New Haven: Yale University Press.

Lasswell, H. D., N. Leites, R. Fadner, J. M. Goldsen, A. Gray, I. L. Janis, A. Kaplan, D. Kaplan, A. Mintz, I. De Sola Pool, S. Yakobson (1949). *The language of politics: studies in quantitative semantics*. New York: George Stewart.

Lasswell, H. D., D. Lerner, and I. de S. Pool (1952). *The comparative study of symbols*. Stanford: Stanford University Press.

Lazarsfeld, P. F. (1941). Remarks on administrative and critical communications research. *Studies in Philosophy and Social Science, 9*, 2-16.

Lazarsfeld, P. F., and A. H. Barton (1951). Qualitative measurement in the social sciences, classification, typologies, and indices. In D. Lerner and H. D. Lasswell (Eds.), *The policy sciences: recent developments in scope and method*. Stanford: Stanford University Press. pp. 180-188.

Lazarsfeld, P. F., B. Berelson, and Hazel Gaudet (1944). *The people's choice: how the voter makes up his mind in a presidential campaign*. New York: Duell, Sloan, and Pearce.

Leary, T. (1957). *Interpersonal diagnosis of personality*. New York: Ronald.

Lee, A. M. (1952). *How to understand propaganda*. New York: Rinehart.

Lee, A. M., and Elizabeth B. Lee (1939). *The fine art of propaganda*. New York: Harcourt, Brace.

Leites, N. C. (1949). Interaction: the Third International on its change of policy. In H. D. Lasswell, N. Leites, R. Fadner, J. M. Goldsen, A. Gray, I. L. Janis, A. Kaplan, D. Kaplan, A. Mintz, I. De Sola Pool, and S. Yakobson, *The language of politics: studies in quantitative semantics*. New York: George Stewart. pp. 298-333.

Leites, N. C., and I. de S. Pool (1942). *On content analysis*. Washington, D.C.: Library of Congress, Experimental Division for Study of War-Time Communications, Document No. 26.

————— (1949). Interaction: the response of communist propaganda to frustration. In H. D. Lasswell, N. Leites, R. Fadner, J. M. Goldsen, A. Gray, I. L. Janis, A. Kaplan, D. Kaplan, A. Mintz, I. De Sola Pool, and S. Yakobson, *The language of politics: studies in quantitative semantics*. New York: George Stewart. pp. 334-381.

Lerner, D. (1950). "The American Soldier" and the public. In R. Merton and P. Lazarsfeld (Eds.), *Continuities in social research*. Glencoe, Ill.: Free Press. pp. 212-251.

Levi-Strauss, C. (1964). *Le cru et le cuit*. Paris: Plon.

Lewin, H. S. (1947). Hitler youth and the Boy Scouts of America: a comparison of aims. *Hum. Relat., 1*, 206-227.

Lewis, H. L. (1960). The Cuban revolt story: AP, UPI and 3 papers. *Journalism Quart., 37*, 573-578, 646.

Lindner, R. M. (1950). The content analysis of the Rorschach protocol. In L. Abt and L. Bellak (Eds.), *Projective psychology*. New York: Knopf. pp. 75-90.

Lippmann, W., and C. Merz (1920). A test of the news. Special supplement to *The New Republic*, **23**, 1-42.

Lorge, I. (1944). Predicting readability. *Teachers College Record*, **45**, 404-419.

Lowenthal, L. (1944). Biographies in popular magazines. In P. F. Lazarsfeld and F. N. Stanton (Eds.), *Radio research 1942-1943*. New York: Duell, Sloan, and Pearce. pp. 507-548.

———— (1949). The sociology of literature. In W. Schramm (Ed.), *Communications in modern society*. Urbana: University of Illinois Press. pp. 82-100.

Lynch, M. D., and A. Effendi (1964). Editorial treatment of India in the New York Times. *Journalism Quart.*, **41**, 430-432.

*McClelland, D. C. (1958). The use of measures of human motivation in the study of society. In J. W. Atkinson (Ed.), *Motives in fantasy, action and society*. Princeton: Van Nostrand. pp. 518-552.

* ———— (1961). *The achieving society*. Princeton: Van Nostrand.

McClelland, D. C., and G. A. Friedman (1952). A cross-cultural study of the relationship between child-rearing practices and achievement motivation appearing in folk tales. In G. E. Swanson, T. M. Newcomb, and E. L. Hartley (Eds.), *Readings in social psychology*. (2nd ed.) New York: Henry Holt. pp. 243-249.

Maccoby, N., F. O. Sabghir, and B. Cushing (1950). A method for the analysis of the news coverage of industry. *Publ. Opin. Quart.*, **14**, 753-758.

McCurdy, H. G. (1939). Literature and personality: analysis of the novels of D. H. Lawrence. *Char. and Pers.*, **8**, 181-203, 311-322.

———— (1947). A study of the novels of Charlotte and Emily Brontë as an expression of their personalities. *J. Pers.*, **16**, 109-152.

———— (1953). *The personality of Shakespeare: a venture in psychological method*. New Haven: Yale University Press.

McDiarmid, M. (1937). Presidential inaugural addresses: a study of verbal symbols. *Publ. Opin. Quart.*, **1**, 79-82.

McEvoy, J., with the collaboration of R. Schmuck and M. Chesler (1966). Letters from the right: content-analysis of a letter writing campaign. Institute for Social Research, University of Michigan. (Mimeo)

McGranahan, D. V., and I. Wayne (1948). German and American traits reflected in popular drama. *Hum. Relat.*, **1**, 429-455.

McLaughlin, B. (1966). The WAI dictionary and self-perceived identity in college students. In P. J. Stone, D. C. Dunphy, M. S. Smith, and D. M. Ogilvie, *The General Inquirer: a computer approach to content analysis in the behavioral sciences*. Cambridge: M.I.T. Press.

McPherson, W. (1964). Lobbying and communication processes. Paper read at American Political Science Association Meeting, Chicago.

Mahl, G. F. (1959). Exploring emotional states by content analysis. In I. de S. Pool (Ed.), *Trends in content analysis*. Urbana: University of Illinois Press. pp. 89-130.

Mann, Mary B. (1944). Studies in language behavior: III. The qualitative differentiation of samples of written language. *Psychol. Monogr.* **56**, No. 2, whole No. 255, 41-74.

Markham, J. W., and G. H. Stempel III (1957). Analysis of techniques in measuring press performance. *Journalism Quart.*, **34**, 187-190.

*Marsden, G. (1965). Content analysis studies of therapeutic interviews: 1954 to 1964. *Psychol. Bull.*, **63**, 298-321.

Massing, I. W. (1963). The image of the Voice of America as drawn in Soviet media. In Matilda W. Riley (Ed.), *Sociological research: a case approach*. New York: Harcourt, Brace, and World. pp. 308-314.

Matthews, B. C. (1910). A study of a New York daily. *Independent*, **68**, 82-86.

Mendenhall, T. C. (1887). The characteristic curves of composition. *Science*, **9**, 237-246.

Merrill, J. C. (1962). The image of the United States in ten Mexican dailies. *Journalism Quart.*, **39**, 203-209.

———— (1965). How Time stereotyped three U.S. Presidents. *Journalism Quart.*, **42**, 563-570.

Merritt, R. L. (1966). *Symbols of American community, 1735-1775*. New Haven: Yale University Press.

Merton, R. K. (1946). *Mass persuasion: the social psychology of a war bond drive*. New York and London: Harper.

———— (1957a). Science and economy of 17th century England. In R. K. Merton, *Social theory and social structure*. Glencoe, Ill.: Free Press. pp. 607-627.

————(1957b). *Social theory and social structure*. New York: Free Press.

Middleton, R. (1960). Fertility values in American magazine fiction: 1916-1956. *Publ. Opin. Quart.*, **24**, 139-143.

Miles, Josephine (1951). The continuity of English poetic language. University of California Publications in English. Berkeley: University of California Press. pp. 517-535.

Miller, R. W. (1967). *An analysis of changes in Chinese descriptions of the Soviet Union using the general inquirer content analysis system*. Washington University. (Mimeo).

Mills, T. M. (1964). *Group transformation*. Englewood Cliffs, N.J.: Prentice-Hall.

Mintz, A. (1949). The feasibility of the use of samples in content analysis. In H. D. Lasswell, N. Leites, R. Fadner, J. M. Goldsen, A. Gray, I. L. Janis, A. Kaplan, D. Kaplan, A. Mintz, I. De Sola Pool, and S. Yakobson, *The language of politics: studies in quantitative semantics.* New York: George Stewart. pp. 127-152.

Mitchell, R. A. (1967). The use of content analysis for exploratory studies. *Publ. Opin. Quart.,* **31**, 230-241.

Morris, C. W. (1946). *Signs, language, and behavior.* Englewood Cliffs, N.J.: Prentice-Hall.

Morton, A. Q. (1963). A computer challenges the church. *The Observer,* Nov. 3, 1963.

Mosteller, F., and D. L. Wallace (1964). *Inference and disputed authorship: the Federalist* Reading, Mass: Addison-Wesley.

Mott, F. L. (1942). Trends in newspaper content. *Annals,* **219,** 60-65.

Mowrer, O. H. (1953). Changes in verbal behavior during psychotherapy. In O. H. Mowrer (Ed.), *Psychotherapy theory and research.* New York: Ronald. pp. 463-545.

Murray, E. J., F. Auld, and Alice M. White (1954). A psychotherapy case showing progress but no decrease in the discomfort-relief quotient. *J. Consult. Psychol.,* **18,** 349-353.

Namenwirth, J. Z. (in press). Some long and short term trends in one American political value: a computer analysis of concern with wealth in 62 party platforms. In G. Gerbner, O. R. Holsti, K. Krippendorff, W. J. Paisley, and P. J. Stone (Eds.), *The analysis of communication content: developments in scientific theories and computer techniques.* New York: Wiley.

Namenwirth, J. Z. and T. L. Brewer (1966). Elite editorial comment on the European and Atlantic communities in four countries. In P. J. Stone, D. C. Dunphy, M. S. Smith, and D. M. Ogilvie, *The General Inquirer: a computer approach to content analysis in the behavioral sciences.* Cambridge: M.I.T. Press. pp. 401-429.

Namenwirth, J. Z., and Lasswell, H. D. (forthcoming). *Changing language in American party platforms: a computer analysis of political values.*

Nixon, R. B., and R. R. Jones (1956). The content of non-competitive newspapers. *Journalism Quart.,* 33, 299-314.

† North, R. C., O. R. Holsti, M. G. Zaninovich, and Dina A. Zinnes (1963). *Content analysis: a handbook with applications for the study of international crisis.* Evanston, Ill.: Northwestern University Press.

Nunnally, J. (1957). The communication of mental health information: a comparison of the opinions of experts and the public with mass media presentations. *Behav. Sci.,* 2, 222-230.

Ogilvie, D. M. (in press). Individual and cultural patterns of fantasized flight. In G. Gerbner, O. R. Holsti, K. Krippendorff, W. J. Paisley, and P. J. Stone (Eds.), *The analysis of communication content: developments in scientific theories and computer techniques.* New York: Wiley.

Ogilvie, D. M., P. J. Stone, and E. S. Shneidman (1966). Some characteristics of genuine versus simulated suicide notes. In P. J. Stone, D. C. Dunphy, M. S. Smith, and D. M. Ogilvie, *The General Inquirer: a computer approach to content analysis in the behavioral sciences.* Cambridge: M.I.T. Press. pp. 527-535.

Ohlström, B. (1966). Information and propaganda. *J. Peace Res.,* 1, 75-88.

Ojemann, R. H., *et al.* (1948). A functional analysis of child development material in current newspapers and magazines. *Child Develpmt.,* 19, 76-92.

Osgood, C. E. (1959). The representational model and relevant research methods. In I. de S. Pool (Ed.), *Trends in content analysis.* Urbana: University of Illinois Press. pp. 33-88.

————— (1962). Studies on the generality of affective meaning systems. *Amer. Psychologist,* 17, 10-28.

† Osgood, C. E., S. Saporta, and J. C. Nunnally (1956). Evaluative assertion analysis. *Litera,* 3, 47-102.

Osgood, C. E., and T. A. Sebeok, Eds. (1954). Psycholinguistics: a survey of theory and research problems. *J. Abnorm. Soc. Psychol. (Suppl.),* 49, No. 4, part 2.

Osgood, C. E., G. J. Suci, and P. H. Tannenbaum (1957). *The measurement of meaning.* Urbana: University of Illinois Press.

Osgood, C. E., and Evelyn G. Walker (1959). Motivation and language behavior: content analysis of suicide notes. *J. Abnorm. Soc. Psychol.,* 59, 58-67.

Page, H. W. (1953). An assessment of the predictive value of certain language measures in psychotherapeutic counseling. In W. U. Snyder (Ed.), *Group report of a program of research in psychotherapy.* University Park: Pennsylvania State College. pp. 88-93.

Paige, J. M. (1966). Letters from Jenny: an approach to the clinical analysis of personality structure by computer. In P. J. Stone, D. C. Dunphy, M. S. Smith, and D. M. Ogilvie, *The General Inquirer: a computer approach to content analysis in the behavioral sciences.* Cambridge: M.I.T. Press. pp. 431-451.

Painter, J. A. (1960). Computer preparation of a poetry concordance. *Communic. Assoc. Computing Machinery,* 3, 91-95.

* Paisley, W. J. (1964). Identifying the unknown communicator in painting, literature and music: the significance of minor encoding habits. *J. Communic.,* 14, 219-237.

————— (1966). The effects of authorship, topic, structure, and time of composition on letter redundancy in English texts. *J. Verb. Learn. Verb. Behav.,* 5, 28-34.

————— (1968). The museum computer and the analysis of artistic content. Paper read at the Conference on Computers and their Potential Applications in Museums.

_____ (in press). Studying "style" as deviation from encoding norms. In G. Gerbner, O. R. Holsti, K. Krippendorff, W. J. Paisley, and P. J. Stone (Eds.), *The analysis of communication content: developments in scientific theories and computer techniques.* New York: Wiley.

Parker, E. C., D. W. Barry, and D. W. Smythe, Eds. (1955). *The television-radio audience and religion.* New York: Harper.

Parrish, S. M., Ed. (1959). *A concordance to the poems of Matthew Arnold.* Ithaca, N.Y.: Cornell University Press.

Parrish, S. M., and J. A. Painter (1963). *A concordance to the poems of W. B. Yeats.* Ithaca, N.Y.: Cornell University Press.

Parsons, T., E. A. Shils, and J. Olds (1952). Values, motives, and systems of action. In T. Parsons and E. A. Shils, *Toward a general theory of action.* Cambridge: Harvard University Press.

Peterson, R. L., and T. L. Brewer (n.d.). The Lasswell value dictionary. New Haven: Yale University. (Mimeo).

Pittenger, R. E., C. F. Hockett, and J. J. Danehy (1960). *The first five minutes: a sample of microscopic interview analysis.* Ithaca, N.Y.: Paul Martineau.

Pool, I. de S. (1951). *Symbols of internationalism.* Stanford: Stanford University Press.

_____ (1952a). *The 'prestige papers': a survey of their editorials.* Stanford: Stanford University Press.

_____ (1952b). *Symbols of democracy.* Stanford: Stanford University Press.

† _____ Ed. (1959). *Trends in content analysis.* Urbana: University of Illinois Press.

Propp, V. (1958). *Morphology of the folktale.* Svatava Pirkova-Jakobson (Ed.), Laurence Scott (Trans.). Bloomington, Ind.: Indiana University Research Center in Anthropology, Folklore, and Linguistics.

Prothro, J. W. (1956). Verbal shifts in the American presidency: a content analysis. *Amer. Polit. Sci. Rev.,* **50,** 726-739.

Psathas, G. (in press). Analyzing dyadic interaction. In G. Gerbner, O. R. Holsti, K. Krippendorff, W. J. Paisley, and P. J. Stone (Eds.), *The analysis of communication content: developments in scientific theories and computer techniques.* New York: Wiley.

Raben, J. (in press). Content analysis and the study of poetry. In G. Gerbner, O. R. Holsti, K. Krippendorff, W. J. Paisley, and P. J. Stone (Eds.), *The analysis of communication content: developments in scientific theories and computer techniques.* New York: Wiley.

Raimy, V. C. (1948). Self reference in counseling interviews. *J. Consul. Psychol.,* **12,** 153-163.

Rainey, G. E. (1966). The American image of peace. Doctoral dissertation, American University.

Rainoff, T. J. (1929). Wave-like fluctuations of creative productivity in the development of west-European physics in the eighteenth and nineteenth centuries. *Isis*, 12, 287-307.

Ramallo, L. I. (1966). The integration of subject and object in the context of action: a study of reports written by successful and unsuccessful volunteers for field work in Africa. In P. J. Stone, D. C. Dunphy, M. S. Smith, and D. M. Ogilvie, *The General Inquirer: a computer approach to content analysis in the behavioral sciences*. Cambridge: M.I.T. Press. pp. 536-547.

Riesman, D., N. Glazer, and D. Reuel (1950). *The lonely crowd*. New Haven: Yale University Press.

Roat, R. (1963). Crisis news in the press abroad. *Quill*, June 1963, 20-21.

Robinson, W. S. (1957). The statistical measure of agreement. *Amer. Sociol. Rev.*, 22, 17-25.

Role of content analysis in opinion and communications research, The (1951). *Publ. Opin. Quart.*, 15, 782-786.

Rosen, B. (1964). Attitude change within the Negro press toward segregation and discrimination. *J. Soc. Psychol.*, 62, 77-83.

Rosenau, J. N. (1961). *Public opinion and foreign policy*. New York: Random House.

———— (1968). Private preferences and public responsibility: the relative potency of individual and role variables in the behavior of U.S. senators. In J. D. Singer (Ed.), *Quantitative international politics: insights and evidence*. New York: Free Press. pp. 17-50.

Roshal, Jean J. G. (1953). The type-token ratio as a measure of changes in behavior variability during psychotherapy. In W. U. Snyder (Ed.), *Group report of a program of research in psychotherapy*. University Park: Pennsylvania State College. pp. 94-104.

Rosi, E. J. (1964). How 50 periodicals and the Times interpreted the Test Ban controversy. *Journalism Quart.*, 41, 545-556.

Royal Commission of the Press, 1947-1949 (1949). Report, Appendix VII. London: His Majesty's Stationery Office.

Rucker, B. W. (1960). News services' crowd reporting in the 1956 presidential campaign. *Journalism Quart.*, 37, 195-198.

Runion, H. L. (1936). An objective study of the speech style of Woodrow Wilson. *Speech Monogr.*, 3, 75-94.

Russell, J. T., and Q. Wright (1933). National attitudes on the Far Eastern controversy. *Amer. Polit. Sci. Rev.*, 27, 555-576.

St. George, M., and L. Dennis (1946). *A trial on trial: the great sedition trial of 1944*. National Civil Rights Committee.

*Salzinger, K., Stephanie Portnoy, and R. S. Feldman (1964). Verbal behavior of schizophrenic and normal subjects. *Ann. N.Y. Acad. Sci.*, 105, 845-860.

Scheuch, E. K., and P. J. Stone (1964). The General Inquirer approach to an international retrieval system for survey archives. *Amer. Behav. Scientist,* **7,** 23-28.

Schneider, L., and S. M. Dornbusch (1958). *Popular religion: inspirational books in America.* Chicago: University of Chicago Press.

Schorer, M. (1949). Fiction and the 'matrix of analogy.' *Kenyon Rev.,* **11,** 539-560.

Schramm, W., Ed. (1959). *One day in the world's press.* Stanford: Stanford University Press.

Schubert, G. (1965). Jackson's judicial philosophy: an exploration in value analysis. *Amer. Polit. Sci. Rev.,* **59,** 940-963.

Schutz, W. C. (1952). Reliability, ambiguity and content analysis. *Psychol. Rev.,* **59,** 119-129.

_____ (1958). On categorizing qualitative data in content analysis. *Publ. Opin. Quart.,* **22,** 503-515.

Scott, W. A. (1955). Reliability of content analysis: the case of nominal scale coding. *Publ. Opin. Quart.,* **19,** 321-325.

Sebald, H. (1962). Studying national character through comparative content analysis. *Social Forces,* **40,** 318-322.

Sebeok, T. A., and V. J. Zeps (1961). Computer research in psycholinguistics: toward an analysis of poetic language. *Behav. Sci.,* **6,** 365-369.

Sedelow, Sally Y., and W. A. Sedelow (in press). Categories and procedures for content analysis in the humanities. In G. Gerbner, O. R. Holsti, K. Krippendorff, W. J. Paisley, and P. J. Stone (Eds.), *The analysis of communication content: developments in scientific theories and computer techniques.* New York: Wiley.

Sedelow, Sally Y., W. A. Sedelow, Jr., and T. Ruggles (1964). Some parameters for computational stylistics: computer aids to the use of traditional categories in stylistic analysis. *In Proceedings of the IBM literary data processing conference.* Yorktown Heights, N.Y.: IBM. pp. 211-229.

Shanas, Ethel (1945). The American Journal of Sociology through fifty years. *Amer. J. Sociol.,* **50,** 522-533.

Sheerer, Elizabeth T. (1949). An analysis of the relationship between acceptance of and respect for self and acceptance of and respect for others in ten counseling cases. *J. Consul. Psychol.,* **13,** 169-175.

Shepard, D. W. (1956). Henry J. Taylor's radio talks: a content analysis. *Journalism Quart.,* **33,** 15-22.

Shneidman, E. S. (1951). *Thematic test analysis.* New York: Grune and Stratton.

_____ (1961). A psychological analysis of political thinking: the Kennedy-Nixon 'Great Debates' and the Kennedy-Khrushchev 'Grim Debates.' Cambridge: Harvard University. (Mimeo).

* ———— (1963). Plan 11. The logic of politics. In L. Arons and M. A. May (Eds.), *Television and human behavior.* New York: Appleton-Century-Crofts. pp. 177-199.

———— (1966). *The logics of communication: a manual for analysis.* China Lake, California: U.S. Naval Ordnance Test Station.

Siegel, S. (1956). *Non-parametric statistics for the behavioral sciences.* New York: McGraw-Hill.

Sikorski, Linda A., D. F. Roberts, and W. J. Paisley (1967). Analyzing letters in mass magazines as "outcroppings" of public opinion. Institute for Communication Research, Stanford University. (Mimeo).

Simmons, R. F. (1966). Automated language processing. In C. A. Cuadra (Ed.), *Annual review of information science and technology.* Vol. 1. New York: Interscience. pp. 137-169.

Skinner, B. F. (1939). The alliteration in Shakespeare's sonnets: a study in literary behavior. *Psychol. Record.,* 3, 186-192.

Smith, M. S., with P. J. Stone and E. N. Glenn (1966). A content analysis of twenty presidential nominating speeches. In P. J. Stone, D. C. Dunphy, M. S. Smith, and D. M. Ogilvie, *The General Inquirer: a computer approach to content analysis in the behavioral sciences.* Cambridge: M.I.T. Press. pp. 359-400.

Smythe, D. W. (1952). Some observations on communication theory. *Audio-Visual Communic. Rev.,* 2, 24-37.

———— (1953). *Three years of New York television, 1951-1953.* Urbana: National Association of Educational Broadcasters, University of Illinois.

Snyder, W. E., Ed. (1953). *Group report of a program of research in psychotherapy.* University Park: Pennsylvania State College.

Sorensen, R. C., and T. C. Sorensen (1955). Proposal for the use of content analysis in literary infringement cases. *Social Forces,* 33, 262-267.

Speed, J. G. (1893). Do newspapers now give the news? *The Forum,* 15, 705-711.

Spiegelman, M., C. Terwilliger, and F. Fearing (1953a). The content of comics: goals and means to goals of comic strip characters. *J. Soc. Psychol.,* 37, 189-203.

———— (1953b). The reliability of agreement in content analysis. *J. Soc. Psychol.,* 37, 175-187.

Star, Shirley A., and Helen M. Hughes (1950). Report of an educational campaign: the Cincinnati plan for the United Nations. *Amer. J. Sociol.,* 55, 389-400.

Starkweather, J. A. (1956). Content-free speech as a source of information about the speakers. *J. Abnorm. Soc. Psychol.,* 52, 394-402.

———— (in press). Computer aids to content recognition. In G. Gerbner, O. R. Holsti, K. Krippendorff, W. J. Paisley, and P. J. Stone (Eds.), *The analysis of communication content: developments in scientific theories and computer techniques.* New York: Wiley.

Starkweather, J. A., and J. B. Decker (1964). Computer analysis of interview content. *Psychol. Reports,* **15,** 875-882.

Stedman, M. S. (1951). Democracy in American communal and socialist literature. *J. History of Ideas,* **12,** 147-154.

Stempel, G. H., III (1952). Research in brief: sample size for classifying subject matter in dailies. *Journalism Quart.,* **29,** 333-334.

———— (1955). Increasing reliability in content analysis. *Journalism Quart.,* **32,** 449-455.

———— (1961). The prestige press covers the 1960 presidential campaign. *Journalism Quart.,* **38,** 157-163.

———— (1965). The prestige press in two presidential elections. *Journalism Quart.,* **42,** 15-21.

Stephenson, W. (1963). Critique of content analysis. *Psychol. Record,* **13,** 155-162.

Stevens, N. E. (1932). The fad as a factor in botanical publication. *Science,* **75,** 286-293.

Stewart, M. (1943). Importance in content analysis: a validity problem. *Journalism Quart.,* **20,** 286-293.

Stock, Dorothy (1949). The self concept and feelings toward others. *J. Consul. Psychol.,* **13,** 176-180.

Stoetzer, C. (1953). *Postage stamps as propaganda.* Washington: Public Affairs Press.

Stone, P. J. (1964). *An introduction to the General Inquirer: a computer system for the study of spoken or written material.* Harvard University and Simulmatics Corp. (Mimeo).

Stone, P. J., R. F. Bales, J. Z. Namenwirth, and D. M. Ogilvie (1962). The General Inquirer: a computer system for content analysis and retrieval based on the sentence as a unit of information. *Behav. Sci.,* **7,** 484-494.

Stone, P. J., D. C. Dunphy, and A. Bernstein (1965). Content analysis applications at simulmatics. *Amer. Behav. Scientist,* **8,** 23-28.

†Stone, P. J., D. C. Dunphy, M. S. Smith, and D. M. Ogilvie (1966). *The General Inquirer: a computer approach to content analysis in the behavioral sciences.* Cambridge: M.I.T. Press.

———— (1968). *User's manual for the general inquirer.* Cambridge: M.I.T. Press.

Stone, P. J., and E. B. Hunt (1963). A computer approach to content analysis. *Proc. Spring Joint Computer Conf., 1963.* pp. 241-256.

Stone, P. J., D. M. Ogilvie, and D. C. Dunphy (1963). Distinguishing real from simulated suicide notes using General Inquirer procedures. Paper read at the Joint Annual Meeting of the American College of Neuropsychopharmacology.

Stone, P. J., with M. Smith, D. C. Dunphy, E. Kelly, K. Chang, and T. Speer (in press). Improved quality of content analysis categories: computerized disambiguation rules for high frequency English words. In G. Gerbner, O. R. Holsti, K. Krippendorff, W. J. Paisley, and P. J. Stone (Eds.), *The analysis of communication content: developments in scientific theories and computer techniques.* New York: Wiley.

Sussman, Leila (1945). Labor in the radio news: an analysis of content. *Journalism Quart., 22,* 207-214.

Taeuber, Irene B. (1932). Changes in the content and presentation of reading material in Minnesota weekly newspapers, 1860-1929. *Journalism Quart., 9,* 281-289.

Tannenbaum, P. H., and B. S. Greenberg (1961a). The effects of bylines on attitude change. *Journalism Quart., 38,* 535-537.

———— (1961b). 'J.Q.' references: a study of professional change. *Journalism Quart., 38,* 203-207.

Tannenbaum, P. H., and M. D. Lynch (1960). Sensationalism: the concept and its measurement. *Journalism Quart., 37,* 381-392.

Taylor, W. L. (1953). 'Cloze Procedure'; a new tool for measuring readability. *Journalism Quart., 30,* 415-433.

———— (1956). Recent developments in the use of 'Cloze Procedure.' *Journalism Quart., 33,* 42-48, 99.

————(1957). Gauging the mental health content of the mass media. *Journalism Quart., 34,* 191-201.

Technical recommendations for psychological tests and diagnostic techniques (1954). *Psychol. Bull., 51,* Suppl., 201-238.

Tenney, A. A. (1912). The scientific analysis of the press. *Independent, 73,* 895-898.

Toch, H. H., S. E. Deutsch, and D. M. Wilkins (1960). The wrath of the bigot: an analysis of protest mail. *Journalism Quart., 37,* 173-185, 266.

Tukey, J. W. (1962). The future of data analysis. *Annals of Mathematical Statistics, 33.*

Walworth, A. (1938). *School histories at war: a study of the treatment of our wars in the secondary school history books of the United States and in those of its former enemies.* Cambridge: Harvard University Press.

Wang, C. K. A. (1955). Reactions in Communist China: an analysis of letters to newspaper editors. USAF Personnel Training Research Center, Technical Report No. 33. HHRI Project: "Chinese Documents Project." January, 1955.

Waples, D., B. Berelson, and F. R. Bradshaw (1940). *What reading does to people.* Chicago: University of Chicago Press.

Warchol, C. (1967). Stamp illustrations and militarism in Nazi Germany. Unpublished paper, Stanford University.

Wayne, I. (1956). American and Soviet themes and values: a content analysis of pictures in popular magazines. *Publ. Opin. Quart.*, **20**, 314-320.

Webb, E. J., D. T. Campbell, R. D. Schwartz, and L. Sechrest (1966). *Unobtrusive measures: nonreactive research in the social sciences.* Chicago: Rand-McNally.

Webb, E. J., and J. R. Salancik (1965). Notes on the sociology of knowledge. *Journalism Quart.*, **42**, 591-595.

Weingast, D. (1950). Walter Lippmann: a content analysis. *Publ. Opin. Quart.*, **13**, 296-302.

Westley, B. H., C. E. Higbie, T. Burke, D. J. Lippert, L. Maurer, and V. A. Stone (1963). The news magazines and the 1960 conventions. *Journalism Quart.*, **40**, 525-531, 647.

Weyl, N., and S. T. Possony (1963). *The geography of intellect.* Chicago: Regnery.

White, R. K. (1947). "Black Boy": a value-analysis. *J. Abnorm. Soc. Psychol.*, **42**, 440-461.

_____ (1949). Hitler, Roosevelt and the nature of war propaganda. *J. Abnorm. Soc. Psychol.*, **44**, 157-174.

_____ (1951). *Value-analysis: the nature and use of the method.* Glen Gardiner, N.J.: Libertarian Press.

White, T. H. (1965). *The making of the president 1964.* New York: Atheneum.

Whiting, A. S. (1960). *China crosses the Yalu.* New York: Macmillan.

Wilcox, W. (1962). The press of the radical right: an exploratory analysis. *Journalism Quart.*, **39**, 152-160.

Willey, M. (1926). *The country newspaper.* Chapel Hill: University of North Carolina Press.

Willoughby, W. F. (1955). Are two competing dailies necessarily better than one? *Journalism Quart.*, **32**, 197-204.

Winick, C. (1963). Trends in the occupation of celebrities—a study of news magazine profiles and television interviews. *J. Soc. Psychol.*, **60**, 301-310.

Wolfarth, D. L. (1961). John F. Kennedy in the tradition of inaugural speeches. *Quart. J. Speech*, **47**, 124-132.

Wolfenstein, Martha, and N. Leites (1950). *Movies: a psychological study.* Glencoe, Ill.: Free Press.

* Wolfson, Rose (1951). Graphology. In H. H. Anderson and G. M. L. Anderson (Eds.), *An introduction to projective techniques.* Englewood Cliffs, N.J.: Prentice-Hall. pp. 416-456.

Woodward, J. L. (1930). *Foreign news in American morning newspapers.* New York: Columbia University Press.

_____ (1934). Quantitative newspaper analysis as a technique of opinion research. *Social Forces*, **12**, 526-537.

Woodward, J. L., and R. Franzen (1948). A study of coding reliability. *Publ. Opin. Quart.,* **12,** 253-257.

Wright, Q., and C. J. Nelson (1939). American attitudes toward Japan and China. *Publ. Opin. Quart.,* **3,** 46-62.

Wyant, Rowena, and Herta Herzog (1941). Voting via the Senate mailbag. *Publ. Opin. Quart.,* **5,** 359-382, 590-624.

Yakobson, S., and H. D. Lasswell (1949). Trend: May Day slogans in Soviet Russia. In H. D. Lasswell, N. Leites, R. Fadner, J. M. Goldsen, A. Gray, I. L. Janis, A. Kaplan, D. Kaplan, A. Mintz, I. De Sola Pool, and S. Yakobson, *The language of politics: studies in quantitative semantics.* New York: George Stewart. pp. 232-297.

Yule, G. U. (1944). *The statistical study of literary vocabulary.* London: Cambridge University Press.

Zaninovich, M. G. (1964). An empirical theory of state response: the Sino-Soviet case. Unpublished doctor's dissertation, Stanford University.

Zinnes, Dina A. (1963). Expression and perception of hostility in international relations. Unpublished doctor's dissertation, Stanford University.

————— (1966). A comparison of hostile behavior of decision-makers in simulate and historical data. *World Politics,* **18,** 474-502.

Zinnes, Dina A., R. C. North, and H. E. Koch, Jr. (1961). Capability, threat and the outbreak of war. In J. N. Rosenau (Ed.), *International politics and foreign policy.* New York: Free Press. pp. 469-482.

Zinnes, Dina A., J. L. Zinnes, and R. D. McClure (in press). Hostility in diplomatic communication: a study of the 1914 crisis. In C. F. Hermann (Ed.), *Contemporary research in international crisis.* New York: Free Press.

Author Index

Abcarian, G. E., 51, 195
Abelson, R. P., 206
Abu-Lughod, I., 52, 195,
Adams, J. B., 50, 130, 199
Albig, W., 47, 48, 195
Albrecht, M. C., 30, 65, 195,
Allen, L. E., 190, 195
Allport, G. W., 17, 29, 47, 52, 70, 71, 130, 195, 202,
Almond, G. A., 31, 51, 112, 195
Alpert, R., 140, 197,
Andrews, T. G., 71, 195
Angell, R. C., 78, 130, 141, 196
Armour, Anne, 196,
Arnheim, R., 119, 196
Arnold, Magda B., 77, 196,
Aronson, E., 22, 81, 196,
Ash, P., 122, 196,
Asheim, L., 51, 196,
Auld, F., 76, 77, 212
Auld, P., 77, 154, 196

Backman, C. W., 135, 196
Badri, M. B., 22, 196,
Bagdikian, B. H., 55, 196,
Baldwin, A. L., 71, 129, 196
Bales, R. F., 23, 66, 112, 196, 218
Bandura, A., 112, 196,
Barcus, F. E., 3, 10, 13, 20, 42, 47, 196
Barghoorn, F. C., 59, 196
Barry, D. W., 53, 214

Barton, A. H., 11, 209
Barzun, J., 191, 196,
Batlin, R., 49, 197,
Bauer, R. A., 88, 197
Becker, H. P., 29, 47, 197
Bennett, E. M., 140, 197
Benson, L., 51, 105, 152, 197
Berelson, B., 3, 6, 13, 20, 32, 47, 48, 50, 58, 69, 90, 95, 110, 111, 117, 132, 144, 148, 150, 194, 197, 209, 219
Berkman, D., 30, 65, 197
Bernstein, A., 159, 218
Bernstein, M. H., 51, 197
Berreman, J. W. M., 62, 197
Block, J., 137, 197
Blumberg, N. B., 49, 197
Blumenstock, D., 59, 208
Boder, D. P., 76, 197
Bradshaw, F. R., 90, 219
Breed, W., 50, 197
Brewer, T. L., 108, 159, 160, 212, 214
Bricker, V. R., 160
Brinegar, C., 86, 197,
Brinton, J., 90, 197,
Brody, R. A., 16, 23, 29, 33, 67, 79, 80, 130, 158, 198, 204
Brooks, M. R., 58, 198,
Broom, L., 50, 198
Brown, W. B., 60, 198,
Bruner, J. S., 29, 47, 59, 71, 130, 195, 198,
Bryan, S. D., 155, 199,

Subject Index

a priori standard, 31, 56
abstraction, 90
"Achievement Imagery," 162-163
Adams, John Quincy, 46
adjective-verb ratio, 76
advertising, 23, 30, 60, 82
aggregate data, 14-15, 32
"alcohol" dictionary, 159
alliteration, 62, 116
American, 65
American business community, 51
American drama, 83
American Illustrated, 60
American Journal of Sociology, 47
American news magazines, 55
American newspapers, 47, 53
American popular religion, 46
American psychology, changing interests in, 47
American Soldier, The, 92
analysis, of flow of information, 90-91
  of life histories, 71
  of literary style, 190
  of psychological traits of individuals, 70 ff
  of variance, 40
antecedents of content, 68 ff.
anti-intellectual bias, 46, 49
anxiety, 76
appearance, measures of, 121
archeology, 15
Arnold, Matthew, 62, 155
art evaluation, 62
Atlantic, 65

attitudes, 101
  measurement of, 164-190
Austen, Jane, 62

Bayesian statistics, 87
best sellers and other novels, 15
Black Boy, 11, 19, 72
Bookniga, 83
botany, 47
British press, 49
Brontë, Emily, 62
Brontë sisters, 72
Bulletin of the Atomic Scientists, 61
business values, 78

campaign biographies, 60
categories, 11, 93, *see also* standard categories
  for analysis of fiction and drama, 113
  for analysis of verbal interaction, 112-113
  based on single classification principle, 100-101
  of bias, 114-115
  construction of, 67
  direction categories, 107
  for ends and means, 110-111
  for evidence, 108
  examples of, 104 ff.
  exhaustiveness of, 99-100
  general requirements of, 95-101
  generality of, 97-99
  independence of, 100

data analysis programs, 161 ff.
data preparation, 160-161, 169-171, 190
decision-makers' attitudes during international crises, 16
decoding process, 27, 35
defensiveness, measures of, 76
dictionaries, 156 ff., 167-9
  for computer analysis, 152
  for middle and lower class language, 159
"disambiguation," 157, 164
discomfort-relief quotient (DRQ), 76
disputed authorship, 17
"document," 1
  personal, 70
doodling styles, 81
Dostoyevsky, F., 33, 72
dream analysis, 101
DRQ (discomfort-relief quotient), 76
Dulles, John Foster, 30, 64, 72, 126, 165

Ebony, 65
editorial support of a political candidate, 15
effects of communication, 88
  perceived credibility of the communicator, 88
  personality factor, 88
  preexisting attitudes, 88
Eisenhower, Dwight D., 46, 47, 55, 63, 92
El Mundo, 82
electoral campaigns, role of the press in, 49
Eliot, George, 62
encoding process, 27
English, 22
Epistles of Paul, 86
equal-appearing intervals (Thurstone's method), 43
evaluative assertion analysis, 124-6, 164
experiment, 14, 16
expert opinion, as a noncontent standard, 58

face validity, 11, 143
"family values," 65

Far Eastern crisis (1930-1932), 43
Father Coughlin, 60
Federal Communications Commission, 84
Federalist Papers, 15, 85, 86, 87, 102, 151-2
fiction, 30, 58
fishing expedition research, 27, 41, 67
flexibility of program, 188
flow of information, analysis of, 90-91
flow of news, 91
folktales, 53, 62, 158, 159
frequency, 6, 7, 9
  measures of, 122
Freud, Sigmund, 154
  dream theory, 47, 93, 107

Galilean, The, 83
Gates, Thomas, 92
general communications, 21
"General Inquirer," 152, 156 ff.
generality, 5
German drama, 83
Gerson, Jean, 85
Goldwater, Barry, 11, 60, 64

Hamilton, Alexander, 5, 85-6, 102, 122, 152
Hamson, Knut, 72, 144
handwriting, 42
Harvard Third Psychosociological Dictionary, 157-8, 169
Hitler, Adolf, 60
  propaganda style of, 60
homographs, 163-4
Hoover, Herbert, 60, 92
hostility, 76
House of Seven Gables, The, 51
Humphrey, Hubert, 19
Hungary crisis, 52

Icarus dictionary, 159
idiosyncrasies of reasoning, 73
Imitation of Christ, The, 85-86
individual reliability, 135-6
inferences, 13, 14
  based on an indirect relationship between symbolic and other forms of behavior, 33

Soviet reaction to Voice of America, 15
space/time, measures of, 121
speech disturbance, 77
St. Louis *Post Dispatch*, 31
Stalin, Joseph, 60
Standard categories and computer content analysis, 103-104
  reasons for the general absence of, 102
standards, of adequacy, 31
  defined by experts, 31-2
  defined by noncontent indices, 31, 58
  derived inductively, 31
statistical methods, 9, 10
statistical tests, 12
Stevenson, Adlai, 46, 63
student attitudes about the future, 52
style, 61 ff.
  and commercial success, 62
Suez crisis, 52
suicide notes, 78, 144
survey, 16
survey research, 14, 23
Swedish newspaper editorials, 60
syntactics, 13, 32
syntax codes, 160-161
syntax coding, 153, 169-170
systematic, 4
systems of enumeration, 8-9, 119 ff.

Taft-Hartley Labor Act, 55
tag tally program, 161
"tagging" of words, 156-157
TAT, *see* Thematic Apperception Tests
Taylor, Henry J., radio talks, 63
television debates, 63, 73
television programs, 47, 53, 54, 58
textbooks, 53
Thematic Apperception Tests, 77
  protocols, 158
theme coding, 160-161, 170-171
Therapist Tactics Dictionary, 159
Thurstone's method (equal-appearing intervals), 43
Time, 55

transmission of rumors, 91
Trends in Content Analysis, 22
True Confessions, 65
True Story, 65
Truman, Harry S., 55, 92
type-token ratio (TTR), 17, 75, 145, 154, 155

Ulysses, 87
UNESCO, 51
unitizing, 136
units of analysis, 116 ff.
unknown authors, identification of, 16
"unobtrusive" research technique, 16
U.S. News and World Report, 55, 61
USSR, 60

validity, 11, 43, 142 ff.
  concurrent, 143, 144-148
  construct, 143, 148
  content, 143
  predictive, 143, 144
value analysis, 60
values, 101
  in children's readers, 28
variance, analysis, 40
Verbally Indexed Associations (VIA) program, 155
Voice of America, 92

WAI dictionary, 159
Wall Street Journal, 56
Washington lobbyists, 51
Willkie, Wendell, 49, 50
Wilson, Woodrow, 63, 115
word count programs, 154 ff.
WORDS system, 154-5
Work Conference on Content Analysis, 13
World Attention Survey, 44
World War I, American entry into, 91
Wright, Richard, 11, 19, 72
Wuthering Heights, 62

Yeats, W. B., 4, 61, 155
Youth's Outlook on the Future, 16